Random Walks
Essays in Elective Criticism

Random Walks includes fifteen lively essays on general problems of literary theory and academic practice as well as the appreciation and interpretation of specific writers and their works.

The first section of the book develops Solway's approach to literature, starting from the assumption that genuine criticism requires the intellectual freedom to range at will across the literary landscape rather than restricting one's direction based on what is current, fashionable, or politically correct. Solway argues that advocating a theoretical school – postmodernism, poststructuralism, semiotics, new historicism, Marxist revisionism, or queer theory – generally involves abandoning the real critical project, which is the discovery of one's own undetermined motives, dispositions, and interests as reflected in the secret mirrors embedded in literary texts. Instead Solway pursues what he calls elective criticism, writing that enables the critical writer to freely discover his or her own "identity" – a concept that he claims cannot reasonably be diluted, relinquished, or deconstructed.

In the second section Solway practises what he preaches, exploring a wide range of authors and subjects. His essays include an analysis of Franz Kafka's *The Trial* as a Jewish joke, a personal memoir of Irving Layton, an interpretation of Erin Mouré's "Pronouns on the Main," an examination of language in William Shakespeare's romances, a reading of Robert Browning's "My Last Duchess" that is sympathetic to the Duke, an assertion that James Joyce has more in common with the traditional novelist than with the professional, (post-)modern alienator, and an exploration of Jonathan Swift's sartorial imagery that contends that form is the source of substantive identity.

DAVID SOLWAY is a poet and professor of English literature, John Abbott College. His previous nonfiction books are *Lying about the Wolf: Essays in Culture and Education* (McGill-Queen's), *Education Lost*, and *The Anatomy of Arcadia*.

Random Walks

Essays in Elective Criticism

David Solway

McGill-Queen's University Press
Montreal & Kingston · London · Buffalo

ISBN 0-7735-1648-4 (cloth)
ISBN 0-7735-1679-4 (paper)

Legal deposit third quarter 1997
Bibliothèque nationale du Québec

Printed in Canada on acid-free paper

McGill-Queen's University Press acknowledges the support received for its publishing program from the Canada Council's Block Grants program.

Canadian Cataloguing in Publication Data

Solway, David, 1941-
Random walks: essays in elective criticism
Includes bibliographical references.
ISBN 0-7735-1648-4 (bound) -
ISBN 0-7735-1679-4 (pbk.)
1. Criticism. 2. Literature – History and criticism.
I. Title.
PR99.S578 1997 801′.95 C97-900395-4

for
Trevor Ferguson
and
Scott Lawrence

Contents

Preface

My problem as a writer is that I have lots of axes to grind and no hatchets to bury. As I survey this collection of essays I am at a loss to find a simple unifying theme or a general subject that proceeds to unfold, whether concentrically or longitudinally. If there is a unity, it would appear to be an emotional one: a certain animus alternating or mingling with a certain love. This tonal swivel or libration may trouble readers and reviewers even more than it does me.

But perhaps I am overstating the case. After all, like any writer, I address myself to the subjects I happen to find of interest without looking for some binding or aprioristic theme that only serves to impose a spurious unity. I follow my inclinations wherever they may lead and try to turn to account whatever may provoke either delight or indignation. More often than not, the text serves merely as a pretext. As both Barthes and Derrida suggest, ultimately what the writer writes is writing itself. There is a sense in which the subject is immaterial, provided it is deeply felt and gives the writer the opportunity to exercise his or her craft. So the principle of unity, if it exists, may also be said to reside in the heteronomous impulse to write per se, which is to say, to write oneself into the world that perplexes, threatens, tempts, and challenges all that is inchoate and dispersed in the pre-reflected self. The need is always to give shape to one's experience, but in order for this to happen what must be avoided above all is a procrustean theory of the world or of any given aspect of it to which experience is made to conform for the sake of an outward or professional coherence. One exercises, in effect, what Peter Sloterdijk (no doubt influenced by Lyotard) calls "kynical thinking," a kind of "floating, playful, essayistic" impulsiveness critical of the grand systems and the rigidity of unifying theory, that tries to redeem all "the little dismembered pieces" neglected by the totality to which we obscurely submit, especially when we think we are at our most authentic. This seems to be how one goes about patiently assembling and fitting together the jigsaw to which one diffidently attaches one's name, before scattering all the pieces again to avoid the distortion of a definitive portrait.

The textual strategy that suggests itself, then, is to write what I am here calling elective criticism, by which I mean, quite simply, to write in such a way that one invests primarily in one's freedom and the subtlest of its literary analogues, stylistic versatility,[1] allowing the scansions and trajectories of temperament to choose the themes, interests, and subjects that attract the attention and to sport with the formal conventions that govern one's presentation. Such a "turn" is becoming increasingly difficult in the current hothouse environment of hydroponic criticism which seems to demand some sort of *parti pris*, a species of ideological cultivation, or a demonstrable affiliation with a given school or movement. Today we do pomo on principle, forcing what should come freely, adopting a stance rather than taking a stroll. Or we *profess* poststructuralism or semiotics or new historicism or Marxist revisionism or queer theory or any of the other routine sublimities, usually couched in some mandatory cryptolect that confers the distinction of unreadability – what I am tempted to call the Homi Bhabha syndrome.[2] But the real critical project entails something radically different, a sort of triple Lutz of the mind: the discovery of one's *initial and consciously undetermined* motives, dispositions, and enthusiasms as reflected in the secret mirrors embedded in literary works; the construction of a coherent and recognizable sensibility, starting with these primitive gradients of the self but shaping them in line with natural impulse into a conscious unity that is resolutely precessional and intimate; and the refusal to accept the resulting configuration as definitive, a decision requiring that the process constantly begin anew but at a higher or at least different level of integration. Genuine criticism is in a certain sense profoundly dialectical, involving an exertion of psychic or intellectual torque, but not necessarily political or "ideological," and *never* institutional.[3]

This project, transposed into the field of critical reflection, may also be seen to owe something to Wittgenstein's refusal in the Preface to the

Philosophical Investigations to force his thoughts "in any single direction against their natural inclination." He preferred to pursue his travels "criss-cross in every direction" and persisted in viewing his "remarks" as "sketches of landscape made in the course of these long and involved journeyings." This is simply another way of describing the "method" of elective criticism which, as such, is nothing new – nor does it pretend to be. It is precisely what Montaigne had in mind when, basing his practice on the precedents he found in Plutarch and Seneca, he proceeded to invent the personal *essai*, plumbing those regions of the self we might conceive as chthonic and scaling up what he detected – the dark elements of appetite and revulsion – into a complex and luminous, textual simulacrum of achieved identity. I am merely applying Montaigne's complaisant modus operandi to *literary subjects* in particular and slapping a new name on this practice or discipline because, trapped in the midst of institutional constraints that are growing more and more wiredrawn and coercive, we have forgotten what it means to be intellectually free: to take random walks across the literary landscape, to choose one's directions in consulting a private, interior compass, to remain indifferent to what is current, fashionable, "correct," or scholastically dominant. And, most of all, to proceed with the sort of cognitive insouciance that pays no attention to any principle of unity that is not implicit. Elective criticism, since it is rooted in the fabular incipience of the personal and the paradox of determinate randomness, will always choose its own script and idiom – prompted by the myriad unsuspected reciprocities and recognitions that are mysteriously and yet somehow inevitably coded into literary works[4] – over the multinational prose of an establishment criticism as exclusionary as it is irrelevant.

Acknowledgments

"Culling and Dereading" appeared in *The Antigonish Review*, 77–8; "The End of Poetry" and "The Word and the Stone" in *Canadian Literature*, 115 and 129 respectively; "Fellatiotics," in somewhat different form and under another title, in *Zymergy* 10; "Pronominal Debris" in *Errata* 1, no. 3; "Framing Layton" in *Matrix*, 38 (reprinted in *Raging Like a Fire*, Véhicule Press and Concordia University, Montreal, 1993); and "Intoxicated Words" in *The Sewanee Review* 95, no. 4.

I wish to thank Eric Ormsby without whose interest, encouragement, and editorial vigour I would probably never have got round to revising and collecting these essays under one cover. I am also grateful to W.J. Keith on whose informed and sympathetic criticism I could always rely and to Martin Battestin for his magnanimous response to the concluding chapter of this book. Finally, I owe a debt of gratitude to Dr Joseph Kornacki who kept me on my feet during the random walks recollected in this volume.

I wish to thank the Conseil des Arts et des Lettres du Québec for its timely and generous assistance in the form of a *bourse de soutien à la pratique artistique* toward the completion of this book.

Foreword

Eric Ormsby

Er war ein Dichter und hasste das Ungefähre.
Rilke, *Aufzeichnungen des Malte Laurids Brigge*

Contrary to popular impression, the essays of a genuine poet can be more exact than the essays of a philosopher or a magistrate or a molecular biologist. This is because the poet's exactitude is never merely factual. A fidelity, almost Linnaean in intensity, to the entire character of words – individual words and words acting in concert – preoccupies the writer of the essays included here. "He was a poet," writes Rilke, "and hated the approximate." The poet and essayist David Solway is alert to the penumbras of words as well as to their more central shadings. His fidelity, his exactitude, is lexical, but it is also emotional. In one of the essays in the present collection Solway speaks of a "lexical radiation of pleasure," but his choice and application of words are never simply lexical. The notion of pleasure in language is surprisingly neglected nowadays and I will return to this later.

At the outset I wish to call attention to Solway's language in these essays, chosen from over two dozen written during the last decade. It is not my intention to examine Solway's works from a literary-critical point of view, nor to situate them within the context of contemporary Canadian literature (though both of these tasks are long overdue). Instead, I focus on a particular and salient feature of his work, his quite distinctive use of language. It would have been easy to dwell on the high moral seriousness of these essays, or to point out how very funny, sometimes outrageously funny, they can be. It would have been an easy matter too to expatiate on the unusual range of the present collection, reaching from the eight essays of the first section that address theoretical and critical concerns (and that constitute, almost *en passant*, a modern poetics) to the seven essays on individual authors that make up the second section and which extend from Kafka to the great Canadian poet Irving Layton (with an interlude devoted to a minute critique – some might think it a vivisection – of the contemporary Canadian poet Erin Mouré) on to Shakespeare, Browning, and Joyce and which culminates in the majestic and utterly original concluding essay on Jonathan Swift entitled "Swift and Sartorism." I have chosen instead to dwell on Solway's language because language at its utmost – what Solway terms "seraphic speech" – is itself a powerful (and conspicuous) protagonist in these essays.

It may seem gratuitous to call attention to Solway's prose. There is scarcely a sentence in *Random Walks* that does not call attention to itself, sometimes slyly but sometimes in the most bravura fashion. Solway's prose, like his marvellous poetry, never resembles the inert, exiguous, virtually comestible sentences of his contemporaries who write a prose so vapid that it dissolves as it is read and, like junk food, leaves neither taste nor nourishment behind. Solway's prose, by contrast, is memorable; it is also lithe, mischievous, shapely, impudent, and ceremonial. His is a style that manages to be magisterial and agitated, in equal measure and at the same time. In my view, this is because Solway presents the distinctive intellectual phenomenon of a stubbornly conservative mind incessantly drawn to risk itself. In Solway's risk-taking, it is form – the shape of a sentence, the shape of a poem – that rescues and exposes him at every moment. This concatenation of such disparate tendencies within a single sensibility lends a sense of danger to his writing. The words in his sentences sit uneasily beside one another like riders on a New York subway car. This is a style, unique not only in Canadian but in contemporary English letters, that bristles with the force and presence of an unpredictable energy. At moments as we read we find ourselves wondering just where these headlong glissandos will land not only ourselves but their progenitor. We have the sense that the author, for all his stylistic control, is hurtling forward as he writes in the momentum of his own surprise.

Open almost any book by David Solway on almost any page and you will be brought up short, before anything else, by the language. There are those famous "$50 words" which an admiring but exasperated fan once wrote to him about. I would place these unusual words at a higher dollar value, but I too could easily fill a page or two of this introduction with examples of such words, the stubborn use of which argues some perverse strategy on the author's part. Among our contemporaries perhaps only in Solway's work does one come across such *rara aves* as borborygm and sordine, anamorphoscopic and nisus, exantlation, lenticular, ipsissimosity, bregmatic, despumated, and (my own favourite) ultracrepidarian. To make matters worse, it is invariably clear when you are reading Solway's prose that the appearance of such words is deliberate, for he is fond of resorting to them when he most wishes to clinch a point. Meanwhile the reader, drawn on to some apparently quite reasonable and even ineluctable assent, is baffled, brought up short. A sense of betrayal begins to take shape. "I've entrusted myself to this author, and *this* is how he treats me? He's used a word I do not, possibly cannot, know, and he has used it purposely because he presumes that I will not know it." Such a reader will not be mollified to learn that Solway also delights in words not to be found even in the twenty-volume *Oxford English Dictionary*.

As soon as these exotic vocables appear, reviewers of Solway's books usually begin spinning their sharpening stones. The predictable response of such reviewers is to complain that this author likes to send us "scuttling" to our dictionaries (others, more ably, "scurry"). That the encounter with a new English word, however recondite, should reduce a reviewer to a vaguely roach-like creature – a semantic Gregor Samsa, as it were – suggests that for such readers words are little more than weaponry to be used in covert power plays. They react to unknown words with the animal panic of infantrymen suddenly overtaken by cavalry. It strikes me as curious that men and women of letters take offence at what is patently a conscious artistic strategy on Solway's part. Even more basically, it is curious that those whose business is words should not rejoice in the discovery of new words. After all, the words unearthed and newly burnished by poets have their own inimitable lustre. We associate trips to the dictionary with a kind of drudgery imposed on us in school when, in fact, the encounter with unknown words should induce a lexical excitation which only dictionaries can assuage.

Solway's prose, like the prose of Nabokov or Joyce, like the prose of Sterne or Donne, says to its readers: *Stop. I am not disposable. I too am a thing among things, a being among beings, a creation among other created things.* Works of art are entities in their own right; they not only deserve, but command, attention. And the essays in the present volume are works of art. In a work of art, nothing is unimportant, least of all the very surface, the texture, of the language in which the work is raimented. "Depth must be hidden," wrote the great Austrian poet Hugo von Hofmannsthal, "Where? On the surface." Moreover, it is one of the cardinal theses of this collection that works of art are "facts of nature" in a very real way, and the prose mirrors and reinforces this thesis. This is what Goethe meant when he remarked that "a work of art is just as much a work of nature as a mountain."

Nowadays, of course, we like our prose plain and unadorned. The high style makes us uneasy. Style itself, like form, is suspect. The commissars have migrated to the West. The Russian novelist Nina Berberova, in her brilliant little study of the Russian symbolist poet Alexander Blok, noted that in the early years of the Revolution, "Russian criticism resolutely separated form from content. Only the subject was considered important ... Form played no more than a modest, auxiliary part. Indeed, the question of form was not even raised with regard to prose. In poetry, the only requirements were to observe the most elementary rules of prosody. All complexity was regarded as superfluous dandyism, all efforts to achieve formal perfection, far from being looked on sympathetically, were denounced as reactionary" (Nina Berberova, *Alexandr Blok* [Manchester: Carcanet, 1996], 12).

Actually, Solway deals masterfully with this predicament in the essay entitled "The Word and the Stone," but he is one of very few to have done so. (The American novelist William H. Gass struggles with comparable issues in his essays and, in fact, seems to me the only writer now active who comes close to Solway's singular achievement. Both Gass and Solway are upholders, and supreme practitioners, of form.) Nowadays, alas, style is associated with privilege or mandarin notions of "class." To many there is something disquieting, even faintly disreputable, in style. Perhaps this is because a pleasure in words, a delight that is not just cerebral but palpably physical – a tactile, even palatal pleasure that can be subtly sensual – can be also, as Barthes pointed out, distinctly libidinous. Nevertheless, one of the comical paradoxes of our *fin de siècle*, in which "sexual liberation" is a piety monotonously intoned, is that the language of our sexual liberators should be so bland, so colourless and capon-pale, so anhedonic. David Solway's freedom from self-censorship is especially refreshing in this respect. He remains unintimidated by the present-day Robespierres, and Robespierrettes, of language.

This facet of Solway's writing is perhaps most conspicuously in evidence in the essay entitled "Never on Sontag," though the hilariously accurate "The Autoerotic Text" runs a close second. The witty title evokes the modern Greek experience so dear to Solway even while it pokes some gentle fun at its subject. There is the playful implication of

Sontag as a resolutely unhermeneutic sensualist, a Melina Mercouri of the intellect; but there is also a serious satirical nip: Sontag is a kind of Sunday sensualist, the way others are Sunday painters, an intellectual trading her birthright for a mess of pottage short on taste as well as nourishment.

The "lexical radiation of pleasure" is not just a matter of words. In these essays good sense prevails; there is a kind of fundamental justice of the eye. Solway loathes cant, persiflage, and obfuscation and he can be scathing, as in "The Autoerotic Text," one of the wittiest demolitions of contemporary literary criticism. This strong rationalist in Solway coexists, happily, with a verbal prankster. On every page there are surprising formulations, as when Solway speaks of an attempt "to spackle the abyss," the homely, household word "spackle" conjoined with "abyss," with its great-vowelled vastness, in a way that is almost apothegmatic. There are also puns, many outrageous, of which "walks the Planck" is perhaps my favourite. At the same time, and often on the same page, Solway can give way convincingly to an exquisite delicacy. What other essayist writing today could suddenly introduce, in an essay on hermeneutics, such a simile as "like pansies in a box of summer savory," or term critics "the belletristic counterparts of the paddle bearers in Japanese subways?"

Indeed, in the end it is the particular and unmistakable voice of the poet which sounds through, again and again, and it is fitting that this voice sound throughout the essays in this volume. As Solway has himself noted, "The essay, like the lyric, is an intensely subjective form, an investigation and expression of the self, but unlike the lyric it is not subsumed under the aspect of pure utterance or (hypothetical) spontaneity." Or, more pithily: "[The essay] carnalizes the indiscernible in the catastrophic body of print." ("On the Essay")

In Solway's prose there is also what I can only term a sweet seriousness, which is deeply characteristic of the rationalist as well as of the verbal craftsman. This quality emerges often in the course of these essays and can be quite moving: "Literature and scholarship, in any authentic sense, have no *raison d'être* if they are not animated through and through by intentionality, if they do not offer to connect, meet, and fructify, if they are not founded on the discipline of literacy and the impulse toward reciprocal intimacy" ("The Autoerotic Text").

Underlying these disparate essays, which range over a huge array of literary works with a delicacy of allusion and reference that is quite remarkable, is a passionate conviction that words matter and that words, like things, are to be honoured and respected. For all the irreverence Solway so wittily displays, there is a profound reverence for language and for literature that is, sadly enough, unique in contemporary Canadian letters. When Solway speaks of "the surprising presence of a genuine vernacular, a lucid unpretentiousness accented by a touch of humour ("Culling and Dereading"), he is describing his own style. In the essay on Kafka, he writes: "One of the great difficulties in life as well as literature is how at the same time to be serious and unpretentious, how to achieve the profound while avoiding the lugubrious, how to express feeling without being sentimental; or, in the Jewish idiom, how to suffer without redundance" ("*The Trial* As Jewish Joke").

And in "The Word and the Stone," a key essay in Solway's oeuvre, and one that constitutes a kind of poet's credo, he writes: "For the great poems inevitably participate in both dimensions of our experience, situated in language that is constantly recuperating itself as something unique, memorable, noble, ophicleidic, resonating, and at the same time urging us outward towards the world in all its beauty and ugliness as something that demands our recognition and involvement."

In dwelling upon Solway's use of language and his choice of words, I would not wish to obscure his many other brilliant qualities. And yet, style is no mere patina gleaming along the surfaces of a thought. Style is the very movement of the mind; words do not clothe thought, they are simultaneous to thought and indistinguishable from it. Just as in a poem one word cannot be arbitrarily subsituted for another without impairing the whole, so too, in these essays; and it is this critical coherence which makes them almost impossible to paraphrase and yet irresistible to quote.

At the outset I remarked that the time was long overdue for some assessment of David Solway's place in contemporary Canadian literature. In actuality, however, I believe that this is too limited a context in which to judge his achievement for he is a thinker and a writer of international scope and import. He is the least parochial, the least regional, of Canadian writers. Of course, one could point to certain undeniable influences, among whom A.M. Klein and Irving Layton might deserve particular mention. But the tracking of influences reveals only what a writer has assimiliated and passed beyond. More importantly, Solway is one of the first Canadian essayists and poets consciously, and with admirable ambition, to envisage and address a global readership, and not merely some local coterie. And it is in this sense that Solway's abiding passion for things Greek may be understood: that is, not merely as an effort to go beyond the confines of present-day "Canadian" experience, but to return to the luminous source of all that is most fully human, the *fons et origo* of all our reasonings as of our musings. That this is invariably and fatally frustrated, however often the attempt be made, that there is in the end no Arcadia, not even in our origins, only goes to show the depth and complexity of his quest. There is a tension in Solway's work in prose as well as in verse, a tension that extends to the very relations between the words that make up his lines and sentences. It is the tension that arises from the inevitable disparity between words and the things that they evoke, between what is hoped for, longed for, and what simply is; but instead of promoting bitterness, this inner disparity spurs his thoughts and gives them immense verve and a nervous elegance which is unique.

This exquisite suspension between the world, as it is given, and language, as it shapes itself in our nerves, brains, and mouths, informs all of the essays in *Random Walks* which, like his poetry, refuse to let go "that eclectic and voluptuous world which art at once creates, transcends, denies, and adores" ("Never on Sontag").

Montreal
January 1997

Random Walks

One does not proceed by specific differences from a genus to its species, nor by deduction from a stable essence to the properties deriving from it, but from a problem to the accidents that condition and resolve it.
Gilles Deleuze and Félix Guattari, *Nomadology: The War Machine*

Consider now a single particle executing a random walk in two dimensions ... All jump directions have equal a priori probability and are uncorrelated with the preceding jumps.
G.J. Dienes and R.J. Borg, *An Introduction to Solid State Diffusion*

Part One

Never on Sontag

"Here is a myst'ry
About a little fir-tree.
Owl says its *his* tree,
And Kanga says its *her* tree.
Which doesn't make any sense," said Pooh, "because Kanga doesn't live in a tree."

A.A. Milne, *The House at Pooh Corner*

The kinds of question we ask are as many as the kinds of things which we know. They are in fact four: (1) whether the connexion of an attribute with a thing is a fact, (2) what is the reason of the connexion, (3) whether a thing exists, (4) what is the nature of the thing.

Aristotle, *Posterior Analytics*, 2. 1

Susan Sontag's celebrated essay "Against Interpretation" continues to exert a disproportionate influence on the study of literature, even in the high-powered deconstructionist world of current criticism and teaching. One reason for its ongoing effect may be that it manages to tap a deep sense of cultural malaise, a suspicion of bad faith, among contemporary intellectuals. Sontag herself refers to "the hypertrophy of the intellect" which vitiates a good deal of what passes for literary scholarship these days. The primary text tends increasingly to become a mere pretext (the wrong kind of pretext) for exegetical acrobatics, a kind of trampoline to sustain the critical evolutions of a troupe of star performers. Literature is gradually being subsumed by criticism, which rejects, as Christopher Norris says, "its subservient Arnoldian stance and [takes] on the freedom of interpretive style with matchless gusto." This is a point which Geoffrey Hartman has stressed with his concept of "answerable style" (the phrase is really Milton's). But the inner, disquieting sense of illicit encroachment remains, a sense of critical poaching on the domain of the artist, which both produces and justifies the anti-interpretive stance adopted by critics like Sontag. The intellect proceeds to "deconstruct" its own congenial program.

A close examination of Sontag's essay reveals, rather surprisingly, that it is really a compendium of some rather slender ideas held up by a kind of stiff indignation, like pansies in a box of summer savory. (As Camille Paglia remarks in "Sontag, Bloody Sontag," in *Vamps and Tramps*, Sontag's essays resemble collages rather than arguments.) It consists of ten sections, varying in length from two involuted pages to one concise sentence, related on the whole impressionistically rather than logically. (One feels that a few of these sections could do-se-do quite freely without serious loss in hortatory power). But for the sake of clarity I propose to review the ten sections in strict sequence, nickel-and-diming my way through the essay to what is obviously intended as its conclusive, ideological payload: erotics replacing hermeneutics.

The ten segments tend to fall into five schematic groupings. Part A (the first three sections) is expository and diagnostic, treating of the origins, nature, and definition(s) of interpretation. Here we find the obligatory reference to the classical notion of art as mimesis, leading to the inevitable separation of content from form and the traditional emphasis on the former at the expense of the latter. This emphasis leads in turn to the curse of intensive interpretation which Sontag understands as a diminution or "impoverishment" of the aesthetic experience, thus a characteristic vice that needs to be expunged. Section 3, the longest in the exordium, provides us with a bit of fine-tuning of the above. Interpretation, as an illustration of a code or convention of reading, is nothing other than "translation," explained by the historical fact of cultural dislocation! The scientific enlightenment of "late classical antiquity" (whatever that may be), by dissipating a pre-existent mythic consciousness, made it necessary to "reconcile the ancient texts to 'modern' demands." Hence interpretation was summoned to ensure the "conservation" of disputed texts in the form of allegory[1] or "alteration," intelligibility being now a function of the disclosure of a true, hidden meaning. Thus interpretation was in effect the sodium pentothol of late classical antiquity.

This first part of the essay concludes with a telling swipe at "new style" interpretation which, unlike the "old style" variety, does not erect "another meaning on top of the literal one" but is essentially archaeological, excavating in order "to find a sub-text which is the true one." What Sontag is alluding to, however, is not really new-style criticism (a misleading term), but *symptomatic* criticism (psychological, economic, or sociological), whose principal sources are to be found in genetic thinkers like Freud or Marx.[2] Sontag's terminology produces an unfortunate confusion with the venerable institution of New Criticism, whose iconic advocacy is, as it happens, diametrically opposed to the presumed "new style" repudiated here.

Part B (comprising sections 4 and 5) oversees the introduction of Sontag's pivotal thesis: the denunciation of "intellect" in the literate world as phlebitic, as displacing "energy and sensual capability" to such an extent that interpretation has become the "revenge of the intellect" upon both art and the world. She then goes on to redefine interpretation as the philistine or vulgarian domestication of art through the agency of the exegetical preposition "about": Kafka's work, for example, is commonly deemed to be "about" divine judgment, "about" the castration anxiety, "about" the emergence of the totalitarian state; Beckett's plays "are read as a statement about modern man's alienation from meaning or from God"; *A Streetcar Named Desire* is misunderstood as being "about ... the decline of western civilization." All this, as she argues, is clearly wrong-headed, yet it is at precisely this point that the essay begins to disclose some of its inherent flaws or inconsistencies. For Sontag does not scruple from offering countervailing interpretations of her own: the phrase "Beckett's delicate dramas of the withdrawn consciousness" turns as a formulation on the barely suppressed exegetical ablative, in the same way as *Streetcar* "being a play *about* a handsome brute ... and a faded mangy belle" does not evade the dreaded interpretive act (italics mine).

Part C (6–7) develops the logical corollary of the preceding, the doctrine of "sensuous immediacy." It continues with the derogation of the modern insistence on meaning and by the consequent promotion of the experience of "pure, untranslatable, sensuous immediacy" as an alternative to interpretation. This explains the change of focus in the essay from literature, via theatre, to the cinema – Cocteau, Resnais, Bergman. This section ends with a charged denunciation of interpretation as turning art into "a mental scheme of categories" or a constellation of "items of content." What matters, apparently, in *Last Year at Marienbad* is not what the film means or signifies, but (1) its sensorial impact and (2) the solutions it proposes "to certain problems of cinematic form." But the term "interpretation" is now growing murky and problematic; what Sontag seems to be decrying is didacticism or pedantry, an intellectual bias that is subliminally equated to the fallacy of interpretation.

Section 7, the longest and densest of the ten, is evidentially crucial to Sontag's argument. It begins by commenting favourably on "the flight from interpretation" exhibited by the most advanced forms of modern artistic endeavour, with condign and predictable reference to non-representational art (or what amounts to the same thing from the reverse perspective, Pop Art) and French symboliste poetry – the advent, I would gather, of redemptive silence in a climate of semantic garrulity.

The confident assertion that follows, that the shift in contemporary taste away from Eliot and towards Pound represents a "turning away from content," is, in the troubled and doctrinaire light of the Cantos, highly dubious if not a trifle pixilated. Sontag then pauses for the space of a paragraph to deliver a swift verbal kick at American fiction for its technical unadventurousness, its lack of an avant-garde, and its tendency to interpretive borborygm.

At this point she arrives at the heart of her constatation, a vigorous plea for the sensuous and immediate, non-interpretable self-sufficiency of art, of which (once again, predictably) the film serves as the cardinal paradigm and exemplar. Thus ensues what was implicit from the very beginning of this highly intellectualized anti-intellectual project, *the apotheosis of the cinema*. The avant-garde film is praised for two reasons, the beauty of its visual imagery and its complex "vocabulary of forms." That is, it appeals both to the senses (and so is non-interpretable) and by implication to "people with minds," who, as it turns out, cannot remain satisfied with sensuous immediacy alone but will eventually need something to go on discussing and analysing. However, it should be evident, I think, that one does not discuss "forms" in a hermeneutic vacuum: forms are related inevitably to intentions – why this particular camera movement, cut, or frame composition and not another? what is the director getting at? – and hence are located squarely in the field of interpretation.

Moreover, the argument now starts to generate a certain uneasiness – in this reader at least. If the film or any other art form is committed to the presentation of sensuously immediate images, sounds, or textures, what ultimately is the point? For such immediacy, *the world suffices*, and art becomes entirely supererogatory. The critique that Sontag is pressing is destructive not only of interpretation but in the last analysis of art as well. I shall return to this issue shortly.

Section 8 (part D) stands by itself. It offers a prescription for an acceptable contemporary criticism, which includes "more attention to form" as the sordine of interpretation[3] (i.e., formal criticism), and, as a modification of this, an "accurate, sharp, loving description of the appearance of a work of art" (i.e., descriptive criticism). This is fine so far as it goes, but presumably any sensitive and intelligent reader, viewer, or listener can do the same thing for himself or herself. Interpretation is quite a different thing. Even at its worst, in its pedagogical or allegorical mode, it involves the presentation of ideas that may not have occurred to one and that – rejected, accepted, or modified – enrich the experience of a work of art. At its best, as it seems to me, its function is anamorphoscopic, disclosing views and perspectives previously unguessed at and lobbying, so to speak, for their integration.

The final instalment E comprises sections 9 and 10, a discussion of the central problem to the solution of which contemporary art presumably addresses itself. Times have changed, and what went down in the past now clogs our aesthetic system. At one time, e.g., for Dante, "it must have been a revolutionary and creative move to design works of art so that they might be experienced on several levels. Now it is not." The mention of Dante here involves the author in a latent and partial contradiction with section 4, in which the late classical and medieval (and no doubt, renaissance) mode of interpretation is airily dismissed as allegorical – level 2 of Dante's polysemous hermeneutic. The implication is that it is the *polysemous* interpreter who is guilty of attempting to conserve a text by altering it, the allegorical project being no more intrusive than the moral or the anagogic. (Sontag obviously preserves the literal level of reading). Polysemous criticism is thus at the same time censured as the rape of the text and acclaimed as revolutionary in its time.

It is interesting to note that Dante's fourfold distinction, developed in his famous letter to Can Grande – to which Sontag accords only perfunctory notice as it works against the grain of her sansculottic argument – goes back at least to St Augustine. In the *De Genesi ad litteram* Augustine recommends that books should be read "*quae ibi aeterna intimentur, quae facta narrentur, quae futura praenuntientur, quae agenda praecipiantur vel moneantur* (as if they intimate eternal things, as if they narrate facts, as if they presage future things, as if they guide or warn us)." The critical quadratic proposed by Augustine might then be designated as the anagogic, the literal, the prophetic, and the moral. Dante's four levels of the literal, the allegorical, the moral, and the anagogic are almost identical. Although this peculiar set of terms may no longer apply in all points to the contemporary experience of reading, its antiquity and its resilience testify to the congenial hunger of the human mind for complexity, richness, and meaning.[4]

This fourfold polysemy is sufficiently venerable to be considered with respect and not to be dismissed as a medieval or renaissance importation whose validity is a function of a transitory critical procedure, or as the nostalgic dream of the *laudator temporis acti*. And when we reflect that such pre-eminently modern works as *Ulysses* and *Finnegans Wake* positively demand the polysemous approach – in fact, cannot be understood without the reader bringing a kind of fly's-eye, multifaceted hermeneutic to bear upon their complex structure – it should become reasonably clear that the argument against interpretation amounts to little more than a rhetorical gesture, an expression of the intellectual fear of the intellect that informs or misinforms Sontag's essay as it does a considerable portion of the modern temper.

At any rate, as an antidote to such allegorical practice (in Sontag's terms) she introduces the category of "transparence" or "luminousness," the experience of "the thing in itself."[5] The thesis on which her category of luminousness is founded is that of the material excess and sensory bombardment from which the modern world demonstrably suffers, the effect of which is the degeneration of sensory responsiveness. The problem is "to recover our senses," and the function of art is now understood as therapeutic, restorative, sanatorial. Interpretation is *non grata*; the critic, I gather, must repaint the painting so we can see it, indicate the formal relations and the surface beauties of a work of art so we can experience or assimilate it. Meaning just clutters. Given this current state of affairs, as she intimates, interpretation becomes sublimely futile, the wrong cure for the wrong infirmity, or an attempt to do more, or other, than the situation either requires or allows – as if Sontag regarded both old- and new-style critics as the belletristic counterparts of the paddle bearers in Japanese subways, stuffing in a clamouring, left-behind significance.[6] But it should be plain that descriptive criticism is not the answer, and will not restore the bleary eye and shell-shocked ear of modern civilization to their original state of supple, pristine responsiveness. Only cultural and environmental modification can do that: less noise, fewer billboards, cleaner air.

I can't say with any degree of confidence or authority what the function of art may be. To represent the world mimetically and thus celebrate or clarify it? To add to the world, varying, complicating, enhancing it? To create, as Sidney suggested in the Defence, a poetic heterocosm as an imaginative substitute for the intolerable imperfection of things as they are? To purge away confusion and reveal the essential nature of our transactions with the world? To slow life down in order to help God observe and remember?

But I suspect that so long as art (whatever it may be or do) continues to exist, some form of interpretation will prove inescapable. Interpretation is a necessary act of the interrogative mind, and although the hermeneutic project frequently degenerates into some sort of scholasticism, the alternative seems equally unappetizing, namely, the programmatic carnality of that splendid paradox, the sophisticated wolf-boy (or wolf-girl), a cross between Mowgli and Mozart. I am tempted to define this problem or complex as the *tathagata*[7] syndrome, which is apparently proliferating in the intellectual world today. Once the artist or critic shows *that* the world is and *how* the world is, then what? The work of art merely shuffles up and takes its place as *one more item in nature* – which is what Sontag means by transparence.[8] This is nothing less than to render art finally unnecessary, *de trop*, an embarrassment, since nature itself provides us with more luminousness, more transparence, than we know what to do with. The market in thatness or thisness, *quidditas* or *haecceitas*, is already supersaturated, as we will find once we have learned to respond erotically, immediately. At this point the essay paradoxically undermines itself.[9] For the insistence on sensuous immediacy and aesthetic reprographics abolishes not only interpretation: it does away with art as well. Art has been assimilated by nature, and interpretation ceases to exist, not because it is harmful or supererogatory but because *there is nothing left to interpret.* One responds to a painting or a poem in exactly the same way as one responds to a tree, in belated fulfilment of Joyce Kilmer's arboreal imperative.

I would argue that although art (and criticism) may contribute to the education of the senses,[10] its program must surely be wider and more inclusive than this, since the human sensibility is by no means co-terminous with the operation of the senses. Moreover, the controlled intake of certain psychotropic substances can produce exactly the effect which Sontag recommends as the primary purpose of art. So can meditation, eurythmics, relaxation techniques, tasteful pornography, jacuzzis, and moving to the country. If the most that we can say for art is that it is a superior form of self-help or a watered-down version of catharsis, the aesthetic analogue of stress management, or a kind of sensory analeptic, we have, I fear, severely damaged our credibility as writers and critics. And, as readers of Sontag's essay, we discover, like Dryden, that we have been cozened with a jelly.

The work of art is neither a sensory emetic nor merely one more item in nature's vast emporium – something that we value exclusively for its sensuous appeal or as an object of silent, restorative contemplation. There is no art without connectedness, a reaching out to the larger world of ideas, facts, events, myths, archetypes – and of course (as Eliot stressed) other works of art. Nor can there be anything resembling a critical discipline without the hermeneutic lust for that eclectic and voluptuous world that art at once creates, transcends, denies, and adores.

Culling and Dereading, or the Pursuit of Absence

> But sodeinly bigonne revel newe
> Til that the brighte sonne lost his hewe;
> For th'orisonte hath reft the sonne his light –
> This is as muche to seye as it was night.
>
> Chaucer, "The Franklin's Tale"

> Analysis of an idea, as it used to be carried out, did in fact consist in nothing else than doing away with its character of familiarity.
>
> Hegel, *The Phenomenology of Mind*

It seems that one can no longer survive in the academic world today unless one has mastered the trick of thinking and phrase-making characteristic of deconstruction. One must first acquire a glossary of key terms and produce them on demand, like a graduate student picking up Anglo-Saxon. Next one must develop a peculiar style of critical writing which is at the same time quirky and obscure, paranomasic and weighty, ostensibly *personal* and yet sufficiently *generalized* to be recognizable as a part of a global phenomenon – a style that, like Horace's Priscus, alternates between adultery in Rome and philosophy in Athens. The infallible "signature" of this writing is the laboured pun (citing/reciting; sense/absence; scene/seen) embedded in a quasi-metaphysical diction. Finally, the postulant must learn to think in paradox and to grasp the elusive, amphibolic logic of literature, namely, that what is is never what it is unless it is what it is not at the moment that it both is and isn't.[1] Thus one becomes capable of handling literary works as if they consisted, in Umberto Eco's phrase, of a "microscopy of indiscernibles." When these three necessary and preliminary operations have been accomplished, the scholar has entered into the curia of deconstruction.

Critical writing in Canada is no exception to this rule. Our journals and reviews bear abundant witness to the spread of deconstruction in an orgy of derivativeness that poses no threat to tenure-track scholasticism, or to what Harry Levin in another context called "the high standard of competent mediocrity." In order to confer that aura of authority on our productions, that illusion of grace, that impression of intellectuality which cannot be countered or questioned, we proceed to wear our writing like uniforms behind which the humble and fallible individual gratefully disappears. The most obscure reviewer writing in *brevier* in the back pages of a magazine with no circulation gravely informs his audience (or lack of it) that a given poem connects its meaning with its absence by formulating a condition of impossibility as its eternally receding source. This is why, presumably, the poem begins with an ellipsis and ends with an aposiopesis. The reader, if there is one, may be forgiven for allowing the article to recede, quietly and inaccessibly, along with its occasion.

What happens when we turn to the more reputable journals? Will we discover writing that does not disguise the plain truth of significant absence with the elaborate fiction of cerebral presence? I take as my litmus test an issue of *The Malahat Review* (no. 83, just arrived in the morning mail), featuring the poetry of Paulette Jiles, Diana Hartog, and Sharon Thesen and including an extensive *apparatus criticus*. Perhaps the cynosure of the essays accompanying the selections of verse is Stephen Scobie's "The Barren Reach of Modern Desire: Intertextuality in Sharon Thesen's 'The Beginning of the Long Dash,'" with its titular implication of mysteries probed and fathomed, of a grand theme magisterially explicated. Having read the piece several times, I regret to say that the answer to my leading question is a non-enthymemic no.

For Professor Scobie's article, ostensibly a critical eulogy of Sharon Thesen's poetry, is really, like much deconstructive writing, a monument to its own questionable existence. There is nothing unexpected here, like the sermon dropping out of Uncle Toby's book on fortifications, to redeem the bristling and predictable nature of a performance that calls attention primarily to itself. The mandatory slashes are there, the incessant puns, the strained effect of bench-pressing rhetoric, and most of the appropriate words, of which "desire" is suitably prominent. In fact, the article orbits around that central, post-Hegelian term, which, since Rene Girard's *Deceit, Desire and the Novel*, has become of francoplanetary importance. Girard's critique was reasonably original and certainly interesting (a close literary analysis of the triangular structure of desire), which is more than one can say for the plethora of minor, derivative studies that have followed in its path.[2] "Desire" as an explanatory term is now of limited value, not only because it is parasitic but because, in its current application, it means what everybody knows it means: *the act of wanting something that is lacking and wanting it badly*. I assume nobody needs Professor Scobie to tell them that "desire operates in terms of lack: gap, void, pause, silence, distance." It is embarrassing to read an analysis of desire as a literary catalyst (or as paradoxically embodied in the *locus* of its own performance) which informs us that "void and margin interact as the site in which the moment of desire takes place." (How much better AE's "Desire is hidden identity.") One has not learned anything of which the buccinator muscle was not fully aware prior to its first contraction.

Moreover, the sort of writing exemplified here is vitiated by the wholesale importation of a jargon and an ideology which it has not offered to change, re-interpret, or "supplement." We find a language taken over shamelessly from the semiologists and the deconstructionists without even the decency of deception – a language studded with terms like "signifier," "trace," "intertextuality," "absence," "inscription," "marginality," "deferral," and the whole familiar rest of it. Thus in Scobie's essay we discover "the complex intertext of Canadian nationality" and learn about "poems that follow, across the intermediate intertexts (frames, parerga) of the book's epigraphs." We are solemnly told that "the moment of 'beginning' is not an absolute one; inscribed in the differential trace of language" (*pace* de Saussure short dash Derrida). We are further edified by phrases like "the ubiquity of intertextual deferral [which] speaks to the continual *inscription* of desire." After the inscription in question has been obligingly "doubled," we stumble across the inevitable "metonymic chain of desire," like those we find stretched between parking-lot bollards. (Why did it take so long in appearing? "Metonymy" is another one of those invariable paleonymics.) Scobie has obviously read not only his Sharon Thesen but his Saussure, his Barthes, his Derrida, his de Man. He has certainly read his Jonathan Culler and his Christopher Norris, which leads me to suspect that all this pseudo-deconstructing or deconstructive reconstructing is merely a form of tirelessly culling from other people's writings on other people's writings on other people writing. Now Barthes is a glorious author, engaging, witty, endlessly insightful; and Derrida is an "original," an Abulafian mystic, whose critical perceptions are based on profound scholarship and theo-philosophical genius. Culler and Norris, for their part, are lucid and brilliant exegetes. But the academic writing that inundates our literary journals in great gouts of terminological viscosity is deadly in its sameness, quantity, murkiness, and intense self-consciousness. As Henry Staten argues in his study of Wittgenstein and Derrida, the pure deconstructive styles of these masters "are so original and powerful that it is easy for those who are drawn to deconstruction to come under their influence and ape their favorite terms and linguistic mannerisms ... But there is nothing so inimical to the basic impulse of deconstruction as the adoption of a canonical style." This "mesmerizing style" will operate "like a Medusa's head [and] turn us to stone," which explains the cohort of over-serious, stony-faced hacks populating our campuses like Easter Island statues. One pleads for the renormalization of critical prose.[3]

What seems to be occurring in critical writing in our country is a displaced version of Benda's *trahison des clercs*. In order to cut it intellectually in today's literary world (now that Frye is bell-bottoming out), we have taken in a big way to the *haute couture* of current critical fashion. This is, of course, almost entirely French[4] (not entirely, since Bakhtin and Gadamer are also chic). Our language, our perceptions, our distinctions, our *ideas* are, let's face it, not ours at all. We talk about "aporetic logic." We are enamoured of absence, misunderstanding, presence, phonocentricity, openness, subversion. We cannot crack a book, let alone write about it, without plunging happily into parergonality, infectious signifiers, the disarticulation of monadic totalities (*pace* de Man), and binary reversals. Merely browse through this harmless edition of the *Malahat*. Clint Burnham praises Susan Glickman (one of our finest, by the way) because "by writing 'subway' [she] deconstructs her romance, its own conditions for being (by including the excluded)" and ends by noting the "*ecriture* possible when the line break is absent." Dennis Cooley appreciates that quality of Paulette Jiles's poetry that "entirely foregoes the attractions of lyric and tilts us through a dizzying series of deictics, markers which normally would locate us in time and place, but which here have become unhooked and spin us therefore into disorientation." (For the model on which this modish kind of writing relies, look up Derrida's article on James Joyce in *Post-Structuralist Joyce*.) Smaro Kamboureli in her commentary on Diana Hartog writes about how a certain word "becomes present by the absence of its own voice" and how a certain lyrical gesture "extends the lyric's formal and structural brevity to include the absence as well as the presence that precedes the verbal enunciation of the lyric poem." Thus, "the reader's traditional expectation of the subjectivity in the lyric is subverted by the poem's intersubjectivity." When she proceeds to comment on "the heterogeneous nature of Hartog's intertextuality," one is permitted to wonder what degree of enlightenment is offered the reader here. Degree subzero, I'm afraid, even in context. For, in effect, nothing at all has been said that could not have been stated in non-criticalese: *a poem echoes.*[5] Brian Edwards (a non-Canadian) entitles his article on Hartog "*Dis-Closures*" – how farouche, as his mentors would say – and goes on to tell us about the "writing's defamiliarizations," about how "oppositions infiltrate one another [so that] they are unstable markers," about that lexical marvel called an "intertextual opus," about "the combination of image and fragmentation that invites attention to gaps between stanzas." That abysmal "gap" again into which our gadarene critics persist in falling. And that trendy "fragmentation" – where have we heard it before? Could it be in de Man who deposes that "deconstruction ... reveal[s] the existence of hidden ... fragmentations"?

In this species of critical writing the underlying objectives are by no means discernible. The bewilderment that an uninitiated reader must experience is not rooted in the personal or idiosyncratic style of the truly individual thinker with whom one feels it essential and rewarding to come to terms. Quite the contrary. What one is dealing with here is a *collective* phenomenon, a stylistic code that can be learned, deployed, and parsed according to a set of complicated instructions. The eccentricity is merely apparent. This "deconstructive style" is in most of its practitioners a superb deterrent to understanding, and one conjectures that its chief function is not to reveal unsuspected truths or esoteric relationships in literary works but to point up the constitutively sibylline nature of the literary enterprise. Those who are involved in it, either as oracles or interpreters, comprise a society of adepts, a cultivated minority distinguished by its unique possession of the appropriate ciphers and symbols and by the presumption of an intelligence to which the merely curious or appreciative cannot hope to aspire.

There is no doubt that critics and scholars have to be pretty smart to generate articles in this mode, even if they work partly by blueprint – but that is exactly the trouble. The essays to which they apply themselves with such busy cortical dexterity turn out to be mainly *parva monumenta*, little attempted masterpieces for which the primary text is seldom more than a pretext. There is thus a sense in which deconstructive writing outsmarts itself, devoured from within by its own vermicular logic. As we know, its definitive method prescribes the reversal of the traditional relation between the central and the marginal, the primary and the secondary, the normal and the deviant, the nominal and the adjectival. But deconstruction stands condemned by its own necessary procedure, since the working out of its implicit logic leads inexorably to terminal self-deconstruction.[6] In treating the text as the pretext for the sake of its own bravura performance, it has also reversed the traditional relation between literature and criticism. Literature as a whole has now become the universal supplement, the accessory and provisional form of lettered writing, while criticism establishes its unassailable hegemony as that for the benefit of which literature has come into being in the first place. Eventually literature must diminish in value and stature and perhaps even cease to exist in any meaningful way as criticism flourishes dialectically at its expense. So literature finds itself reduced to the status of an elaborate puzzle or game, marked by the same basic dispensability, the same accidence and gratuitousness, that has troubled the critical program from its beginnings.

This reversal has already been candidly admitted and endorsed as a benign function of criticism *in general*. When we read an important poet, for example, it is not the poet *sui generis* whom we engage but the *construct* of a particular influential critic or school of critics. Wordsworth today is largely Geoffrey Hartman's "Wordsworth," if by that name "we understand an array of concerns, formal properties, influences, and so on." It follows that "the work to be done" on any significant writer "is not what the [critical] institution responds to but what it *creates*."[7] There is a sense, then, in which the literary work does not precede exegesis and interpretation but necessarily tails it.

This relation is in effect a psychological truism: we see in part what we have been taught to see. But deconstruction tends to exacerbate the tension between literature and criticism by tampering with the *gestalt*, fixing the figure-ground flipover in such a way that the relation between the constituents is permanently reversed. It is no longer a question of creating what we recognize but of both repressing the potential value of a literary work as it addresses the central concerns and experience of the reader *and* "subverting" its formal and ontological priority, thus turning it into a pretext for the exercise of a set of critico-philosophical procedures which become their own *raison d'être*. What we are witnessing is a kind of revanchist takeover in the literary field.[8]

The logical outcome of this chronic reversal is a criticism that must boomerang back upon itself if it wishes to persist, a condition that is gradually coming to pass as more and more critical essays and articles and books devote themselves to other critical works. Deconstruction, thriving on the arbitrary, paradoxical, and inconclusive, proceeds to deconstruct itself in a way and to an extent never envisioned as part of its original project, since the self-destructive quality of deconstruction is not a reflection of the fey or problematical cast of mind on which it prides itself. It is rather an integral and involuntary function of its essential nature. Ultimately it will attain to the condition of the Swiftian spider that spins its complicated web out of its own churning entrails, giving no sweetness and no light.9

In any case, while the deconstructive habit still addresses itself to high literature, its practitioners, in order to justify their effort, must imply that their chosen authors are (unconsciously, potentially, or actually) as clever, deft, mischievous, subtle, and ratiocinative as they are themselves – otherwise why bother? But such charity is tainted. Its purpose for the most part is neither to honour the writer they engage nor the reader they subdue but to guarantee the critical project, to establish credit. The real victim is literature itself, willy-nilly transformed into a sort of intertextual Rubik's cube which only the virtuoso can satisfactorily manipulate.

The problem is further vexed in countries where colonial insecurity in its second stage tends to undermine the belief in "local" intellectual resources. The first phase of such insecurity consists of a strident and insular self-infatuation bringing with it a host of evident dangers including the loss of a sense of reality. In the second, the centripetal focus is replaced by a programmatic cosmopolitanism equivalent to the fury of the newly converted, a passionate embracing of styles, techniques, fashions, attitudes, and ideologies that appear authoritative precisely because they are not domestic and thus not contaminated by self-distrust. In the intellectual domain the result is a kind of levitical attempt to out-mentor the instructors, to adopt a pose, method, and tone, a stylistic enunciation, that not only resembles the tenor of the master but tries valiantly to perfect it. But as it happens, the striving for perfection generally exhausts itself in repetition since the genuine resources that exist are neither tapped nor encouraged. The same goes, of course, for an *authentic* eclecticism based on the confidence of personal vision and the courage to develop a truly expressive and incunabular language: it, too, is easily squandered.

As a result, we tend to rely on the rare and yet necessary eruption of genius, the sudden and continuing presence of the star performance. This is because Canadian criticism has no endogenous tradition of critical inquiry, no recognizable community agreeing on fundamental principles of analysis and argument. There are competing schools and regionalisms of critical endeavour, of course, but these do not seem to function within a larger consensus regarding the nature of subject, the norms of inquiry, and the premises of the discipline itself. We fall back on one or two great names, a Northrop Frye or a Marshall McLuhan, whose influence is chiefly sectarian. It should be no surprise, then, to find that what often passes for criticism in this country is really an exalted form of controversy in which legions of Canlit graduates take up their "positions" in the universities under the banner of one or another revered mentor.

The alternative to the persistent camp-following that subs for autonomous inquiry seems to be a sort of branch-plant submission to the foreign multinational, Structuralism Inc. or Deconstruction Fiduciare – once again under the auspices of the great name. In either case the consequence is not genuine criticism but apostolic repetition. In the second case, the repetition is of a mainly *verbal* nature, the blatant subsumption of a shiny new lexicon which disguises the damning absence of original ideas. Criticism is reduced to a species of lexical gadgetry that when deployed produces a triple victim: the designated text which is neither invented nor discovered but assumes an ancillary status whose function is secretly understood as merely provocational; the local variant of the critical enterprise whose existence is parasitic on both literature *and the dominant form* of the critical enterprise (itself parasitic on its literary host) – thus the *deuteros* gradually replaces the *protos* in a kind of saturnalian reversal of established priorities; and thirdly, the very language itself which is used not to communicate, enact, or evoke but in large part to obscure. So the deconstructive style in its widespread adoption is the contemporary avatar of epideictic or demonstrative rhetoric which is meant to procure assent by suppressing content, *producing* content, or, as the case may be, by elaborating the self-evident if the latter is deemed to be unpersuasive on its own merits. It is hard to imagine anything more futile and self-defeating, more *insecure*, than these blazing yet empty graphotechnics.

The deconstructive style as it is practised by too many of our reviewers, critics, and writers is a reflection of this insecurity and bad faith. It is like the proverbial poor trade in baseball in which a promising player in the farm system is exchanged for the big name who survives mainly on his reputation. I am not saying that deconstruction *in itself* is a snare and a delusion (that is, had it not been exalted and legitimized into a movement torn apart by its internal contradictions but remained in the speculative territory of a handful of original thinkers). I *am* suggesting – to change the metaphor – that those who blithely and unreflectingly repeat its congenial rhetoric begin to resemble the members of the *Neminiana secta*, founded by the thirteenth-century Frenchman Radulfus who, having the idea that the Latin word for no one, *nemo*, was the name of an actual person, came to the conclusion that Nemo was the son of God and established a sect of worshippers. In the interests of fairness, let it be said that two or three of the thinkers now associated with "structuralism" and "deconstruction" are admirable and provocative, non-Radulfian writers. Many of these glitterati, however, are perilously close to Radulfian status. They owe their celebrity to their challenging obscurity (ask yourself this question: do you *honestly* understand Lacan?)[10] and to their deployment of a bizarre and attractive critical idiom whose chief property is that it renders the self-evident formidably abstruse. Their appeal is largely to the sense of election. Some of their American disciples, like de Man, Hartman, and Hillis Miller, can be lively and interesting, though verging on the sectarian.[11] But surely we do not ennoble the literature and thought of this country by becoming professional cullers and dereaders, the Trekkies of the literary and academic communities, neminianic imitators of the admittedly fascinating but, in a sense, entirely *singular* "philosophical" critics of other nations. So we continue to ape the manners of the foreigner. We use his terminology, ply his discriminations, dress up our critical and literary prose in the fancy rhetorical vestments of the new aristocratic *salon*, and as a result grow even more resolutely provincial than we were before. What exemption can we plead? There is not even the mitigating circumstance of altering or transforming what we have so blatantly assimilated. Who, finally, are we really trying to impress?[12] The presbyters of deconstruction would probably be offended or amused, or perhaps gratified, and the "common reader" only mystified, irritated, or bored – and not because he or she is patiently viewing bliss from the Barthean shore of pleasure. Critical writing and thinking in this country can only benefit from the non-aporetic absence of deconstructive analysis and the surprising presence of a genuine vernacular, a lucid unpretentiousness accented by a touch of humour, a kind of sartorial modesty and practicality (in which a certain dash and verve may also find an appropriate place[13]). For the emperor's new clothes were made in France, and nakedness is fatal in the Canadian winter.

The Autoerotic Text

Reflections on Barbara Johnson's "The Frame of Reference: Poe, Lacan, Derrida."

> I had seen her – not as the living and breathing Berenice, but as the Berenice of a dream; not as a being of the earth, earthy, but as the abstraction of such a being; not as a thing to admire, but to analyze; not as an object of love, but as the theme of the most abstruse although desultory speculation.
>
> Poe, "Berenice"

> It's a case of Aaron's rod as the incredible shrinking dildo.
>
> Camille Paglia, *Sex, Art, and American Culture*

INTRODUCTORY NOTE

As I do not wish to multiply quotations unduly, I would refer the interested reader to the article in question (or, indeed, if the reader is unfamiliar with the genre, to just about *any* "deconstructive" text). Presumably, like me, he or she will start looking for hidden clues, gypsy patrins, a few leaves arranged deictically at the ends of sentences, to help us find our bearings.

Or to switch metaphors: the common reader (assuming he or she has not been professionalized out of existence) is like the prince in *Sleeping Beauty*, trying to kiss the text awake. But one can no longer penetrate the wall of thorns that bristles around the enchanted castle in which the text continues to slumber. The wicked fairies of deconstruction, who were not invited to the feast of life, have seen to that.

The standard justification for such turbid and repellant language is that, as Catherine Belsey argues in *Critical Practice*, "New concepts, new theories, necessitate new, unfamiliar and therefore initially difficult discourses." Such discourses must struggle to reveal and purge the ideological contamination inherent in lucid, discursive writing, the bourgeois myth of verbal transparency, of prior meanings shining through the clear pane of discourse – which naturally requires the new theoretician to be as provocatively opaque as possible. The occasional clarity to be found in the expository texts, of which Belsey's is a good example, is airily confessed as "contradictory" and left at that, as if confession guaranteed absolution in criticism no less than in religion. Further, the somewhat befuddled reader is surely entitled to ask from what perspective or vantage point the critique of ideological discourse is being launched, if not from that of another ideology equally "given," preconstituted, unconscious, and thus thoroughly polluted with a set of prior, unreflected assumptions? The "b" is still in "subtle" for all its subtlety.

One longs, finally, for a species of critical writing that resembles the communicative style of Jane Austen's Catherine Morland, who "cannot speak well enough to be unintelligible."

My Lord, my Lord, the French have gather'd head.

I Henry, 6.4

Having just finished Barbara Johnson's analysis of Jacques Derrida's intervention in Jacques Lacan's Seminar on Edgar Allen Poe's "The Purloined Letter," I feel compelled to mutter an objection to the entire, endlessly deferred, self-infatuated head game these coy literary specialists are so indefatigably playing. For that is basically what these avatars of cerebrality, these masters and mistresses of psychocritical writing, are doing: *imagining the act of transitivity*, shamelessly practising the textual BJ, disseminating meanings without conceptual fruition, multiplying paradox upon paradox, the ultimate effect of which is one of mutual cancellation or dispersion. What is taking place here is a style of critical writing and thinking resembling the sterile manipulations of a pure, encysted, libidinal hedonism, the cupidity of the self in its quest for absolute self-possession. This is ironically all the more so in proportion as it affects to "decentre" or "problematize" the subject, to undo the logocentric habit or bracket the autonomy of the besieged, deprivileged self. And it averts the peril of solipsism only insofar as it seeks to communicate by specular repetition, reproducing the gestures, manner, and rhetorical strategies it has seen enacted by other solo practitioners of the art. I am doing what you are doing, it says, but we are not doing it together; we are merely repeating one another's moves and gestures – a phenomenon that Murray Schwartz in his essay "Critic, Define Thyself" describes as "a domino theory without gravity: everyone leans on everyone else, but nobody falls!" (One thinks also of Charlie Chaplin with his trayful of glasses, rushing forward to keep himself from falling.)

My *initial* objection is not to the convoluted nonsense perpetrated by Lacan[1] or to the cryptic, sterile, and profoundly expendable exegeses[2] that call the genius of Derrida into question, but to the torpid and disingenuous writing of Barbara Johnson,[3] an American sufferer *par excellence* of the "new" French disease. Compare, for example, the lucid essays of Richard Wilbur on Poe's mystery stories in *Responses* – clear, sensible, modest writing – with Johnson's characteristic obfuscation of the same subject. Wilbur writes: "There is a decided [note: not "undecidable"] duplicity, then, in Poe's presentation of Dupin; he is in one aspect a master detective who, as A.H. Quinn was persuaded, 'proceeds not by guessing but by analysis,' and in another aspect he is a seer who infallibly knows ... Like Roderick Usher and the divided William Wilson, Dupin has two distinct speaking voices, one high [his "vaticinal treble"] and one low." Wilbur then proceeds to offer a crisp, intelligible explication of these stories' allegorical structure. Barbara Johnson, presumably disintricating the complex interplay between Freud, Lacan, and Derrida with glancing reference to Poe (all of which has something to do with the assumption that the purloined letter is the mother's missing phallus which is eventually returned),[4] writes: "when the observation of the mother's lack of a penis is joined with the father's threat of castration as the punishment for incest, the child passes from the alternative (thesis vs. antithesis; presence vs. absence of a penis) to the synthesis (the phallus as a sign of the fact that the child can only enter into the circuit of desire by assuming the fact that both the subject and the object of desire will always be substitutes for something that was never really present)."[5] Johnson then concludes in part that the whole process involves the incessant repetition of an act that never occurred. Where Wilbur is concerned with the essentially allegorical structure of Poe's vision ("Allegorically, the action of the story has been a soul's fathoming and ordering of itself"), Johnson is preoccupied with Lacan's notion of the letter as signifier and of *this* story as "a kind of allegory of the signifier," and so it goes until the reader is virtually shredded by all these signifiers and signifieds whirring through the air of commentary like Ninja throwing-stars.

There comes a point when one begins to lose confidence in the febrile ingeminations of this species of writing, its erotic declensions arrested always in the locatives of the flesh. We all start off castrated, it appears, but the missing phallus will eventually return to the mother by twinning or repetition in the scene, no doubt, of Castoration. The beat goes on in Marie Bonaparte, Luce Irigaray, Ellie Ragland-Sullivan (who appears to have coined the adjective "penian"), Jane Gallop (cf. her "Phallus/Penis: Same Difference"), and, of course, in the discursive jacqueries of the current Franco-American revolt against reason and lucidity and the decency of good writing.

One should not allow oneself to heed the seductive come-on of this psychocritical and deconstructive *debossage*. It is all conducted in an atmosphere of problematic brilliance, in a pleasure dome of infinitely reflecting mirrors in which the antinomies and paralogisms of an onanistic logic proliferate with indecent and endless abandon. The reader is often impressed and bedazzled by this impure play of the autoerotic intelligence but is rarely entertained or instructed. For ultimately it says nothing, gives nothing, leads nowhere, remains resolutely nonpuerperal, produces no discernible effects except those of pedagogical power based on the lonely, hypertrophic gratifications of an educated infantilism. It is perhaps time now to cancel this "felicific calculus," to give the much-manipulated phallus a long-overdue rest, to cease this febrile erection of delusory theories of the text, the reader, the literant, the author, the scriptor, of masculine metaphor and feminine metonymy, of the sender who receives and the receiver who sends, of the unsent message endlessly returning, of lack as difference and difference (or différance) as the non-substantial substitute, of transcendental signifiers and floating or drifting signifieds, of the immense Enclitic of contemporary criticism – and get down to thinking clearly and writing readably once again. It is perhaps time to enter into an honest, reciprocal, and *genetic* relation with the baffled reader who for some time now has been forced into the role of the unwilling voyeur of cerebral excess.[6]

D.H. Lawrence's notorious attack on Poe as a sort of intellectual vampire dedicated to knowing *rationally* what should be felt in the blood and experienced in the flesh would seem to be somewhat unfair to Poe but applies with uncanny precision to the contemporary school of critical diddlers for whom Poe is a prime elective affinity.[7] One can't help wondering in a Laurentian way about the sex lives of such presumably seminal thinkers (about Freud, the transcendental Sigmundifier, the record speaks for itself). It takes only "a little elementary psychoanalysis," as the education historian H.I. Marrou suggests, to reveal "the unsuspected repressions tucked away in the souls of our scholars." And, we might add, the naiveté as well. Had Lacan, for example, acquired authentic knowledge of human sexuality, how could he have located the phallus in the voice (and B. Johnson have written so earnestly about this new unequivocal signifier) without recognizing the implicit bad joke about deep-throating that leads to an inadvertent and embarrassing *mise en abyme* (just as the fact that Lacan's Freudian School was serendipitously located on the rue Claude Bernard, no. 69, goes unnoticed)? And how could they continue writing about Poe's poor abused story without at some point realizing that their texts are radically "problematized" by the force of a repressed and displaced sexuality – *per loins* that have not been sufficiently stimulated and caressed by the real presence of another? For Lacan, the phallus is that privileged signifier "where logos is joined together with the advent of desire." This definition is the fruit of a century of Laocoon-like psychoanalytic theorizing. Should we not finally acknowledge that the "phallus" is simply an *idea* which analysts, literary and psychological, have been excessively fondling into the maturity of their disciplines – an idea derived from the penis, a rather common physical appendage that people have been using for pleasure and reproduction since the first beginnings of hominid prehistory? (Yes, yes, we know all about the Lacanian distinction between the Phallus, which everybody lacks, and the penis, which everybody wants). Let us not be overly prudish or decorous about this matter. Such writing as dominates a considerable portion of the scholarly community today bespeaks a radical disorder of the psyche founded on sexual repression of truly staggering magnitude. Whether the origins of this dysfunction are political or social or educational, it is something other than neurotic repression libidinally deflected in the direction of the cultural enterprise. It is the orgy of the individual subject abetted and inflamed by the spectacle of the chosen other, the interlocutor, and who projects the image of solitary and complex involutions in order to be seen and to see in turn. Existence is authenticated not in the experience of mutuality but in the proof of influence, allowing the practitioner to continue unnatural textual practices with impunity while affirming his or her being at several removes, in effectual isolation. Masturbation continues unabated in a Gulliverian rejection of the world (cf. Swift's Master Bates, Gulliver's benefactor), delusional entities called ideas are indefinitely pursued, and new, refined, solitary, unreal pleasures discovered and indulged. But it all takes place in the imagination, the scene of this kind of writing, in which the pursuit of the desired object, itself in pursuit of *its* desired object, may continue unabated.

The spectacle of grown-up, intelligent people still playing theoretically with their widdlers, real or imagined – what Lacan calls the "transcendental signifier" and Derrida the "universal phallus," which is poked indiscriminately into all available "signifying lacunae" (Derrida) – gives one pause for wonder, to say the least. Regardless of how the polysemous and ever-protean dick is transformed and reinterpreted (or reappropriated), whether as Derrida's *calcul de la mère* (*Glas*) or Marie Bonaparte's Freudian thesis of the missing phallus of the mother (the women are irresistibly drawn to it as well, obviously), the reader is nevertheless confronted with a massive form of object-cathexis, a lifelong obsession with the *membrum virile* in all its permutations and combinations, that must ultimately discredit the ostensibly neutral or disinterested character of the analytic quest. What we are witnessing is something we might, a little frivolously, denominate the Isis complex, the perennial search for the lost or absent organ that would integrate and re-animate the body of the scholar's irretrievable, unfulfilled and still-desired past – a need whose satisfaction is displaced and projected onto the medium of the analytic text. At the level of the text, the art of masturbation can be endlessly indulged without guilt or shame, as the attempt to recover a dissipated mastery, a primal self-sufficiency, proceeds under the auspices of the dispassionate inquiry or the quasi-medical etiological study, like a child under the bed.

The text in such cases serves a double function: it is both an attempt to retrieve the past and the locus of a re-enactment of the past in the safe and unacknowledged form of an analytical pursuit. For the object of the psychocritical or psycholiterary quest is, as with the child fondling his or her genitalia, both pleasure and control (another kind of "pleasure of the text"), as well as the pleasure *of* control.[8] There are scholars as we have seen whose analytic discourse veers perilously close to the forbidden topic, replaying in *words* what it can no longer tolerate or simply enjoy in *deeds*, practising the critical form of telephone sex, as if to tempt recognition the better to disarm it under the fiction of scientific immunity.[9] And there are others, or the same writers at different times, whose prose appears detached and immaculate, decently zippered up, yet whose typical mode of inquiry and speculation involves the indefinite pursuit of circulating images, phantasmal centrifugalities, the flickering reflections of evanescent abstractions, that lead them into the deepest recesses of narcissistic reverie from which they emerge – if their prose serves as reliable testimony – in the swooning and perithanatic state of Lady Madeline Usher. In either case the aura of scryptographic prurience is embarrassingly plain. As Auden puts it in "Lullaby":

An abstract insight wakes
Among the glaciers and the rocks
The hermit's sensual ecstasy.

We are treating, apparently, a species of writing that mirrors the discontinuities, insularities, and self-aggrandizements of an age devoted to the quest for instant gratification. And such gratification is most readily attained by the projection and reabsorption of images.[10] One might consider the increasingly popular "mode" of the rock video as the laic analogue of the structural-deconstructive-psychocritical form of discourse. The rock video deals in "pure" intransitive sexuality, images of the contorted physical self endlessly multiplying in that favourite device of the medium, the mirror (the reflecting sun-visor, the polished sequin, the shuffled snapshot, the gleaming hubcap). The "deconstructive" article purveys the tainted goods of "pure" textuality, the product of the gyrating intellectual self, the reflection of reflection, penetrating ever more deeply into the nothingness of the ubiquitous gap (Johnson quotes Hartman's joke about the whodonut), teasing itself without remission into the furthest reaches and intricacies of rarefied self-abuse, yielding a new species of pleasure that even a des Esseintes would find outrageous. This is the return of Clifford Chatterley with a vengeance, the sterile ecstasy of the unsext, repairing stealthily to their libraries, turning absence into a nominal substantive, and publishing the results for the delectation of the carnally arrested.[11]

This is not a question of a radical supplementarity in its work of perfecting a supposedly original and natural plenitude of experience. The textual evidence or evidential textuality at our disposal suggests rather that such an original plenitude was never wholly entertained or assumed to begin with – *not because it is logically (or phenomenologically) impossible but because of an empirical or accidental deficiency in the body of developing experience itself.* Something is missing (oddly, *penia* is the Greek word for "lack"), not necessarily in the constitutive *structure* of experience but in the raw pragmatics of concrete sexual union and the emotional integrity of response. The famous gap or lack is really nothing more than a libidinal as well as a cognitive disorder: an insufficiency of *genetic* experience (insufficient either because of failed opportunities or distorted attitudes or both) and a subsequent repression of the awareness of displacement, of the operations of transposition. The autoerotic text bears witness to the narcissistic absorption of genuine affectivity, the containment of the vector of desire, within the intuited, shadowy "body" of the self.[12] Here we are presented with a clue as to the real nature of the purloined letter, the somatic text of which the psychocritical report is little more than an indefinitely extended and reappropriating, epistolaphagous postscript, the commentary that devours and replaces the argument.

> I'm gonna sit right down and write myself a letter
> And make believe it came from you.
>
> Fred Ahlert

The mechanical and contingent nature of such writing becomes glaringly evident when one compares the extended version of Johnson's essay, which appeared in *Yale French Studies* (1978) and was reprinted in *The Critical Difference* (1980) with the abridged version that concludes editor Hartman's *Psychoanalysis and the Question of the Text* (1978). Whole paragraphs are lopped off with casual disregard, often without the slightest attempt at constructing a semantic bridge between the segments newly joined or forced into unexpected contiguity (a caricature of metonymic sexuality). For example, the third paragraph of the original simply vanishes and the reader must leap from second to fourth, a feat that an athletic "literant" may perform without too much difficulty. But suddenly the abyss opens between paragraph 4 and paragraph 10 (the latter moderately revised), and the reader, if sufficiently lynx-eyed, can descry across a vast space equal to five deleted paragraphs a long (three-page) quotation of "Derrida's quotation of Lacan's paraphrase of Poe's quoted narrations" (original version).

One must do something like hitch a ride on Dante's Geryon to get over to the other side of the citation, where with considerable relief one finds *almost* two paragraphs intact. A slight effect of revision towards the end of the second then brings the giddy reader tottering to the brink of a canyon stretching across a space equivalent to twenty-five paragraphs (some very short, others extensive), including several more citations and a prolonged discussion of Lacanian numerology one (sic) would have thought central to the issue, since Johnson is treating the notion of Dupin's doubleness, Lacan's famous distinction between imaginary duality and symbolic duality, and the problem of how, if 1=2 (symbolic bifurcation), can 2=1+1 (imaginary doubling). These seismic disturbances continue to shake and devastate the text.

What has in effect happened is that whole sections of the essay, entire passages of Johnson's letter to the reader, have been ruthlessly purloined by none other than the author, our highly respected Professor Dupine herself, for the obvious purpose of fitting the piece into the space allotted in a collection of diverse critical writings. Or we might say it is the queen herself who has filched the letter and hidden it in its original place where no one who was not informed, who did not stoop to read the fine print in the footnotes, would think to look. Thus the queen's guilt is expiated by her manifest innocence: the purloined letter remains on the writing table, and the theft or disruption of the message has not occurred either because it has not been noticed or because larceny can always be mistaken for paraphrase. But the fact remains that, at the very least, a portion of the letter has been lifted, perhaps as many as a third of its pages, without the "receiver" necessarily experiencing its loss or a jarring disruption of meaning. This can only suggest that the entire letter is equally dispensable, equally inessential – a conclusion of which the queen herself must remain unaware by arranging to have the ministerial unconscious purloin the indelible script of recognition. For the letter which is stolen by the queen is also written by the queen – to herself.

Without getting too fancy about this little bit of intellectual criminality, one might reasonably suggest that the *real* purloined letter is the fundamental *literacy* of a "deconstructive" text that can be so readily dismembered or disremembered without its author presumably suspecting that its meaning may be impaired. Worse, if its meaning can be said to exist only in the play of endless dissemination, in a perpetual *metaludicity*, then there can be no essential meaning at all, no seminal lucidity, to be disrupted or clouded over in the first place. We are dealing with a fundamentally *illiterate text*, its illusion of grammaticality only serving to complicate and obscure the semantic void upon which it is predicated – its constitutive disconnectability, its epistolary autism. And autism reproduces the structure of illiteracy on the level of the message as it obliterates contact on the level of transitivity. It is precisely here that a baulked textuality meets a thwarted and arrested sexuality, in the *lack* of connection, the *absence* of reciprocity (to use those words), the failure of literacy.

If the reader, despite Lacan's hints, can never know the contents of the purloined letter, he or she may enjoy better luck with regard to Johnson's essay by returning to the longer original and re-inserting the missing passages into the expurgated version. But there is no escaping the irony of illiteracy or of mirrored self-encryptment. *The letter has never existed* or, what amounts to the same thing, has "always already" been purloined – but not in the Derridean sense of the differential trace and the perpetually receding source. It never existed not because it was never written by a unitary, self-present subject (a typical "deconstructive" argument) but quite simply because it was *never properly written* in the first place, in either of its quasi-independent forms. Letters are originally meant to communicate, to transfer meaning, to specify coordinates – which is the only reason they are capable of deceiving or mystifying in the first place. A genuine scholarly essay has at least this in common with a genuine literary work: it is intended to convey or evoke meaning, to produce effects, to touch instrumentally on the practice of life, to clarify perception and thought – otherwise it is not dissemination but pure dissimulation. A French letter is meant, on the contrary, to interrupt the flow and prevent conception. And onanism is merely that letter without the envelope. Literature and scholarship, in any authentic sense, have no *raison d'être* if they are not animated through and through by intentionality, if they do not offer to connect, meet, and fructify, if they are not founded on the discipline of literacy and the impulse toward reciprocal intimacy. But texts whose very existence is predicated exclusively on the rampant proliferation of metaphysical paradox are the analogue in the literary domain of an erotic narcissism practised by a group of super-intelligent children whose fascination with the penis and the clitoris argues nothing less than the textual displacement of infantile compulsions. What is at stake here is what goes on between the covers.

As Robert Scholes has conclusively demonstrated (in *Textual Power*, quoting to good effect from W.V.O. Quine's *Word and Object*), the concept of reference inevitably entails the "interaction between perception and a 'coordinate system' ... or a 'frame of reference.'" Signifieds are not arbitrary but are at least "partly grounded upon phenomena." Quine covered this territory somewhat earlier (in *From a Logical Point of View*), rigorously establishing "how identity and ostension are combined in conceptualizing extended objects," a procedure from which we may extrapolate to the conceptualizing of feelings and presuppositions – psychological objects – whose practical and behavioural effects argue for their validity. The writing table and the bed are interchangeable metaphors for the "frame of reference" uniting two orders of reality – words and things, the cry and the experience, lover and beloved, human being and world – and which rescues our textual productions from absolute circularity or ouroboric self-containment. The letters that are assembled into words, no less than the words that are assembled into letters, produce that relation of kinship, of affinity, of resemblance between differentials *without which the entire structure of assumptions actual life is predicated upon would collapse.* The letter is always to some extent a love letter.

Although the letter has been purloined, it has not been lost. Presence, union, and reciprocity may be possible, if only fleetingly and intermittently – in genuine orgasm, in the rare meeting of the eyes, in moments of illumination and understanding, in reading and writing at their best.[13] The proper use of the bed re-enacts in one dimension of experience the sincere attempt to clarify and communicate in another – *literally*, on the writing tablet, the *dipthera*, from which *littera* is itself most probably derived. It is precisely where this effort fails, where the letter in the loins is misconceived, and where the writing table is the transposed image, or the structural reproduction, of the solitary, misconstrued bed, that meaning is lost in the textual ejaculation, falling on barren ground. Finally, the writing table is assimilated to the sort of bed that curiously resembles Kafka's four-poster torture machine whose single occupant is written into a state of ecstatic though sterile enlightenment and ultimately, quite simply *written to death.*[14] For the letter that is constitutionally incapable of being sent, or what amounts to the same thing, is strategically misaddressed and returned to the sender, is in effect a *dead letter*, one that never arrives – the letter that killeth the spirit of communion which is the very condition of its existence.

On the Essay, or the Jubilation of the Lambda

An interrogative move is relative to a subtableau sj. It consists of a question addressed to nature. The presupposition of the question must occur in the left column of the subtableau. Nature must provide a full answer. Let this answer be Ai. Then Ai is added to the left column of sj.

Jaakko Hintikka, *The Sign of Three*,
ed. Umberto Eco and Thomas A. Sebeok

For though he cannot fly, he is an excellent clamberer.

Christopher Smart, *Jubilate Agno*

ARGUMENT

In his report on the postmodern condition, Jean-Francois Lyotard speculates that "the essay (Montaigne) is Postmodern" – a simple assertion which operates as a one-sentence insertion, a kind of phrasal shim, between two longer paragraphs. What he means is far from clear, unless he is suggesting that the essayist works without "pre-established rules" or "familiar categories," in the mode of the future anterior that presumably qualifies the postmodern sensibility. In a more general sense, what a literary object is, or is understood to have always been, is precisely that which comes in its own unprecedented way into eventual existence. At the same time, it can only *substitute* for that which it ostensibly represents, conferring existence by intimation. The writer in our time attempts "to invent allusions to the conceivable which cannot be presented," a formulation sufficiently radical to obscure its unobjectionable content. The completed work stands, as a digest or pandect of the laws that govern its own creation, in the splendour of sheer heteronomous existence. And the laws to which the essay in particular conforms, one would assume, are the laws of the productive self which, although imperceptible, remains nevertheless conceivable – and therefore consolatory. Similarly Edward Said in *The World, the Text and the Critic* privileges the essay form for a somewhat different yet related reason: short, investigative, sceptical, the essay is the organ of secular rather than hermetic thinking, its very unsystematic nature rendering it "the principal way in which to write criticism" in an age given over to the disenchantment of the stable pieties. And what Said says should perhaps be taken seriously, as the name of the form is inscribed phonetically in the first two letters of his surname (an aleatory enhancement of authority which may be the only permissible variety still to be found), and the source of its power indicated by the last two.

The essay form is generally assumed, of course, to have originated with Montaigne, who found his congenial antecedents in Seneca and Plutarch. But what he found there he refined and subliminated, purging the classical template of its, so to speak, objective features and turning it into a trial (or rather triage), an assaying, probing, weighing, appreciating, testing, and separating-out of the psychological fragments that comprise the knowing self. The essay, like the lyric, is an intensely subjective form, an investigation and expression of the self, but unlike the lyric it is not subsumed under the aspect of pure utterance or (hypothetical) spontaneity. It is, rather, a *deliberate* attempt to penetrate into the depths, to discover the epistemic substance of which the self consists: in short, *to find out what it is one really thinks and knows* and therefore who one is.

Thus Montaigne could write of his collection, in "Of Giving the Lie," that it constituted "a book consubstantial with its author, concerned with my own self, an integral part of my life," so that the essay, by a kind of mystical homoousios, presents to the father (or author), in an act of graphic recognition, the lineaments of the son who is none other than himself, knowing now what he always knew but didn't know he knew. The essay renders the subjective objective, externalizes the internal, or – more appropriately phrased in accordance with the thought patterns of a pre-analytic age – carnalizes the indiscernible in the catastrophic body of print: "I have painted my inward self with colours clearer than my original ones." The spirit which is made flesh so that it can recognize and know itself becomes in a peculiar equation isomorphic with the self that is made print for precisely the same reason. Spirit is to flesh as self is to print, in the sense that the localized self, in virtue of the act of writing as recovery or anamnesis, perceives, acknowledges, and confirms itself in the literary form of the essay. If literary creation occurs for the purpose of baptismal speculation, the reflection of the face that broods upon the face of the deep, hauling its bright, lenticular image out of the darkness into the light of conscious recognition, then the essay is the most effective of all the literary genres. And it is this infralapsarian retrieval, this desperate exantlation of identity, that leads to the jubilation of the lambda.

PERFORMANCE

For I will consider the critic Geoffrey, who in *Saving the Text* treads to all the measures upon the Derridean music and celebrates with the sonic and paronomastic resources of the alphabet Smart's hoary Hebrew *lamed*, the sign of the celestial. Of great importance to begin with is the central note or phoneme which Derrida condenses out of Hegel as *Sa*, or *Savoir absolu*, which is no longer playable or ployable or pre-hensible in our post-*Sa*ussurean epoch, the sigla of a totalizing consciousness foundering on unbridgeable differentials. *Sa*, Hartman deposes, has now become a tachygraphic abbreviation doing double or even triple duty, that is, doing the splits as sigla for *Savoir absolu* on the one hand and as an abbreviation for the infamous, eternally vanishing, metonymic *signifiant* on the other. To make matters worse, Saussure's text as a signifier collapses into the gulf that divides it forever from itself as a signified, yielding us the homophonic *ça* – whatever *it*, the text, may be – and two *Sa*'s. Hartman concludes: "Ça is too sassy."

No, sah! Sa essays far sassier sashays than Hartman says it does. The *Sa*. The *Savoir absolu*, forever unattainable but perpetually beckoning, to be vigorously pursued, as Wallace Stevens puts it in "The Plain Sense of Things," before we come "to an end of the imagination, / Inanimate as an inert savoir," modulating thence into the *Savoir agonist* which struggles mightily with all that is elusive, recessional, taunting – a *Savoir asymptot* inspired by the Horatian dictum (taken over by Kant) *Sapere aude*, and continuing to invite all manner of playful manipulations.

As for example: we take the S and draw a vertical line through it, which gives us Lacan's emblem of the subverted subject who does not know he is dead, compelling him to continue writing in order to stitch and patch that epistemological thrust into the vitals, to *create* knowledge in order to repress knowledge. Dare to know in order not to know. But we also have with this decisive stroke the representation of the dollar sign where, as James Merrill writes, "snake and Tree of Paradise entwine," the vertical pole of immortality subverted by the serpent promising knowledge and final apotheosis, tempting us to explore the heights, or the inverted depths, of the Creation, to achieve an eternal solvency – the other face of infinite bankruptcy.

But the "a" also clamours for attention, requiring its capitalization into equal significance, and as the A, reinforcing the Promethean imperative by embodying what Kandinsky called the "movement of the triangle" to which he compared the "life of the spirit."[1] The triangle rises slowly and invisibly: "What today can be understood only by the apex and to the rest of the triangle is an incomprehensible gibberish, forms tomorrow the true thought and feeling of the second segment" which lies below. The vertical slash through the S permutes into the horizontal bar across the A like the rail in an eternally ascending elevator which we grasp with affected nonchalance as we rise gradually, inexorably with it. The A, agonistic and asymptotic, iconic *lambda* (with horizontal bar) moving upward through the *grammata* of gnosis toward the distant, redemptive, and quasi-teleological alpha represented trans-alphabetically as A, is also the processional tapering toward a cognitive point of intersection which stops precisely there before the Λ becomes the Chi, X, the dissipation of self in the infinite. But the *lift itself* must continue to rise, gradually, to allow for the passing of time, the condition of knowledge. A sudden acceleration or a simple arrest may prove fatal to its occupants.

The essay. The S, eh? But what does the S – the first fragmentary signal received by Marconi – have to say, if not what the A strives to be, knowing what it is, that is, desires to be, by putative self-reflection, receiving at least a portion of the message it valiantly composes and sends? Yet it is precisely here that the heroic effort falters. This gradual climbing to the summit of the *montaigne*, this jubilation of the lambda, this driving up the hairpin road toward the high pneumatic lookout as *lamed*, sign of the celestial, twists into *sigma*, sign of the self, in a vision of digraphic unity or sameness, this laborious and exhilarating dream of the heights, this brave attempt to spackle the abyss may in the last analysis plummet clumsily and predictably into the spectacular rift between the letters like Gibreel Farishta and Saladin Chamcha quarreling over palingenesis: the creation of knowledge to suppress knowledge. The essay is the postmodern form *par excellence* because it is weightless, non-narrative, specular, Lego-centric, the reflex of the *Urverdrängung*, chimerical, self-important, but also mere lexical camouflage. Lyotard is right up to a point, dancing in his sequined tights as did Montaigne to enact a brilliant performance upon the void, the stage on which the unpresentable is presented. But the performance cannot console; it can only preoccupy or distract, as what it presents is nothing other than the unimaginable, the incommensurable, that which may not in fact exist. The essay is the form that invents that which cannot reliably be discovered, that brings into fugitive existence the virtual particle of the self before it walks the Planck back into the vacuum from which it emerged. The essay is the child of the vasectomy, the interval smaller than time, the progeny of the impotent serpent whose promise is as unfulfillable as it is necessary. In writing about others, we write about ourselves, but in writing about ourselves, we write always about the Other, which continues to resist the assayer's instruments and scales.

Thus, upwardly mobile in the realm of Spirit, the Λ remains on the conceptual go, leading toward the attempted divinizing of the self – the sign, as Bulwer-Lytton remarks in *The Coming Race*, of the Supreme Being "symbolized by what may be termed the hieroglyphic of a pyramid, Λ."[2] Or, closer to home, Einstein's notorious lambda factor or cosmological constant designed to stabilize the equation for a static universe. There is no contradiction here: a static or completed universe is precisely that toward which the A perpetually tends in its endless desire for (what Nietzsche called) *ipsissimosity*, very ownness, accomplished selfhood. (The same notion can be found in Hayden White's *Metahistory*, where we learn that a chronicle of events may be "transformed into a *completed* diachronic process, about which one can then ask questions as if he were dealing with a *synchronic structure* of relationships.") Thus the *lambda* and the *sigma*, the transposed A and the completed *lamed*, turn out to be identical, a perfect tautonym. The sigla enacts an identity that continues to recede and torment.

For, as Pierre Klossowski observes (in *Un si funeste desire*), the identity principle is a representational sham: the same is always the other posturing as the same. The "authentic" version of the textualized self is always the translation of an aprioristic desire to summon unity and completeness by the magical act of writing it down, by allowing the alphabet or any segment of it to coalesce into a single letter that functions as an embodiment of the same. Thus the fragments of the self, the *disjecta membra* of subjective experience, are made to cohere, reflected in that which is at the same time the source and agency of its *manifest* intelligibility. (As Pound ironically comments in "Canto CXVI" – the cantos are, of course, primarily essays – "it coheres all right / even if my notes do not cohere.") And this is why the essay, both representational and interrogative in its textual deportment, is the most effective and thoroughgoing form of imaginative fiction, a category it ostensibly repudiates. On the one hand, by virtue of its objective and methodical style, it appears to stanch what Jean Beaufret called the "haemorrhage of subjectivity"; on the other, it remains preoccupied with the determination of a prior and composite, productive unity – finding (to use

Swift's Tubbian language) in *totidem syllabis* what it desires in *totidem literis*. By enunciation, it delivers annunciation, turning the syllables of critical articulation into the pattern of an intuited self. In the end, the essay craftily re-establishes the principle of identity which its air of neutrality and disinterestedness, of candid inquiry, renders immune to that corrosive doubt with which it began and which continues secretly to motivate the performance. The most personal of genres, its strategy of apparent impersonality, its technique of analytic rigour and impartiality, enables it to achieve without fear of detection the subtle dissimulations of literary practice, to slip a Nintendo cartridge into the faculty that constructs its picture of the world and therefore, employing the grammar of implication, of the self that is its reflex and obverse. As Archer remarks in *The Beaux' Strategem*, "You can't counterfeit the passion without feeling it." Or as with Benjamin Constant's hero in *Adolphe*, the feigning of love for the purpose of seduction leads to the "real" thing itself, experience founded in conviction. The psychology at work is basically essayistic.

CONCLUSION

The personal, voluntaristic, and essentially *arbitrary* nature of the essay form was early recognized by Malebranche who, in his *De la recherche de la vérité*, saw it as the formal displacement of rhetorical excess, as infected by hyperbole and metaphor which "persuade only by stunning and dazzling the mind." The essay as practised by Montaigne effected a sleight-of-mind transition by which the *entretien* of logical argument and close reasoning was erased and supplanted by the insidious faculty of the imagination. Descartes, equally suspicious of Montaigne and the impressionistic manipulations of the essayistic sensibility, composed his *Discourse on Method* in part as a response to such dubious procedures. Both Malebranche and Descartes understood that the essay, which purports to describe and record, to investigate and discover, in fact invents, constructs, projects, and ultimately *persuades*, and is therefore to be classified as a branch of rhetoric rather than of philosophic method. And it is perhaps most deceptive in its guise as an objective account or analytical inquiry, which only serves to obscure the interior *nisus* or drive toward the fashioning of a tenable point of view, a recognizable and defensible self which, unlike the Cartesian *cogito*, is not the origin of reflection but the resultant, the purpose and end-point of the entire rhetorical operation. That is, self-persuasion attains to self-assertion, or Sp (*Savoir partiel*) merges with the Sa (*Savoir absolu*) to establish a concluding, not an originary, *cogito*. Behind the stalking-horse of dispassionate technique and an attitude of sceptical detachment, the essayist proceeds to trace the contours of a patchwork, gradually assembled self which translates perspective and parallax into an entity *positioned by implication*, that is, into a *pied-à-terre* that cannot be doubted. The essayist is one who is always looking for a place to stay, a condo for the psyche.

The essay, then, is the work of the dedicated fragmentarian, the secular Kabbalist digging in the realm of the shells for the bits and pieces of an assumed and originary identity, a constructer of crosswords and jigsaws the resolution of which promises the recovery of a word that has been lost or an image that has been radically dispersed. Its documentary form – rational, ordered, intelligible – is intended to counter the recognition of its fundamentally impressionistic nature and its character as a quest for an "absolute" knowledge of the self that paradoxically comes into existence only as a function of the quest itself. For regardless of the nominal subject to which the essay addresses itself (literary-critical, political, sociological), it continues to trace, directly or indirectly, the outlines of an assumed originating sensibility, to plot the trajectory of the desired, imagined ego, and to amortize a self that has been injured and dismembered, *(bl)essé*. This element of the contingent, the variable and internally shifting, is italicized by Burckhardt, who begins his great work by claiming that it "bears the title of essay in the strictest sense of the word" – this strict sense entailing nothing less than the notion of subjective parallax and the determinant position of the recording self. "This work might easily, in other hands, not only receive a wholly different treatment and application, but lead to essentially different conclusions." There is nothing objective about the essay despite the sceptical, dispassionate pose it affects; it is, on the contrary, the most *interested*, the most personal and committed of forms, as well as the most *assertive*.

The essay thus eschews diegetic or narrative shape in order to evade the taint and accusation of fiction while it pursues what appears to be a logotherapeutic recuperation of meaning, a form of ophthalmology[3] – sane, modest and clear – whose purpose, however, is to ensure the redemptive blindness without which, in Marlow's words, "it would have been too dark." Like Hawthorne's "railroad bibliopolist," the essayist makes the journey bearable by providing the material with which to construct an alternate, epicyclical journey, projecting *kairos* upon *chronos*, establishing a year and an origin to authenticate the illusion, *floating the label*, pretending expertise. *Sapere aude*. But also: *Sumere apertus*. Navigating cleverly between the lyric utterance and the narrative impulse,[4] the essay achieves a semiotic authority attesting to a founding structure – "I have had to fashion and compose myself so often to bring myself out," writes Montaigne, "that the model itself has to some extent grown firm and taken shape." The model may not exist in actuality (and even if it did, would remain indiscernible, which in some epistemologies is tantamount to non-existence) and yet survives even the most subversive attempts against its integrity, for the very reason that such attempts presuppose the very form and the conative drive which powers it. Or to put it differently: the essay finds itself installed as the postmortem form because it operates as nothing more or less than the *backing* of the Lacanian mirror, that which guarantees the imaginary and keeps it always in place precisely as the dead underwrite the unborn, and the past remembers the future, as the necessary illusion of the *esse*.

SOMMAIRE ALGEBRIQUE

1 Whatever one writes about, it is always about the self.
2 But the self one writes about cannot be properly said to exist; it is *brought into existence* in the act of writing.
3 The self that is brought into existence in the act of writing about the self is always an *analogue* of the self which presumably does the writing and which cannot be properly said to exist.
4 The writer then proceeds to identify the *primordial self* (which must remain indiscernible and which may be essentially incoherent) with the *analogical self* (which convinces by its apparent wholeness and integration but remains essentially a construct).
5 The literary form or genre that accomplishes the task of analogical transposition most effectively is the essay, owing to its deceptively cool, sceptical, investigative, and dispassionate manner. It always appears to be directed towards *another object*, even if that object is confessedly and demonstrably the writing subject itself. And when the object is plainly exterior to the self, it serves nevertheless a displaced and cryptographic function, resisting yet inviting decipherment. *The essay is the medium of the implied "subject"* (a term that, in conflating self and object as nominally opposed into a single unifying word, subsumes the essential project of the essay).
6 The apparent success of this operation is the obverse of its real failure. That is, the Sa (*Savoir absolu*) is at best merely absolute knowledge of the As (Analogical self) – both a tragic peripety and an ironic reversal.[5]
7 Sa x As = Σ> = $ or A(= Λ + handrail)[6]

The End of Poetry

> Our native Muse, heaven knows and heaven be praised, is not exclusive. Whether out of the innocence of a childlike heart to whom all things are pure, or with the serenity of a status so majestic that the mere keeping up of tones and appearances, the suburban wonder as to what the strait-laced Unities might possibly think, or sad sour Probability possibly say, are questions for which she doesn't ... in her lofty maturity any longer ... care a rap, she invites, dear generous-hearted creature that she is, just tout le monde to drop in at any time.
>
> W.H. Auden, *The Sea and the Mirror*

> A baleful quasi-doctrine of omnism seems to underlie this sort of poetry: everything goes, everybody can do it, everything is as good as everything else ... Did you notice a chip in your cup this morning? Make a poem of it. That chip is as good as the Crucifixion. Did the rain soak your newspaper? Make a poem of it. Did the girl at the lunch counter smile at you? Make a poem of it. Her smile was sour, was it? Another poem. Is your beat-up station wagon blue? Did your shoe come unlaced? Did a ray of sunlight fall on your geranium? Poem, poem, poem.
>
> Oscar Mandel, *The Book of Elaborations*

Despite the state of fratricidal strife that exists among poets and the schools they are associated with, there is a common and implicit assumption about the poetic calling in the modern world that unites them. It has now attained to the status of an unchallenged dogma, which can be syllogized as follows. First, if a poem is to be a vital and meaningful comment on or analysis of experience, it must to some extent reflect that experience. Secondly, experience in and of the contemporary world is a reductive phenomenon, fragmented, anarchic, pulverized. Consequently, any poem that pretends to authenticity or authority must reflect the discontinuities of the life we are compelled to live by virtue of the fact that we are living *now*.

This series of postulates has much to recommend it and is obviously persuasive. For one thing, who can doubt the critical placebo that poetry must, in one way or another, reflect the structure, quality, or contours of the age in which it moves and has its being if it is to retain its vitality? Otherwise, must it not be hospitalized, kept going by elaborate life-support systems, surviving intravenously in a state of archival nostalgia? Poetry must be *in* its time in order to be *of* its time, and it must be of its time if it has any intention of lasting, since only through a vigorous participation in the temporal can it presume to achieve eternity.

For another thing, the analysis of contemporary experience as disintegrative is now little more than a blatant truism. Hardly anyone questions any longer the psychological commonplace that a sense of alienation, loss, and despair is the essential factor in the modern experience of the world. The only absolute we acknowledge is the speed of light; as for the rest, the Heraclitean flux has escaped the confines of a pre-Socratic apothegm and threatens to swamp us all in every aspect of our lives. If God died in the nineteenth century, as Nietzsche tells us, religion promptly followed in the twentieth, taking with it our only viable guarantee of a now mainly worthless moral currency. The spectre of instant annihilation robs us of our seriousness in our dealings with one another and with posterity. Political life has broken down as has the humanist faith in reason, and even the ultimate cohesions of speech have been syntactically undermined. It is not just that monologue has replaced dialogue but that the monologue has become largely unintelligible. The precarious balance of whatever ecology we wish to consider has been upset beyond, as many suspect, the possibility of restoration.

If this is the condition of life poets confront, then (assuming that the creative élan has not abandoned them, that they have not been reduced to silence, which may be the only honest response to such irremediable devastation) it follows that the poems they set about composing, repressing the conviction of futility beneath the surface of their narcissism, must reflect the chaos, the rootlessness, the violence, the disruptions, the spiritual centrifugalities of the world they are condemned to die in. And this evidently means that the poems they may be condemned to live in must be rid of all historical ballast and of all those traditional beatitudes of form, order, and intelligibility invoked by the more fortunate poets who still lived in the age of innocence between Pericles and Hitler.

Such, put simply, is the modern poetic creed. Obviously, the issues it raises are more complex than its mere formulation might indicate. For example, does not a poetry that *resists* its time, opposing lucidity to obscurity, order to chaos, sense to senselessness, by that very token indirectly or elliptically participate in its time, if only through the medium of a problematic recognition? Is not its actual practice implicitly diagnostic? May not rhyme, let us say, constitute a plea for harmony and not an atavistic ineptitude?[1] May not the very existence of, if not metre, then a discernible cadence suggest the need for internal continuity and psychic momentum rather than the ineffectual hope of dim Arcadian symmetries? In short, may there not be historical periods in which poetry, if it wishes to survive, is compelled to live *in partibus infidelium*, carrying on a sort of guerrilla warfare against the pervasive assumptions and dominant "realities" of the day? The relation of literature to its time is not necessarily one of strict equivalence and the commitment of the former to the latter is often paradoxical or rebellious.[2]

We are touching on the insoluble dilemma of the relation between art and life which I do not want to resurrect here. Suffice it to say that neither pole of the equation can substitute for the equation itself. The self-contained world of art is at best a dubious refuge from the confusions and banalities of raw experience, bringing with it the dangers of inanition and preciosity. On the other hand, the sheer, voluminous flux of experience into which artists are regularly advised to plunge in order to revitalize their flagging energies will more likely than not leave literary corpses washed up on the beaches of respectability, academia or, if the artist is thorough, in the churning surf of an African exile or the intellectual morgue of gangsta rap. But each must nevertheless judge which pole of the equation diffidently to approach in the service of an unforgiving muse if the work is to avoid becoming parodistic or inconsequential.

To return to the development of our theme: despite the almost infinite permutations the subject permits, the theory of poetry reduces (as does that of art in general) to the theory of imitation taken in its widest conceivable sense. And imitation is conceived in basically two ways. The artist is required either to imitate "nature," which can mean anything from landscape to manners to interior or psychological configurations, or is exhorted to the imitation of the traditional forms of literary endeavour in appropriate language, in which case what is "copied" is not "nature" but one or another of the formally established ways in which it has been agreed that nature may be copied. In the first instance, the artist's imagination must be governed by his or her apperception of reality or, in the complex refinements of later speculation, by its own intrinsic laws as it conspires with the external *materia* to produce reality itself. In the second case, imagination must be subordinated to a social and critical consensus regarding the appropriate forms of literary representation, whose pedigree dates from the *Republic* and the *Poetics*.

The operative terms are, of course, to be understood with a certain generous latitude. Literature is not slavishly mimetic; it is also inventive and analytic, and no genuine writer is concerned with photographic verisimilitude. The writer does not copy so much as interpret. Similarly, the antithetical terms "nature" and "tradition," notwithstanding the venerable polarity into which they have been historically locked, are susceptible of endless modification. But the two "moments" of the antithesis can never by entirely eluded, and the thrust of the writer's creative temperament moves in one or another of these ancestral and inevitable directions. In this sense it may be valid to claim that beneath the profusion of individual modulations we can distinguish these two fundamental impulses toward the imitation of "nature" on the one side or the imitation of established "form" on the other. That is, we may speak either of the "laws" the creative temperament must obey or of the "norms" to which it must conform.

The two impulses are not at bottom diametrically opposed, as the social doctrine implicitly assumes that reality is not infinite and there accordingly exists a definable number of expressive forms which correspond to its limited permutations. Of course, the classical world is extinct, and the neo-classical sensibility was hijacked by industrial capitalism, but the simple fact that we continue to accept the rhetorical distinction between poetry and prose, that poets (somewhat heedless of their innovative practices) tend to leave the customary margins on either side of the page and are also given to declaiming or chanting their verses rather than merely *reading* them, is evidence of an abiding belief in the formal difference between the two media and therefore in the general validity of the classical idea. "Form" is grounded in "nature" and is solidly associated with a repertoire of legitimate strategies for the expression of different kinds of experience.

The blunt fact remains that the theory of poetic convention has fallen on evil days and is widely regarded as superannuated. The classical idea of poetry as requiring elevated diction – as commanding a unique language distinct from both prose and ordinary speech, equipped with a peculiar set of rules, conventions, and formal exclusions – is now considered as an exercise in Brahmanic arrogance or anachronistic fatuity. It simply does not meet the brazen imperatives of contemporary experience and is as unseasonable or ludicrous as mixing a Molotov cocktail in a Ming vase. When Ortega y Gasset defines poetic language as a "hovering" medium, raised above the abrasions and rugosities of current speech, he is looking back to the traditional conceptions of epic, drama, and the prophetic literature. But even the conversion of the hoary emblems of the winged steed or magic carpet into that of the lexical helicopter does not redeem his formulation from the charge of antiquarianism. Poetic conventions are passé: rhyme is obsolete (did not Milton consider it a barbarism?); metre is infantile, and even the stress-count is a throwback to Anglo-Saxon artlessness. The stanza form continues to be used but more as a logical convenience, an adaptation of the prose paragraph, than as a part of the traditional architectonic; and the language itself must avoid archaic "heightening" or "point" as it scrupulously democratizes its mandarin inclinations in the direction of the idiomatic, the colloquial, and the ubiquitous. Poetry can now be dialled on the telephone and read on the bus sandwiched between advertisements, as if Wordsworth's Preface were actually to be taken seriously.

The prevailing dogma is clear and unmistakable. The doctrine of the imitation of traditional form is defunct, relegated to the limbo of a classical irrelevance. A poetry that honours the canons and attitudes of its masonic past, reveres the illustrious predecessor, recognizes degree and precedence, and deploys a complex, formally appropriate, and distinctively memorable language is dismissed as either hieratic snobbishness or creative senility. The proper use to which this kind of poetry can be put was determined by Congreve's Mrs Millamant, who curls her hair with love letters, but "only with those in verse ... I never pin up my hair with prose." And the poets who continue to practise these ancestral sanctities are patronized as elegant but pitiable old fogies mourning the end of their feudal prerogatives. The world has passed them by. The careering motorcar has flung the yellow caravan into the ditch and poets who wish to survive must shake the dust out of their knickers and dream of magnificent onsets into a levelling future. Thus the principle of mimetic form is no longer adequate to the explosiveness and terror of the modern world and must be abandoned if we are to come to terms with the nature of our experience, the superluminal chaos of our event-horizon. Otherwise, along with religious faith, good craftsmanship, diplomatic immunity, and other such vestigial remnants of a vanished order, poetry cannot hope to escape obsolescence. This, more or less, is the creed to which the majority of poets now subscribes.

But if the imitation of form, the hallowing of poetic convention, has been tossed onto the scrap heap of outmoded pieties, we are left with the imitation of nature as the only theoretical foundation on which to ground the poetry of the modern era. The forms we must devise or discover in order to mirror, contain, or inflect the volatilities of our experience must inevitably correspond to that experience. In consequence, form moves toward the paradoxical assimilation of formlessness, and poets begin to conceive of their work as a sequence of ambiguous strategies to reflect the sense of confusion, homelessness, and disruption (or of mere indifference) with which the world persecutes them. Honesty, they assert, compels them to write directly – eloquence is suspect, inherited form the result of quaint artisanal compulsions, and time too valuable and fugitive an inheritance to waste on laborious composition. A poem can no longer claim the luxury of evocativeness, and the sense of its commitment to pressing, immediate needs or the anarchic qualities of our experience invalidates its allegiance to its own constituent materials, an activity it can only regard as an untenable hedonism or technical encapsulation. The predictable effect of all this is that poetry comes increasingly to resemble prose.[3]

The poetic modes that flourish in our climate of misinformation are clearly the descriptive narrative, the documentary, and the personal reminiscence (often deflected pronominally into the third person to evade the accusation of lyrical infatuation). These modes of poetic discourse are seen as unobjectionable from the standpoint of the contemporary milieu and even as adventurously experimental. And they are accompanied by the feverish search for structural models: the memoir or diary is high on the list of acceptable templates, but a quicksilver backing can be scraped together from almost any paradigmatic quarter, provided it is non-poetic in origin, such as the TV script, the recipe, the memo, or even the telephone book. (The fact that Villon, among others, used the testament in precisely this way partially explains his resurgent popularity.) The point I am making is that today the tendency is almost universal and by no means a maverick or eccentric gesture. The technical vacuum left by the extinction of conventional form has been surreptitiously filled by the substitution of prosaic or documentary prototypes, since the poet must get structural patterns from somewhere. The element of disingenuousness arises from the conflict between the proclaimed conviction that form must be internal and organic and the obsessive practice of ransacking (to use Samuel Johnson's word) the world of common, unmediated experience for exemplars and paradigms. There is no escaping the ironic conclusion that the contemporary notion of form, where such may be said to exist, is at least as external and artificial as the literary conventions that the traditional poet is routinely denounced for applying.

But there is a further and more corrosive irony at work in the matter under discussion. The imitation of inherited form is widely construed as archaic, reactionary, and inappropriate; heightened language is regarded as artificial (once a term of approval, now dyslogistic); order and restraint are dismissed as hangovers from a pastoral and genteel state of mind, now understood as historically incongruous or irrelevant. But the imitation of nature or of the given state of affairs that underlies contemporary practice is in effect the province of the novel, as has been the case since Robinson Crusoe domesticated his island and Moll Flanders picked the pockets of the contemporary scene. And when it comes to holding the mirror up to nature on Stendhal's dusty highway or in Hamlet's theatre (or holding it up to the self, like the little mirror Ibsen glued to the inside crown of his hat to comb his hair with), poetry is out of its league and cannot compete with its formidable opponent. The novel is just too compendious, too all-embracing, too versatile and flexible and omnivorous a genre to defer in its analysis of experience to the right of poetic primogeniture. Moreover, to add injury to insult, it is capable in its lyrical mood of actually swallowing and digesting its traditional rival, so that the only place where we may still encounter poetry in its old-fashioned guise of evocative speech is in the body of the novel itself – an irritable Jonah, a lying Pinocchio, whistling in the depths of the leviathan. And as if to administer the coup de grâce, modern criticism has deposed that the novel is not a continuation of the classical tradition, the descendant of the epic, but is the unique literary expression of modern society deriving ultimately from the Puritan reformation of the sixteenth and seventeenth centuries and the industrial upheavals of the eighteenth.

This irony is not only inescapable but possibly terminal as well. Poetry, approximating to the novelistic parallax, ceases to be "poetic" and grows more and more prosaic in structure, content, and language. The idea of "decorum" did not wither away, however, with classical and Renaissance literary values. Decorum may be defined as style accommodated to subject, means to ends, idiom to intention. Thus the idea of poetic decorum in today's literary environment exacts an extortionate price from the practising poet who must now bring the poem into line with the novelistic perspective on the world and adopt the techniques and strategies of an alien genre in order to retain or regain credibility. So the truth stares us glumly in the face. The poet goes on multiplying narrative upon description upon documentary in odd linguistic constructs called poems that scarcely anyone bothers to read except other poets and an entrenched minority of academic critics – without whom, be it said, the medium would quickly succumb to literary entropy. Meanwhile it manages to maintain itself prosthetically.

If the imitation of nature is the privilege or the proper sphere of the novel, and the imitation of disciplinary or parietal form has been consigned to oblivion, it seems reasonable to assume that poetry is confronted with only two options, namely, it must be either prosaic or irrelevant. There is no *tertium quid*. It reflects and participates in the modern experience of universal chaos and predictably disintegrates, becoming discontinuous, haphazard, and aleatory, or variously smuggles an extraneous concept of order into its performative ambience and so reduces itself to a parasitical and undistinguished existence, encroaching on the terrain of the novel only to be wiped out or incorporated. This is where the imitation of nature inexorably leads it. The other alternative is equally depressing: it opposes the experience of violence and anarchy and stays equally clear of the giantocracy of the novel, setting up a small, countervailing linguistic system predicated on order and continuity. Thus it becomes instantly obsolete and intensely private, the formal expression of nostalgia for a lost coherence.

The modern poet navigates in the straits between the Scylla of the irrelevant and the Charybdis of the prosaic, and there is every sign in the apocalyptic moment we inhabit that this epic journey is about to be cut short, if it has not already ended. And if, as many believe, the novel is itself endangered by the graphic and electronic revolutions inspired by a triumphant technological barbarism, prose will soon confront its own set of complementary options: to become irrelevant as its predecessor, or somehow cinematic and instantaneous as its successor. (It is, of course, rapidly becoming audiotronic.) In which case it is possible that poetry will be deprived of even its posthumous survival in the body of the novel, one more minor, unremembered casualty in the collapse of the past.

CONCLUDING REMARKS

In a certain sense, poetry (or the improbable act of writing and reading it) has more in common with science fiction than with any other branch of prose literature, given the "Coleridgean" proviso that science fiction (of the cruder sort, at any rate) is popular since it relies on the familiar operations of fancy, and that poetry is paradoxically remote, since it is based on the rigorous principles of the imagination. The traditional poem and the SF story construct codified worlds which in terms of consistency and intelligibility provide a fleeting alternative to the feeling of dispersion and the experience of triteness we associate with contemporary life. At the same time, it is obvious that science fiction cannot be diffracted through the medium of verse (although this has been inadvisedly attempted) without the reciprocal annihilation of the two genres. The poem in its quest for poise and equilibrium is immediately crippled by an orthopedic self-consciousness while the science fiction story in its need for spectacle and narrative expansiveness chafes in frustration at the formal and rhetorical limitations imposed upon it. But it might be worth suggesting that poetry was the science fiction of the ancient world, not in the sense of detailing implausible adventures in the epic (or even Lucianic) mode but rather in describing an implicit trajectory that overarched and to some extent negated the world of daily experience. Poetry once provided, as science fiction does today, the significant alternative to the commonplace.

We might also note that poetry has been crowded out of the aesthetic field not only by its brawny, mimetic competitor, the novel, but by its once-pliant, former handmaiden, music. Eric Havelock tells us in his *Origins of Western Literacy* that as the written word gained its identity and became "increasingly prosaic," it was freed from its previous bondage to mnemonic verse rhythm. But this emancipation had the concomitant effect of releasing rhythm from its subservience to poetry, allowing it to be conceptualized in pure sound independent of diction and "increasingly thought of not as an accompaniment to words but as a separate technology with its own laws and procedures." Thus both the mimetic and phonetic functions of verse have been taken from it by the disciplines of fiction and music, which are better adapted to the respective modalities of verbal imitation and rhythmic sound than is their ostensible predecessor.

There doesn't seem to be much the poet can do about these generic macerations except, perhaps, to move to Ireland.

It may be useful to consider in somewhat finer detail the vexing problem of poetic form. The *concept* of poetic form is, like the *practice* of modern verse, permissive and accommodating. We can mean almost anything we like by it and still feel that we are being rigorous, consistent, and responsible in its application. We can speak, for example, of inherited form, by which we intend that traditional repertory of shapes and rules that give us recognizable *types* of poems – sonnet, sestina, etc. – as well as those internal devices and conventions – syllable or stress count, metrical requirements – that constitute the *grammar* of poetic language. Again, we may have a peculiar kind of *diction* in mind, which is meant to distinguish the language of poetry from that of common speech and narrative or discursive prose. This distinction cuts across the idea of form as architectonic, since heightened or "formal" diction (or what Yeats called "lyric cantillation") may be found in charged or rhythmic prose while remaining dormant in those verbal artifacts we call poems. The difference is usually expressed as that between verse and poetry which Sidney developed in the *Defence*, "verse being but an ornament and no cause of Poetry, since there have been many most excellent poets that never versified, and now swarm many versifiers that need never answer to the name of poets." The principle that distinguishes poetry from verse would appear to be a double one: ethical fervour and metaphoric power generating memorable language which can leaven either verse or prose into that higher form called poetry.

By "form" we can also mean the model, the supervening structure or template that governs the overall conception of a poem, e.g., the testament, the letter, the film script, which helps the poet order both ideas and presentation. It is this third notion of form that seems to dominate contemporary practice in its effort to ground the poem in an accepted rhetorical genre which confers legitimacy by virtue of both its ubiquity and its utilitarian nature. Like Matthew Arnold's Shakespeare, the paradigm is institutional and need not abide our question. It also simplifies the poet's job considerably by offering a blueprint or a set of instructions while at the same time acting as a permanent scaffolding to keep the poem from collapsing on itself. But the real issue here is the sense of formal legitimacy the poet derives from the model.

The way in which the term "form" is used – whether to designate shape, technical conventions, diction, or structure – depends very much on the context in which it appears. Both reader and writer must remain vigilant to ensure that the word does not become an excuse for shoddy thinking, a euphemism for mediocrity, or a justification for imaginative repression and neurotic tidiness. But it seems to me that the love of form in the old aurgentitive sense demands knowledge of, respect for and discipline in both the *craft* that is professed and the *language* that is deployed. The problem with much contemporary poetry may then be defined as its "formlessness" in these two degrees and its correspondent triviality, technical poverty reflecting thematic slenderness.

Many serious poets would take exception to the preceding or wish to modify the argument I am pressing. As a poet friend observes in a recent letter to me, taking issue with some of the contentions in this essay, "poetry needs to use everything at its disposal to reclaim ground lost to the novel or the drama. There is also a subtle, internal music, based on the concept of rhyme, which eschews the obviousness of end-rhyme for those fine repetitions of sound embedded at the level of vowel and consonant – not blatant alliteration, but a much more subtly spaced and modulated accretion of identical or merely similar sounds." The point is well made. The technique of internal resonance or echo, "based on the concept of rhyme" but eschewing "the obviousness of end-rhyme," has long been an indispensable part of the poet's repertoire of phonetic strategies. The great master of this technique is of course Shakespeare in whose plays, even more than in the early poems or the sonnets, coherence and resonance are established precisely "at the level of vowel and consonant," as in Hamlet's famous speech. In our own century no poet has surpassed Wallace Stevens in the art of tonal modulation and the subtlety of "musical" effect. But Shakespeare and Stevens were extremely "formal" poets: they counted syllables, weighed the effect of phonetic repetitions on a Troy Weight scale, and at the same time meditated the grand, avoirdupois themes that, as the mathematician Steven Weinberg remarked with respect to the questions posed by cosmological research, "lift human life a little above the level of farce, and give it some of the grace of tragedy." Consider also in this connection the concluding stanza of Richard Wilbur's strictly end-rhymed "Ceremony," the title poem of his prize-winning volume, in which the poet contemplates his relation to the muse:

> Ho hum. I am for wit and wakefulness
> And love this feigning lady by Bazille.
> What's lightly hid is deepest understood,
> And when with social smile and formal dress
> She teaches leaves to curtsey and quadrille,
> I think there are most tigers in the wood.

Or for that matter the painting on which it is obviously based, Frederic Bazille's *Reunion de famille*, 1867 (now in the Musée d'Orsay), in which the lady in the striped dress seated to the viewer's right of the larger, central grouping of characters seems both to tilt and compress the canvas like a propulsive force, so that the observer is insensibly constrained to step back and keep a respectable distance. Form is power. As for "those fine repetitions of sound," they are certainly effective and potent when they work, but I sometimes suspect that they often remain undetectable even at the level of the unconscious or that they tend to occur inevitably as a function of the limited number of phonemes the language puts at the poet's disposal. Those poets who pride themselves on their phonetic subtlety may occasionally delude themselves as to their poetic power.

We should also remember that poetic energy, poetic impact, derives to an equally great extent from the *power of the phrase*. Memorability is a function of highly charged language which can only live within the phrase, but whose continuity, be it said, cannot be indefinite: language can support only so much intensity without burning up, like the seraphim who can chant "holy" only once before being consumed by the fires of their devotion; similarly the mind is always limited by imminent exhaustion. But language and mind unite in sustaining intermittent bursts of semantic and aesthetic incandescence – a fusion subtended by the poetic phrase or passage. This is the seraphic language in the absence of which poetry reduces to the condition of mere verse or neutral prose, pedestrian and safe. Seraphic language, however, does not ignite in the void; it depends partly on the mysterious gift of the poet, partly on the poet's training in the grammar and syntax of this peculiar discourse. The complex of reasons that determine or explain memorability must always remain at least partially obscure, but few readers, professional or amateur, can deny that if they have emerged with anything from their experience of poetry, it is with a few lines here and there, and sometimes whole passages, that have branded themselves upon the memory. It is precisely this seraphic speech, this quality of memorability, that is lacking in the bulk of contemporary poetry – the reason being, I suspect, its uncritical fondness for a debased, "prosaic," undistinguished use of language grounded in the prudential piety, the unexceptionable poetics, of that lower order of angels, the ofanim, who can chant "holy" as often as they like and live to tell about it without a trace of combustibility about their speech.

The Word and the Stone

Is dicust ollis popularibus olim
Qui tum vivebant homines atque aevum agitabant
Flos delibatus populi, Suadaeque medulla.

Quintus Ennius, quoted in the *Attic Nights* of Aulus Gellius, book 7

To be sure, the sculptor uses stone just as the mason uses it, in his own way. But he does not use it up. That happens in a certain way only where the work miscarries ... To be sure, the poet also uses the word – not, however, like ordinary speakers and writers who have to use them up, but rather in such a way that the word only now becomes and remains truly a word.

Martin Heidegger, "The Origin of the Work of Art"

As Robert Scholes comments in *Textual Power*, developing a theme we now associate with Russian Formalism but which is native to the western literary tradition as a whole, "Much of our poetry has been written ... to remove the veil of language that covers everything with a false familiarity." The Romantics, as we know, embarked upon the same defamiliarizing project,[1] Coleridge remarking in the *Biographia* on Wordsworth's noble attempt to strip the "film of familiarity" from our perception of the world and Shelley picking up the same phraseology in the *Defence*: "Poetry lifts the veil from the hidden beauty of the world, and makes familiar objects be as if they were not familiar."[2]

The Romantics, of course, hold no monopoly on this restorative function of poetic language, which is an effect of the best poetry whenever it may be written. Dr Johnson, commenting on the distinguishing qualitites of Pope's work in his *Life* of the poet, similarly observes with approval that "familiar things are made new."[3] Although today we speak of dehabitualization, "ostranenie," the Brechtian *Verfremdungseffekt* or simply the A-effect, displacement, estrangement, and so on, modern formalism has basically articulated a standard and venerable insight into the essential nature of the poetic transaction with the world in a renovated (i.e., critically defamiliarized) idiom that enables us to grasp an old truth with renewed vigour. But the identical insight persists, from Plotinus in the third century neoplatonically affirming "that the arts do not simply imitate what they see" but reproduce the *logoi*, the original and pristine forms of the Creation, to the protocols of imagism, futurism, and formalism in our own time. One thinks of Pound and Williams strenuously "making it new," Viktor Shklovsky exorting us to "make the stone stoney"[4] (oddly reminiscent of Husserl's famous cry, "Back to the things themselves!"), of Susan Sontag prescribing the recovery or the erotic rehabilitation of the senses through art, and J.L. Austin advocating the use of the abnormal to "throw light on the normal," thus penetrating "the blinding veil of ease and obviousness."[5]

But there is a complementary impetus as well in the western tradition that asserts that poetic language finds its central purpose in purifying the dialect of the tribe, renovating the medium not only to enhance and clarify our perception of the world but to purge and intensify our relations with language itself. Mallarmé and Eliot are by no means theoretical pioneers in this regard, and the preoccupation with language *per se* has always been an inalienable portion of the poet's linguistic patrimony, as was recognized, for example, by Heidegger in his late essays when he defined the function of poetry as *an intercession on behalf of language*, the house of Being.[6] These two aspects or moities of poetic practice are neatly summed up and paralleled in Michael Riffaterre's distinction between the two forms or stages of reading, the "heuristic" in which signs function in a chiefly referential fashion, and the "retroactive" in which certain difficulties, obscurities, "ungrammaticalities," that may arise in a text defeat a mimetic reading and require a new, *depreconceptional* approach.[7] Or as Scholes puts it in his comment on Shklovsky's dictum about making the stone stoney, poetry may "at least make language itself visible ... [that is] ... make the word wordy."

These are the two ideological poles, the limit points between which poetry has always shuttled and still continues to oscillate in its recognition of its own peculiar nature and purpose. It sets language in place between the frames of its margins like a clear pane through which we are meant to glimpse the problematic grandeur of existence. Or it presents us with a stained-glass window which foregrounds its own colour and design, diffracting the light that irradiates the world outside in order to accentuate its own intrinsic luminescence.[8] At one extreme, poetic language tends to efface itself, to become invisible, literally *unremarkable*, decarnalized, and to subordinate itself to the greater and more memorable discourse of the world to which it directs our attention;[9] at the other extreme, the world itself fades toward the status of ghostly back-up or is, at least, *reduced* to offering the minimum support necessary to sustain the verbal artefact and allow it to be perceived. The most exorbitant formulation of this latter tendency is probably Alfred Döblin's "Poetry is categorically opposed to rational scribbling that is subordinated to external ends."

Within this general bipolar context the poem takes up its position. But the metaphor of the window works only insofar as the poem moves conspicuously towards one or another of its limiting conditions. As soon as a poem is perceived as embodying *both* functions, the visual metaphor is probably best replaced by an aural one, in which the notion of harmony or counterpoint renders its dual nature with greater adequacy. For the great poems inevitably participate in both dimensions of our experience, situated in language that is constantly recuperating itself as something unique, memorable, noble, ophicleidic, and resonating, and at the same time urging us outward towards the world in all its beauty and ugliness as something that demands our recognition and involvement. Great poetry is both *in language* and *in the world* simultaneously, dividing our attention into two complementary halves and then reuniting these halves stereoscopically or stereophonically so that our experience is one of depth or immersion. In such cases, form, style, period, and all taxonomical considerations fall away, so that whether we are reading Pope's "The Rape of the Lock" or Wordsworth's "Resolution and Independence," we find ourselves in the presence of a poem in which language and world, sound and sense, *logos* and *cosmos* are wedded and reciprocally amplified.[10] We find ourselves moving in two directions at once without experiencing the disabling sense of contradiction – we are in the condition of dream – to arrive if only for a moment at the centre of an exaltation, a reaffirmation of language and world in which neither is sacrificed for the sake of the other.

Thus in the presence of the great poem we gradually become aware of an aspect of language that generally escapes our attention. The illumination of the world in all its fullness, that is, of our experience of the world in its rich multidimensionality, necessarily involves the *privileging of language in itself as well.* For language, complex and insoluble phenomenon that is,[11] does not only reflect or influence the world, thus fulfilling an exclusively agential function. It is also *a part of the world* in which we live, as "real," as objective, as manifest as mountains, dreams, dictatorships, diseases, weather, tables, sunsets, and curbstones. It has not only an instrumental significance but enjoys an ontological status as well. And it is the peculiar and historical nature of poetic discourse to inflect this double nature of language as both tool and object, implement and substance, *at the same time.* When language proceeds to blue-pencil itself, disappearing effortlessly into its function, it may succeed in opening a portion of the world to our inspection, but it obscures and suppresses another equally vital aspect of our experience – in fact, precisely that which distinguishes the mind from the animal plenitude of the Creation. Heidegger tells us that the malfunctioning tool, the breakdown of equipment, restores our awareness of Being by startling us out of the sleep of smooth functioning.[12] The *success* of language in drawing attention, not only to the world but to itself (and thus, to ourselves as well), is equivalent on the ontological plane to the *failure* of equipment: it restores a significant portion of the world and the intrinsic stratum of our existence to our attention. (Or what amounts to the same thing: the success of language on the ontological plane is predicated on the failure of language as equipment, that is, language on the purely instrumental or utilitarian plane.) When poetic language commits what C.S. Lewis calls "verbicide," profaning its high or scansorial nature, it does not go alone but takes an innocent victim along with it, a constitutive element of *both* the poem and the world which is lost in the sleep of eudaimonistic or functional efficiency.

The claim that poetry violates its historical nature and its constitutive value by dispossessing language *qua* language or rendering it transparent does not imply that it fulfils its "mandate" by going to the opposite extreme of rhetorical opacity or by a programmatic thickening of its lexical pigmentation. A language that delights mainly in expressing an ultimate inexpressibility, not disappearing tamely into the inaudible hum of function but congealing grumously into substance, shutting out the world by virtue of its own precedent visibility, produces a poetry that is distressing once again for its fractal one-sidedness. (However indiscriminately we employ the acoustic and pictorial metaphors here, the point remains equally well or ill taken. The poet's slam-dunking words phonetically on the page or splashing them about with *tachiste* abandon amounts to the same thing – an attack of disabling lexemia.) Swinburnian excess is no antidote to metalinguistic transparency. The poet who emphasizes the wordiness of the word, the sheer facticity of language, at the expense of subject, theme, passion, or insight, comes to resemble Swift's nonplussed geographer in "On Poetry" who, poring over an empty map of Africa, places elephants for want of towns. It *should* be clear that poetic language is – to continue the metaphor – an elephant one rides *on the way* to the town and that the poet is not only a (Swiftian) geographer but a mahout as well.

Thus, when Yeats writes in "The Man and the Echo,"

Did that play of mine send out
Certain men the English shot?

he is turning to account the double nature of poetic language. On the one hand, the poem directs our notice to a significant issue *outside* the poem, to an event in the world which the poem reflects and about which the poet reflects, broods, meditates; on the other hand, metre, rhyme, and the sense of strong verbal charge draw attention to the lines themselves as language consciously manipulated inside the poem. The attention that the poem calls to itself establishes it as an inalienable part of the larger event it both queries and describes, adding to its complexity and underscoring its composite, multi-layered, interrogative force. It is precisely this curious, dream-like sense of being in two places at once, both inside the poem minding its language and outside the poem reconstructing the event towards which it points, that accounts for its acknowledged power to move us and perhaps even to change us.

Contemporary English-language poetry has by and large forfeited the power to move by its determined attempt to factor language out of the poetic equation.[13] It is not *on the whole* a poetry that insists on its status as word, and it no longer tends to define itself, as Derek Attridge says in *Peculiar Language*, "in terms of its difference from natural language." As it converges increasingly on the idiom and cadence of prose and, even further, begins to echo the flat, indolent, and anonymous rhythms of normative speech, it proceeds to obliterate the *objectivity* and *viability* of language as an essential and miraculous part of the larger world that it presumably describes, questions, opposes, or underwrites. The poem begins to disappear into its subject, drawing away from itself, sacrificing its own incommutable nature as noble or memorable "speech" and thus paradoxically impoverishing the experience it is intended to clarify or enhance. Especially is this the case in contemporary Canadian poetry in which many of our most talented writers, in bringing us close to the object of their concern, render their language transparent and inoperative as language *in itself*. It is almost as if the very intensity of their feelings, the depth and legitimacy of their preoccupations, their moral integrity as such, has dimmed the vitality and power of the language in which they are constrained to work – a language that has fallen victim to the enormity of the event whose distance from the imagination has been effectively cancelled. When Michael Harris in his award-winning "Turning out the Light" brings us almost bodily, as it seems, to the bedside of his cancer-stricken brother and allows us to watch him die, the horror and pathos, utterly genuine as they may be, proceed to bury a poem that has just died before our eyes, turning out the light on its existence *as a poem*. Most readers are not aware of this because they are not aware of the poem. The poem has abolished itself as language and thus effaced language itself for the space of our reading as that part of the world that transcends its occasion. I am not suggesting that certain themes and subjects should be proscribed as too dangerous, too "real" for poems to handle safely (which may in fact be the case for most "holocaust poems" written by poets who have not experienced the unimaginable). Rather, the poem should simultaneously demand recognition *as a poem* in the face of even the most outrageous and irreducible of experiences – as does, for example, Dylan Thomas's "Do Not Go Gentle," villanelling its way past its subject in order to *centralize* itself as a linguistic and aesthetic artefact. Otherwise it is deprived of its distinctive mode of existence as poetry and can be readily assimilated to anything else that works as well in re-enacting or transmitting the experience it confronts: effective journalism, moving prose, intense or persuasive conversation, psychotropic telepathy. But when Irving Layton writes of the death of his mother in "Keine Lazarovitch," the reader may suffer an induced vicarious anguish, be quite literally moved to tears, and re-approach the poem only in fear and trembling. At the same time *the poem affirms its own existence as a poem* and continues to resonate verbally in the imagination, surviving the death it mourns by virtue of its "peculiar language" – lines like "the inescapable lousiness of growing old," "how / She had loved God but cursed extravagantly his creatures," and "her youngest sings / While all the rivers of her red veins move into the sea," insisting on their own poetic autonomy as *lines*, as a collocation of memorable and glorious *words*. The poem has refused to surrender to the mortality it laments.

Or considering the scandal and terror of dictatorship as described in Gary Geddes's recent *No Easy Exit*, once again I find my response troubled and somehow devitalized. It may seem frivolous to lodge an objection to poetic technique in the face of the manifest horrors perpetrated in Pinochet's Chile and recorded in the poems in this collection, yet the *literary* response is an integral part of the total experience of which "the poem" is both catalyst and medium. Emerging from a reading of the book, I am overwhelmed by disgust and indignation at the events transcribed therein but somehow unmoved by the poetry (very much as with some of the work of Carolyn Forché, especially her El Salvadorian "Return"). The poet is invisibly present throughout as an honest and sensitive observer, as an authentic conscience, and the depth of his moral concern must affect even the most callous of his readers. But – possibly as just such a callous reader – I have almost no recollection of any of the words and lines of which the poems are constructed. I retain certain images and sensations, but I retain none of the poems. I am aware that the poet may take precisely this seizure of linguistic amnesia as an indication of the success of the book, but once again I stress that such an effect is producible in many other ways that have nothing to do with the peculiar nature and power of poetic language, including a visit to Chile. What is going on inside the poem does not appear able to escape the gravitational radius of the event horizon into which it has plunged. As does not happen, for instance, with Wilfred Owen who, recording the horror of war from the trenches, about as close up as one can get, will conclude:

My friend, you would not tell with such high zest
To children ardent for some desperate glory,
The old lie: Dulce et decorum est
Pro patria mori.

– giving us in this poem not only a vivid and immediate representation of a soldier in a gas-attack "gargling from the froth-corrupted lungs" but also a skilful and perhaps even magisterial deployment of poetic language in which two Latin words are made to march in English military rhyme, another line ("To children ardent for some desperate glory") which imprints itself indelibly upon the memory, and a clever hemistich which brings the entire piece to a cold, blank, snapped-off closure that echoes on ironically in the imagination in aftertones as moving and significant as Hopkins's latreutic "Praise Him."

Readers find themselves inhabiting a very different *poetic* territory on turning to the works of Geddes and Harris which I have singled out for consideration.[14] For example, the former's "Little Windows":

a number killed at the air-base
others thrown into the sea
from helicopters, stomachs opened ...

When they break her eyes
images remain.
Sound of the helicopter

recedes. Sea is a window
above him, water
tongues the red from his stomach.

Or the latter's "Turning out the Light":

He is tired of the shame
of wetting his bed; he wants
the wheelchair toilet ...

Even the sound of the softly opening door
has him cry and gag
on the dregs of his vomit.

The morning drip
eases red cells
into the bloated arm.

Individual words, lines, and stanzas melt into their correlative circumstances, dissolving into the experience rather than crystallizing out of it. More to the point, however, is the general *cumulative* effect of the longer sequences, in which the pain, the anguish, the sense of magnitude experienced by the reader even at a second remove erase the poems *qua* poems from his or her awareness and may equally be said to sublate the poems from themselves. When the distance from the recorded event is collapsed, the awareness of language, the distinctive essence of the poem, is also wiped out, whereas in reading the previously cited poems of Yeats or Owen or Layton, a paradoxical *linguistic joy* is felt to accompany the sense of sombre empathy evoked by these pieces, owing to our recognition of a certain aesthetic control, a self-conscious lexical and architectonic mastery. It is almost as if the voluptuous delight the poet takes in mastery of words is communicated directly to the reader, who cannot help but share in a sort of lexical radiation of pleasure.

It is the *linguistic* effort to establish the poem's countervailing reality, its gritty, heteronomous respeaking of the world – an effort enabling us to recognize not only the subject or the event but the aesthetic object as well – that generates the composite experience we insist on coming back to, on remembering, on *delighting in* despite what may be its frightful or melancholy theme. Without this peculiar species of reality-matching, of linguistic equity or cardinality, the poem ceases to exist as a poem and becomes something else, a pure transparence, a verbal enzyme, a form of cinematic immediacy. It is, strangely enough, as if such writing fulfils the condition of the good translation, which succeeds best when its disappears entirely from view. What this sort of "poetic language" gives us, in effect, is a *translation* rather than a complementary and autonomous *aspect* of the real. But the defining and promethean claim of all genuine poetic language is simply that it is as real in its own stubborn, energetic way as the real itself. Or to change the metaphor, if the poem moves across in its entirety from its status as language to take up its position in or *directly beside* its subject, then discourse and event find themselves on the same side of the seesaw – depriving the work, as well as the reader, of that strange and distinctive sense of aesthetic exhilaration we associate with good poetry. This soaring emotion may have something to do with the tragic function of all serious art, the "Lapis Lazuli" vision of the world *sub specie aeternitatis*, but it need not flow from anything so philosophically austere as Aristotelian catharsis. The reaction of delight or euphoria in the presence of works treating of catastrophic subjects may strike the more ethically rigorous as disturbingly sadistic, but the skilful or magian deployment of the aesthetic medium induces that sense of wonder, appreciation, and joy enabling the mind to resist sentimentality or despair.[15] And the aesthetic medium in which poetry moves and has its being is, after all, language in all its resident complexity. The poem, then, as it confronts its subject, attempts to make not itself but the world transparent, accessible to meaning, communicable: *it tries to make the stone wordy*. Concurrently, in rendering its theme with all the resources at its disposal – rhythm, image, form, tone, and especially diction (or what Edward Said calls "linguicity," an all-inclusive category) – it tries to render not the world but itself as solid, lapidary, mosaic, or, if one likes, as *Demosthenean* as the rhetoric of enunciation permits, *it tries to make the word stoney*.[16] And both at the same time.

Thus when I read Yeats, Owen, Layton, my response to the solemnity of the events called forth by the poems is not diminished but enhanced by my complementary appreciation of the language manipulated on the page. Such an experience is rich and complex, deepened by the consummate verbal skill that does not only articulate itself *in vacuo* but *preserves the event* as well,[17] preventing it from dispersing with the inevitable gases of an immediate visceral reaction. This is the paradox of poetic language[18] which preserves the world only if it survives its occasion, belonging to the world about which it writes, in which it is written, and of which it forms an indissoluble part as an object of writing. But poets in the English tradition today, with a few notable exceptions, have tended to succumb to the ideology of the real, betraying language in its poetic or *aculeated* function in order to honour a commitment to "fact" or to the "real" as it impinges upon the personality. In contemporary Canadian verse especially, the stone has battered the word into a condition of insensibility, as even the merest acquaintance with our recent productions should make distressingly clear. But it would be a mistake to assume that language must necessarily falter and submit before reality, glumly reconciling itself to a harsh, rupiculous existence. Amidst the upheavals and sufferings of a country very much subject to the depredations of the reality principle, the work of George Seferis, for example, sensuous, digraphic, and superbly crafted, continues to be read and recited *as poetry*,[19] as much for the language it commands within the poems as for the experience it invokes and memorializes outside them – as if in proof of the children's game in which paper always covers stone:

Οπου και να ταζιδεψω η Ελλαδα με πληγωνει
Στο Πηλιο μεσα στιζ καστανιεζ το πουκαμισο του Κενταυρου
γλιοτρουσε μεσα στα φυλλα για να τυλιχτει στο κορμι μου
καθωζ ανεΒαινα την αντπφορα κι η θαλασσα μ ακολυθουσε
ανεΒαινονταζκιαυτησαντονυδραργυροθερμομετρου
ωζ που να Βρουμε τα νερα του Βουνου

Although the best poetry will avoid both ends of the sliding scale of its performative ambience, the petrifactive and the verbifactive,[20] it understands, intuitively or consciously, that a strong, lithic, corrugated language is what distinguishes its own existence as poetry and that such language remains an integral part of the world it addresses. "With good authors," writes Alfred Döblin in a less doctrinaire moment, "language always wins."

Fellatiotics: The Relation between Surface and Depth

> Play is always lost when it seeks salvation in games.
>
> Jacques Derrida, *Dissemination*

> Given the importance of surfaces in such accounts, it is surprising that philosophers of such a realist bent have said almost nothing in detail about surfaces, about what it is that we see directly in acts of veridical perception.
>
> Avrum Stroll, *Surfaces*

Newsstand pornography, still a controversial matter in many parts of the country, has an analytic significance we have scarcely begun to appreciate. Though its *blatant* appeal is in the realm of the erotic, it also serves as a kind of cultural indicator, an index of "latent" or imaginative life in the latter's primary function of the constitution of experience. I am not referring to the mere existence of pornography itself or basing a cultural analysis on the incidence of pornographic displays – such an audit would lead, as it has done in the vociferous press, to conclusions that are inescapably banal, sentimental, and morally obtuse. Rather, what can accepting pornography as a social fact that is in itself morally neutral, as something that is always with us in one form or another whether implicit or explicit – what can it tell us about the relation of imagination to experience in a given cultural period? Differently put: what is the relation of pornography to ontology, and how do small, progressive changes in pornographic representation signal comparable adjustments in the reality-continuum whose subjective limit is the "intention" and whose objective boundary we call the "act"?

The pornographic item providing the clearest indication of epistemological variation – not simply in terms of cultural attitudes but in terms of the *perception of reality* – is heterosexual fellatio. A sociological study of cultural norms would, of course, find it necessary to draw attention to the obvious: that the exhibition of male homosexuality is confined to specialized magazines which must be sought out in the darker corners of the cultural system; that lesbian encounters are represented more or less openly and in considerable detail; and that cunnilingus has long been a staple, the bread and butter of the trade. These are facts that testify both to the inferior position of women in the culture – they are *objects* whose sexual manipulation is implicitly permitted – and to the continuing history of the Pauline subversion of sexuality in a civilization that persists in seeing the erotic as a degradation, as a brute reduction of human dignity. Until very recently on our public newsstands, the male organ has been ascribed VIP status, rarely seen, doing God's work in secret, a kind of "spiritual" agent, whereas the female genitalia, as with the rosebud anus, has been generously exposed to visual traffic.

The recent emergence of the *membrum virile* to visible prominence may imply a new, debased egalitarianism – as if to suggest that in our enlightened epoch, equality between the sexes works *downward*, that women have not been elevated to the status of subjects but that men have been debased to the condition of objects, have been *feminized*. But as we are engaged here not in sociological but epistemological analysis, we are to study the new adventures of the membrum ("new" in the sense of going public, coming out of the closet) as a philosophical indicator, a needle pointing in perceptual and ontological directions. "And stand up tall! Straight. I want to see you looking fine for me," as *Finnegans Wake* has it.

When the phallus first came to newsstand prominence (in conservative cities like Montreal, where I write), it was almost immediately displayed in various degrees of vaginal insertion and occasionally in simulated anal penetration – although in the latter case, in the typical Derridean form of presence by absence. (The organ was, so to speak, lopped off and the viewer had to imagine the event with the aid of visual cues: anatomical positions, the expression of delighted agony on the face of the woman turned full camera, etc.) The situation was very different and inherently more interesting when it came to the practice of fellatio. In the incunabular stage, the phallus rested fully erect two or three inches from the woman's mouth, which was only slightly open, hesitant, reflective, as if uttering a muted exclamation of surprise. The censor, apparently, had no quarrel with this graphic representation of the *vita contemplativa*. When this phase of the erotically tentative had been successfully negotiated, the woman was then permitted to open her mouth widely and extend her tongue, closing the distance to a tantalizing inch. In successive issues of the magazines, the tongue was allowed to stretch further and further, curling upward at the tip like a surrogate organ (cf. the "classic" Greek postcard of the ithyphallic god), suggesting on one level of implication the innocent pleasures of ice-cream but on another the primacy of the phallocratic sensibility. The censor had no objections.

The third phase of the operation soon followed. Now the tongue came to rest on the head of the patient, longaninimous penis or gingerly probed the circumcision ridge in an ideal, static, Parmenidean felicity. These representations were ordered by a rigid geometry of straight lines: tongue, penis, and the rapt, catatonic gaze of the woman extending to a point of intersection at the trivium of an encounter still controlled by the dynamics of postponement. The whole procedure resembled an illustration in Euclidean erotics, an abstract delineation of an act that was happening and yet not happening, a textbook diagram that escaped the organic or the empirical by virtue of its rigorous linear organization. It might just as well have been a technical design or a Renaissance exemplification of the mechanics of perspective.

As the censor continued silent, the covers of these magazines finally crossed the labial Rubicon into the fourth stage. Now the glans was permitted haustorial entry and disappeared from view into a mouth that had remained open for almost two years. "Only connect," said one of Forster's characters. The moment had arrived, genuine contact had been made, the act of fellatio, after such long deferral, publicly achieved. All one had to do was reach up for a copy of *Adult Pleasures* coyly reposing behind *Popular Mechanics* to enjoy the graphic reproduction in full publicity of an act troubled by generations of panic. The puritan sensibility and the indignation of the moral majority had at last been neutralized. Reality had come into its own, publicly acknowledged.

But the situation is by no means so simple. Why the apparent dissatisfaction among the clientele, leafing surreptitiously through the pages of the magazine and either replacing it on the shelf with ill-concealed gestures of frustration or buying a copy of *Scientific American* to appease the stern and judicial demeanour of the cashier? The affordable representation of fellatio had been eagerly awaited; now that it had arrived (my inquiries among a large number of newsstand vendors indicated), it produced dissatisfaction and irritation in a considerable proportion of the voyeurship, paradoxically contributing to the sale of the reputable periodicals.

Evidently, fellatio (which a statistical survey conducted by a celebrated journal established as the chief, male sexual pleasure) had somehow *not occurred*. The glans was in the mouth but the shaft wasn't. The oral depths of the proverbially willing female had not been sufficiently penetrated. The rounded lips, the pucker in the cheeks implying intake and suction, the oral screening of the circumcision trace seemed inadequate to convince. How much, one is tempted to ask in the purest Kinseyan spirit, of the penis must be ingested before the jaded observer is prepared to admit that fellatio is indeed taking place? Half the shaft – in the inevitable fifth stage of manifestation? Will he be satisfied then? Three quarters? What degree of visual dismemberment serves as fellatic authentication?

For the fact remains that by the standard definition of the act fellatio had indubitably taken place: "a sexual activity involving oral contact with the male genitals" (Webster). In the fourth stage of representation glossal contact had been plainly superseded and replaced, not simply by oral "contact," but oral penetration. There can be no doubt that what is occurring on the cover of *Adult Pleasures* (and a host of similar productions) is a manifest blow job. (Or at the very least, what the Romans distinguished as *irrumatio*.) Moreover, in the more expensive photojournals the promise on the cover is amply fulfilled behind the prophylactic cellophane wrapping, as the exposed shaft of the penis, while not necessarily vanishing to the hilt, enjoys increased oral sheathing, the female mouth translated into a veritable condom. Yet the voyeur continues to feel cheated, deprived not only of the pleasure but the reality he has been promised, compelling him to return to the newsstand and turn the pages of the other magazines on the top shelf with renewed priapic dedication. The search for laryngeal fabliaux goes on.

We are confronted here with a peculiar and instructive dilemma. The quest of the voyeur will never be satisfied because the act he wishes to observe or to enjoy vicariously, or the *reality* in which he desires to participate like Plato's highly trained philosopher, can no longer occur. By a strange kind of psycho-logic, the represented existence of a thing is undermined and cancelled by its very existence in itself. This is a phenomenon native not only to newsstand pornography but to the entire scope of contemporary experience of the world, and especially to literary or textual experience. An event has no reality for us unless it can be priapically validated, which is to say the object of our desire, the knowledge we wish to attain, has become a function of imaginary depth. As Jacques Barzun laments in *The House of Intellect*, in the pornosophic climate that prevails today, "the search is for essences. Not externals, depths. The taste for psychologizing takes it for granted that depths are more real than surfaces ..."[1] We are no longer content to experience a surface, which we are persuaded suffers from a *deficiency of reality* precisely to the degree in which it remains a surface (witness the derogatory connotation of "superficial") or, what amounts to the same thing, to the degree in which *it must be imagined in order to exist for us*.

Our experience with textual representation of the world has come increasingly to resemble the voyeuristic experience of reprographic fellatio. The *act*, blatantly undeniable, has receded to the level or status of an *intention* (i.e., a textual, not necessarily an authorial intention). The labially embowered glans is only a sign or a promise of an event that has as yet to take place. The signified has been *debarassé* of its own existence and retreated to the status of a new signifier in what threatens to become an endless, Lacanian process of empty signification, of perpetual deferral and sterile dissemination. What is is not what it is but has become the expression of an intention – but an intention to become nothing but itself, the thing it already is and always was. And when reality is reduced to the level of mere promise, act to intention, signified to signifier, existence to exponent, event to indication of event, the imagination is displaced from its visionary function and is called in to take the place of perception itself. We are in that condition Swift anatomized in *A Tale of a Tub*: "when a Man's fancy gets astride on his Reason, when Imagination is at cuffs with the Senses, and Common Understanding, as well as Common Sense, is Kickt out of Doors."

The voyeur cannot persuade himself that what he sees on the glossy print before him is a representation of actual fellatio; his anxiety diminishes only to the extent in which he is capable of imagining the event that is in fact statically enacted before his very eyes. The event is unreal for him because it lacks *depth*, not just abstract three-dimensional but simulated, *invasive* depth. The imagination is consequently summoned to represent entry as invasion, insertion as penetration, one depth as another, the glans as the shaft, the shaft as the testicles, the genital apparatus as the entire body, the body as ... the series has no final term. But this much seems to be the case for the sensibility under discussion: 1) what is must be imagined in order to be what it is; and 2) the specific property that must be imagined is invasive or penetrative depth. That is to say, because the object or event to be perceived lacks depth – or, more accurately, the representation of depth – it must be imagined, preferably in depth *but even in its apparent lack of depth* if it is to be assigned substantive existence;[2] and secondly, it will continue to lack depth because no depth, presentational or imagined, is deep enough to satisfy the sensibility that has lost touch with the surface of its experience or with the credal validation of that surface, that is, with what Derrida calls somewhere "the pellicular essence of being."

The experience of reading today has lost touch with the textual surface of its object. I am not referring to "superficiality" in its regrettable or pejorative sense, reading as mere eye-balling, the passive consumption of readerly texts, airplane reading, Harlequinizing, etc., but to the kind of reading regularly performed by the specialists – to, for want of a better term, hermeneutic reading. In the contemporary analytic milieu no serious text is sufficient to itself, is "deep" enough to gratify the hard-core appetite for substance, meaning, operative significance, or underlying reality on the part of the new breed of textual voyeur flourishing amongst us. The text must be imagined or visualized in ever-expanding (or is it narrowing?) concentricities of spiral *profondeurs* in the complacent assumption that the ninth circle will one day be discovered and explored – leading no doubt to purgatorial classifications and ultimately to celestial insights. An author is one – to employ a male metaphor – who projects in his text an erect phallus insufficiently swallowed; it is up to the reader if he or she is to valourize the textual representation, if it is to seem real, to descend passionately, in imagination, upon the implied author. It is up to him or her to re-imagine the experience "encoded" in the text in terms of what is not seen: an "actantial function," a deep "semic transformation," a mysterious "differential trace," a profound "ideologeme" or frame of collective discourse, a semiotic "matrix," an invisible "hypogram" or "paragram," units of "libidinal investment," etymological *diakresis*, molecular evasion and schizophrenic disruption, and the sliding signified (set in motion by the floating signifier). Add to all this the collapsible galleries of (De-Manxean) rhetoricity among the rubble of which we must probe and sift to specify the precise cause of referential cave-ins; intertextual (Kristevean) termites tunnelling through the wordwork; allegorical excess and ironic deficiency always and inevitably complicating the picture; tropological modes that underlie even the preconceptual experience of writer or reader; the archival vault of exclusionary and transformational rules which cannot be unlocked or dynamited – in other words, the variety of forms assumed by the deep structure of signification requiring that every serious reader become a kind of Jacques Costeau to explore or chart a text satisfactorily. The sensuous response to the texture of experience, whether of life or of literature, has yielded to the zealous and rather lugubrious plunge into the depths – which, of course, continue as always to recede. Compared to the modern or postmodern reader, someone like the medieval exegete Andrew of St Victor (d. 1175) seems a positively evolved negotiator of texts, insisting as he did upon reading *iuxta superficiem littere* (i.e., according to the letter). It is as if today we have forgotten how to enjoy ourselves or even how to live, let alone how to read, in the obsessive and Nemo-like search for the deeper strata of meaning. (Nor should the customary emphasis on the *ludic* nature of the investigative project, on the playful hermeneutics of indeterminacy and disseminative spillage, deceive us from recognizing the almost perverse earnestness of the operation. When people become serious about their pleasure, pleasure is the first thing that escapes their grasp. The "deconstructive surface" is only a metaphor for an unbalanced and deregulating pursuit of the invisible.)

Thus plot, character, passages of fine writing, the rich and carnal aesthetic surface of the prose and the narrative cease to exist in their own right or to be accredited as a form of primary textual experience. The shaft remains in view; therefore the "Joy of Reading" is effectively thwarted, which is like saying an alphabetical letter is not a letter so long as kern or serif remains exposed. Which amounts, in effect, to the radical decarnalization of literary experience.

We must exercise a little care here. I am not arguing that "depth" is unimportant or illusory *tout court*, but I am suggesting that the current preoccupation with substrata insensibly produces a climate of response in which actual experience, the perception of textual events and their ripple effect in the imagination, suffers gradual attenuation and is ultimately lost. The text ceases to exist in exact proportion as the text itself must be laboriously re-imagined in order to receive the gift of existence (rather than serve, as it was originally intended, as a *stimulus* to the imagination). In the imagination which remains *unconscripted* and free to engage with all that is not immediately present[3] but surrounds it like a nimbus, that is, with *the continuum of the world*, character and event are progressively elaborated. Fictional people and real people are permitted to mix freely, Hamlet figures in one's dreams as significantly as one's friend or brother, Jonathan Swift steps from his grave and holds converse in the Glubdubbdrib of his reader's imagination. The sense of the world is immeasurably enriched, as the dead, the fictive, and the actual, all invited to the party, arrive to swell one's acquaintanceship. And it is precisely this "sense of the world," this affirmation of felt reality, this redemptive function of the imagination as it addresses itself to the task of broadening (not only "deepening") the continuum of experience that enables us to say, "I saw eternity the other night." *The other night*. What will we see tonight? Tomorrow night?

This sense of the opulence of the world, of its plurality and magicality, of the concrete intensity of potential experience, begins to waver and falter, to "wallow faint and sudden everywhere," as Richard Wilbur puts it, once we allow ourselves to be cut off from the surface of the presentational and are forced to invoke the imagination *to reproduce a text for us*. It is the fascination, *the obsession with "depth" as a substitute for presence* that debars us from perceiving the depth that is already there and which will always be there as an integral part of the surface. (Since surface and depth, to apply Taine's celebrated metaphor, bear the relation to one another of recto and verso.) No surface is flat or one-dimensional unless we make it so, unless we have grown incapable of naive and joyful response. This does not constitute a plea for prescriptive superficiality; contained or enfolded depth is also an aspect of reality, as anyone who has studied physics, enjoyed fellatio, or simply *read a book* can attest. But it is the principal tenet or axiom of the modern age that nothing is substantively real unless it can be *imagined* in depth, unravelled, penetrated, deconstructed, dismantled, and definitively *revealed*.

Thus we have become so jaded that we are now in the incongruous position of having to imagine what is given. The imagination no longer fills in the blanks or completes a pre-indicated trajectory or populates absence. *It reproduces what is present as if to compensate for a failure of perception*. We have to bring an increasingly moribund imagination into play not even to constitute experience but merely to *recognize* it, to *italicize* the given in order to establish its prior existence. The object or phenomenon whose depths we are vigilantly probing, reconstructing, and imagining must now be (re)imagined *as the object or phenomenon that it is*, if it is not to vanish from our purview or if it is to retain its perceptual meaning and integrity for us. What is, isn't – until we subject it to intensified scrutiny, to a theoretically infinite *commentary*, what we like to call an analysis *in depth*, which only then enables us to endorse and posit its veridical existence as an object of perception and as *an experience for us*. The surface, we have been taught, is an illusion. We cannot understand the function of language, for example, unless we disinter its hidden, deep structure, just as we must remain forever innocent before the complex significance of a literary work until we penetrate to the level of its semic or structural operators. Literary experience remains callow and superficial until we have developed the appetite for analytic deep-throating or deep-thrusting. At that moment, presumably, the experience is valourized and the reader has taken in the text, subsumed it, and in the same instant established its reality. The possibility that the reader or critic has only participated in the process of what

Derrida calls *invagination* or in what Swift described in the *Tale* as merely one more vestimentary textual layer, exposing merely one more surface in a progressive and endless sequence of unveilings, has apparently escaped his attention. For human experience is always a function of the surface, is always, as it were, epithelial in its nature no matter how "deep" we are prepared to go. This is not to imply that we cannot or should not strip away manifest content in order to reach the barometric levels of latent significance but rather that we should realize such a process is theoretically infinite and always to some extent arbitrary. Even if we should one day succeed in splitting the hadron bag and observing quarks in action, we must still see that our experience of reality is inevitably skin-deep: the quark is nothing but another integument, another phenomenon of the surface which in turn "contains" infinite Blakean worlds whose "profundity" as we understand it is entirely metaphorical, a way in which the human mind re-interprets infinite laterality (or what Todorov called "lateral transcendence.")

All this is to suggest that we are as well served in observing as in *delving* and that we might profitably consider the renewed importance of focusing on the content of our experience, its contours, lineaments, and substantive presence. Reality as surface is always with us and need not be bracketed in the mistaken attempt to uncover the explanatory essence of things – which very likely does not exist, or if it does, must remain, in Owen Barfield's sense of the term, "unrepresented." What is on the "surface" may be partially accounted for by what lies "beneath," but what lies "beneath" is only another surface that imperiously demands further unmasking or demystifying.

I am not for a moment suggesting that the entire process ought to be abandoned. Reality is evidently structured, laminated, sedimented, intrinsically complex in nature, as the physical, mathematical, and (to some extent) the social sciences have made inescapably clear. But I am suggesting that the accompanying metaphysics, the intellectual predisposition to regard the nature of reality as *profound* rather than complex, leads to a misconception of "truth" and a devaluation of actual experience – which always occurs on the surface *wherever we happen to locate it*. The result of the current misconstruction from which we suffer is the progressive marasmus, the debilitation of actual *productive* experience which is now confined to the mere *reproduction* of the existent, to, let us say, a reprographic function. What stands before us has been discredited, deprived of existential vigour and substance, requiring the imagination to substitute for perception – or rather, for the belief in the world which hypostatizes the selectivity of the perceptual transaction. The act of perception that guarantees our experience of the world has been gradually reduced to the status of an *intention* that proposes to accomplish that which already exists. Which is to say that our *attention* has been distracted, weakened, and finally undone so that "experience of life," as of the text, has become a kind of ghostly epiphenomenon, the phantom of the opus, imprisoning the imagination in the function of gross restitution of the pre-existent rather than granting it its ancestral function of sketching alternative configurations of the real, of making proposals that lead to new experiences of the surface which has not yet been explored or mapped. The imagination working at its ideal limit tests the possible and brings it into the circle of the real, renovating not only by replacement but by extension.[4] But it rapidly grows exhausted if it is dedicated to italicizing, underlining, stressing the non-observable as the foundation of the observable which, since it is improperly observed, must be recreated in imagination – a service it is constrained to perform once we have neglected to attend to the superficies of our experience.

By the recommended "set" toward the voluptuous surface of things I do not refer to that mode of explanatory hypothesis whose purpose is "to save the appearances," into which Owen Barfield inquired. There is a sense in which we can never get beyond appearances or shed phenomena, no matter how "deep" we go. I am talking about perception, recognition, and pleasure, a form of sensuous experience that is whirled away and swallowed up in a kind of vertical Coriolis effect of endless structuration. This uvular pursuit of the truth, even if it results in the blithe dismissal of truth as a slippery undecidable, distracts us from experiencing the world in which we live, reduces our vitality and ardour, and diminishes that pleasure which Wilde says, in *The Soul of Man under Socialism*, "is Nature's test, her sign of approval." The preeminent philosopher of the surface, who stresses the importance of attending to the superficial aspect of things, is Jonathan Swift who, for example, while attacking the fraudulent nature of nominal Christianity (the "Argument against Abolishing Christianity") implies through his consummate irony its ultimate necessity. Similarly, in his "Project for the Advancement of Religion," he acknowledges that the best we can hope for is a nation of hypocrites who are content to observe the common forms of Christian behaviour. It is especially hazardous to interrogate the notorious *Tale* whose satiric intricacies continue to baffle even the most astute scholars, but may there not be a glimmer of authorial intent in the ambiguous praise of credulity: "so far preferable is that Wisdom, which converses about the Surface, to that pretended Philosophy which enters into the Depth of Things, and then comes gravely back with the Informations and Discoveries, that in the inside they are good for nothing." Or, in our context, that they are too good, too *precieux*, for the world in which it is our privilege and need to live.[5]

In treating of this surface/depth distinction, one must be careful, as indicated above, to keep the semantic gasket in place. For example, Barthes, as is well known, praises Robbe-Grillet precisely for the latter's surface qualities. Robbe-Grillet suspends narrative continuity, demotivates his characters, and impedes the production of meaning, thus keeping the reader on the surface of his descriptions which themselves provide only a "superficial" transcript of the world. But the sort of analysis Barthes conducts, like the kind of writing Robbe-Grillet deploys, is precisely that which is engaged in unmasking, demystifying, exposing, re-evaluating, refocusing; that is, it is a species of Revelation that discloses a panorama of unsuspected events, obscure or mazy practices, profound disruptions, constructions, "realities," or "truths" the reader might otherwise misconstrue or ignore. Thus the programmatic cancellation of depth requires an odd sort of depth analysis which renders the whole procedure paradoxical and "profoundly" suspect.[6]

The Greek dramatists knew what they were about when they completed their trilogies with a satyr play which functioned as an imaginative corrective, subjecting the analysis of the human condition carried out by the tragic cycle to unsparing and remedial mockery. Life is tragic; life is also absurd and farcical. If we look too deeply, laughter is abolished. The catharsis of pity and fear may lead to a state of serene acceptance or resignation, perhaps even to aesthetic joy, but it will not lead to restorative laughter. We must also attend to the surface where, so to speak, the jokes get told. Gods, demons, and the impersonal voice of Fate do not exchange one-liners or collapse in merriment. We need not disregard the findings of depth analysis, but should we not also affirm the importance of Greek fourthplay?

ADDENDUM

It is a curious fact that structural, semiotic, and deconstructive studies continue to proliferate as fewer and fewer people apply themselves to reading, writing, and even speaking coherently. While structuralists are busy investigating synchronic systems of meaning, while linguistically oriented critics are devising semiotic rectangles and pursuing glossematic analyses, while deconstructors are contriving new theories of textuality, intertextuality, and literary discourse in general – the text has become obsolete. Inveterate film-goers, video freaks and screen-glazed computer zombies are flocking into our colleges in ever greater numbers, very few of them having read more than half a dozen books *voluntarily* in their entire academic careers (according to a recent survey of student reading habits conducted among the English community colleges in Quebec). And the wider public reads less and less as the video outlets multiply. It is precisely in this ambience, in which the written word is dying and the spoken word is paralysed, that new and labyrinthine theories of the text flourish and ramify. I wonder if this is not a sign of the end, of a paradoxical sort of *absence* not envisaged by current "deconstructive" thinking. Our literary scholars appear to be retreating into a new Alexandrianism in which they can go on devising ever more complicated theories of linguistic transference or develop ever more intricate accounts of literary discourse in complete ignorance of the central phenomenon of our time: the death of the book.

Barthes with his proairetic and hermeneutic codes, Greimas with his semes, lexemes, sememes, and classemes, Bloom with his tropes, defences and cabbalistic ratios, Deleuze/Guattari with their molars and moleculars, Derrida with his traces and *iters*, Jameson with his ideologemes, etc. etc. – all this at the same time that enormous numbers of students are graduating incapable of parsing a Harlequin romance. The disproportion, the gap is cataclysmic.

Ironically the "subject" whom our theoreticians are busy "decentering" or "dispersing," showing how he is an effect, a construct, a semantic grid of interpretive conventions and not a unified, self-present, initiating self, has nonetheless as an unabashed and undivided entity consciously decided to stop reading books and certainly to pay no attention whatever to semioticians and deconstructors. Introducing Greimas's semes and sememes to a group of poetry students one day, I reluctantly had to admit the justice of their sceptical laughter. "Can't compare with meems and sheems," one of them said. And in the last analysis, I'm not so sure the joke is on the students in this particular case. Current theory, as Camille Paglia has spunkily proclaimed, is really a hothouse product of English postgraduate departments and self-serving critical journals like PMLA, both safely ignored by the world outside.

Notes on Lucianic Satire

ARGUMENT

1 Lucianic satire is the literary form of intellectual prophylaxis. It protects the self from the vices it attacks, such as pomposity, self-righteousness, or the sclerosis of absolute conviction, by undermining its own critique and calling its own authority into question. Thus, there is usually an element of self-parody to leaven the moralizing seriousness of its burden.

2 But it is also meant to protect the self from the inevitability of disappointment and therefore must inoculate its deposition with the serum of irony and self-mockery. It seeks at least a partial immunity against the crushing despair associated with the failure of its attempt to reform the world.

3 Consequently, Lucianic satire acknowledges both the fallibility of the self and the belligerence of the world, subjective weakness and objective barbarism. It knows both that the self can be infected by the disease it proposes to cure *and* that the disease will never be remedied. It must fight on two fronts at once, resisting contagion and holding off despair.

4 The mock encomium is a technique of intellectual survival ("irony" has "iron" in it), a form of self-defence, and one of the subtlest of the martial arts of the mind in its nimble deployment of ambiguity and paradox. But it is also a form of intellectual adventurousness insofar

as it can recognize the incorrigibility of the world and the moral dubiousness of the reforming self while continuing to venture forth, in Samuel Butler's phrase, as "a kind of Knight Errant ... to relieve the Distressed Damsel Virtue." Because it is aware of the defects it can neither avoid nor finally correct, it is characterized essentially by an inner poignancy all the greater for the rhetorical camouflage it generates. It is perhaps best exemplified by the passage from Proverbs: While the mouth is smiling, the heart is sad.

5 Lucianic satire might be summarily understood as a pose, an elliptical stance, a way of confronting experience at an angle. It is wary and spry, the intellectual equivalent of Parthian cavalry, for which the motions of advance and retreat are identical. The species of irony attached to this form of satire is double-edged as it is intended to cut both ways, its object being the self-world dyad. And it is whimsical in tone precisely because it lives in the emotional region of the subjunctive or the counter-factual, which is also the region of bitterness. It realizes that freedom is ultimately a function, as it is a victim, of the imagination which, as Johnson said, "preys incessantly on life."

COMMENTARY

The idea of self-defence can be interpreted in a number of ways. In its most obvious sense, defence is exterior. The satirist knows that he may be either misconstrued or, as the case may be, understood all too clearly, and therefore that he may find himself in considerable danger. Thus Juvenal, to evade the hostility of powerful adversaries and especially the lethal vindictiveness of the Emperor Domitian (who, Seutonius informs us, "came down heavily on authors who lampooned distinguished men and women"), refuses to name the objects of his indignation and rather transparently declares, "I shall try my hand on the famous dead" in order to protect himself.

In Lucianic satire, as I understand this particular category, defence is interior, proprioceptive. It is a way of heading off despair at the pass. As an illustration of the point, one might consider the scene in *Cyrano de Bergerac* in which the hero practises a sort of delaying tactic. Knowing that he is doomed to the loss of Roxane, who is within-doors being married to his rival Christian, he invents a Lucianic moon-tale to delay the nefarious Comte de Guiche whose presence in the house would interrupt and prevent the wedding of the girl Cyrano loves. The point is that the tale is so amusing, so charming and imaginative, that it is both literally and figuratively diverting. The comte, who is bent on achieving the seduction of the beautiful Roxane, finds himself for a brief, critical moment more interested in the consummation of the tale than of his lust. And Cyrano, whose heart is breaking while he ensures the completion of the ceremony that will put the woman he loves forever out of his reach, is *inwardly* diverted by the production of his own unstanchable fantasy. The success of his purpose involves the failure of his desire, but the sting of loss and deprivation is temporarily blunted, and even perhaps anaesthetized, by the fecund whimsicality of his invention. At this instant he is the impeccable Lucianic satirist, the man in the moon whose peculiar brand of lunacy enables him to resist the gravitational tug of inevitable defeat and the dejection of spirits that goes along with it. The story is so good, so fertile and flamboyant, that the world and its dependencies are momentarily eclipsed.

Our satirist thus moves on two parallel yet antithetical planes, or in two opposite directions at once. On the one hand his commitment to the remedial is absolute; on the other, the iridescence and vivacity of his performance substitutes in some measure for the checkmate of his deepest convictions. The success of the story neutralizes, at least partially, the failure of his hopes.

Generally speaking, the same is true of Swift, who on the whole probably endorses the Brobdingnagian king's famous peroration. If humankind is the "most pernicious race of little odious vermin that nature ever suffered to crawl upon the surface of the earth," then the only therapy that remains is total extermination – which would at any rate exempt the satirist from the labour of composition. But when the writer reaches this extreme of vituperation and contempt, he is no longer a satirist but a misanthropist. The trick is to be able to acknowledge the recalcitrance of the world or the malevolence of humankind while simultaneously attempting to amuse, reform, and improve it, an act that requires the psychological equivalent of the Charley Chaplin back-kick or the ability to keep travelling when the world has shrunk to the size of a gallstone. Lucianic satire is a technique of survival and the satirist must with one part of his mind assume the habits of the Laputan aristocrat by turning one eye inward and one eye toward the zenith. The event can be counted on to strike him emphatically with a pebble-filled bladder; meanwhile he is consoled by music and mathematics, or by the prosodic harmonies of his tale and the acrobatic figurations of his wit. Infidelity is rendered harmless with the assistance of paper and implements.

If this analysis is correct, one would have to say that an essential part of the psychology of Lucianic satire is mural and protective, and the tale is among other things an elaborate gesture of self-defence. The perspective towards the world which our satirist adopts is, one might say, a machicolated one as he peers through the opening in his mental parapet at the onset of the inevitable. But the buoyancy of the tale serves as a consolation for the leaden weight of personal defeat.

As we recall, the infirmity against which the satirist has to protect himself is twofold. It is not only against the wreck of his hopes that he must gird his heart but also the taint of moral contamination that he must effectively resist. When Lucian in *The True History* has Rhadamanthus threaten Socrates with banishment from the Isle of the Blessed because he is "ruining the atmosphere of the party with his peculiar brand of irony," the reader is entitled to speculate on the author's motives in framing this curious passage. We remember that Socratic irony consists in the feigning of ignorance for pedagogical reasons. Is not Lucian, like Socrates, protesting the purity of his intentions in deflating the hyperbolic travel literature of his day? Is he not in reality striking at the inordinate credulity of the common reader, of the earthbound imagination, which underwrites the everlasting popularity of romantic or escapist literature? The issue is still with us as irresponsible and sub-literate Othellos continue to prate of Anthropophagi and Blemyae, to which decoctions credulous Desdemonas, as always, "seriously incline." The passage in question is a clear indication that Lucian regards the satirist as pari passu a professional spoilsport whose tenure in any society is always insecure. And he is briefly calling attention to his own practice, "flashing" as it were, pointing out that beneath the ostensible capriciousness of his performance, the exaggeration, the high good humour, the absurdity of it all, abides a serious moral intention whose effect can occasionally be lacerating and mordant.

But this only as far as the Lucianic satirist can keep company with the redoubtable Socrates, who may be facetiously compared to a Silenus, who can take on the didactic function of the fool, and whose guiding principle is "Know Thyself." For Socrates, despite his elenchial brilliance and dialectic rigour, never truly considered himself a fool, or as innately corruptible, but our species of satirist is theoretically aware that he is liable to the same accusations his ballistic wit directs at his chosen targets, be they people or attitudes, individuals or abstractions. In a certain sense he knows himself better than Socrates ever did and consequently cannot allow his moral fervour and didactic insistences to obscure his own fallible humanity. His ridicule is partially deflected toward himself in the oblique recognition that he shares the patrimony of the ludicrous with his intended victims.

Thus Thomas More, knowing that the Latin transcript of his surname means "folly,"[1] confers the name of "Hythlodaeus" (meaning roughly "expert in trifles") on his protagonist, calls the governor of his ideal polity "Ademus" ("peopleless"), the senators "tranibors" ("gluttons"), and the assemblymen "syphogrants" ("silly old men"). Similarly Rabelais shelves among the books in the library of St Victor's the flatulent text, *Ars honeste petandi in societate* (or *The Art of Farting Decently in Public*) by the scholarly Hardouin de Graetz. Which reminds us that Rabelais was himself a scholar and a physician as well. As for the name of his chief protagonist, "Pantagruel" apparently derives from a mystery-play in which a diabolical Panthagruel attended incorrigible drunkards to stimulate their thirst. Moreover, there can be little doubt that Gargantua is with equal seriousness and frivolity proposed as the contemporary incarnation of Plato's philosopher-king. As Gilbert Highet affirms in *The Classical Tradition*, "he is educated in a manner befitting a descendant of Plato, and ultimately endows a community which partly resembles that of the Guards in *The Republic*." And the letter that Gargantua sends Pantagruel is a primary document in Renaissance theory of education.[2]

The Lucianic satirist possesses a double-jointed sensibility[3] or even what we might tentatively denote as a meta-sensibility. At the same moment that he scatters tacks under other people's feet, he strews banana peels beneath his own. In this way he avoids the occupational hazard of the moralist, the proctor of common values, which is a tendency to the shrill, the declamatory, the pontifical. There is, of course, no guarantee of ultimate immunity, and the satirist whom indignation drives to verse, as Juvenal proclaims in his poem and Swift on his tombstone, lives very near the dangerous edge of things. Lucianic satire is as much a protection against Juvenalian satire as it is an assault on the follies and absurdities of mankind.

SUMMATION

It is, I would suggest, at least possible that the idea of self-defence I have proposed is one of the subliminal strands of meaning in the *Praise of Folly* of Erasmus who, as we know, translated Lucian with Thomas More in 1506. We are aware that Erasmus had a profound distaste for, if not a deep horror of, extreme positions, entrenched orthodoxies, ideological intolerances. This would explain his own sense of helplessness and frustration as he found himself caught in the crossfire between the reforming animus of Luther and the hidebound, persecuting moralism of the established Church – between, in effect, competing fanaticisms. His own plea for moderation and flexibility, for mutual accommodation, earned him little but the hostile suspicion of both sides. Although the *Praise of Folly* was written before the dispute had erupted into an apocalyptic confrontation, it contained an element of accurate prescience in its recommendation of a kind of saving monkeyshine. Life, Folly tells us, is akin to theatre and requires a willingness on the part of the actors to play their roles without ruining the illusion: "It's all a sort of pretence, but it's the only way to act out this farce." People must, she proclaims, "have the sense to turn a blind eye and sweeten life for themselves with the honey of folly."

The *Praise of Folly*, then, is to a large extent an entreaty to its readers not to take life and themselves too seriously, or as we would say today, to eschew ideological extremes. Theatre avoids the irreversible. A death on stage is performed, not suffered, and one could imagine the confusion and discomfiture of an audience presented with, so to speak, a real live corpse on the boards. Erasmus is hinting that the aesthetic inappropriateness of an actual death occurring on the stage is tantamount to torture, banishment, and execution in life itself as the result of political or theological convictions whose validity can never be conclusively proven. A pope is to some degree also acting the papal role, and a reformer or zealot is equally playing the part of the reformer or zealot in the religious drama for which he has auditioned. It is not, as Eliot said, that humankind cannot bear too much reality, but that too much reality destroys the performance.

On a more modest level of inquiry, one might submit that Erasmus is prescribing as well for the committed satirist. For Folly, the great benefactress of mankind, is also acting out the part of Folly, and the satirist by the same token playing the role of the satirist. It would be pure folly, then, in the dyslogistic, unErasmian sense, for Folly to take herself too seriously and set herself up as an infallible legislator or an ideological crusader. Only in this way can the satirist, the Lucianic thespian, protect himself against the infection of the absolute and the fatal discouragement of his noblest aspirations.

The theatre metaphor is explicitly urged by "Thomas More," the character in the dialogue (whose views at this moment are probably very close to his creator's), when he opposes Raphael's abandonment of the political world by citing "another philosophy that is more urbane, that takes its proper cue and fits itself to the drama being played, acting its part aptly and well." This passage sounds like a paraphrase of the celebrated twenty-ninth chapter of the *Praise of Folly* in which Erasmus argues that one does not question the part an actor is playing or pose inappropriate, ontological queries (a dig at Socrates?). "Nothing is so foolish as mistimed wisdom." Again, Swift in his scathing "Digression on Madness," once the ironical component has been factored out and "placed," seems to be quite seriously suggesting that men should not "reckon among the high points of wisdom the art of exposing weak sides and publishing infirmities – an employment ... neither better nor worse that unmasking, which, I think, has never been allowed fair usage, either in the world or in the playhouse." What I am getting at is something a little different, a modification or permutation of the theatre metaphor, which I apply to the *psychology* of the satirist and not to the peculiar manipulations of experience which he recommends. This formulation accounts for half the case I am making – humility as a means of exemption. As for the other half, the need for diversion in the face of inevitable failure, I am tempted to quote Livy (book 7, chapter 2) who, in discussing the origin of satire, alludes to the desire for "scenic entertainments" as a distraction from the plague that would not abate. The satirist is aware that the plague of mortality with its attendant defects and vices cannot be dissipated, and takes refuge in the entertainment he provides himself in the midst of his best, therapeutic efforts.

Part Two

The Trial As Jewish Joke

The thought that there is anything fresh to be said of Franz Kafka's *The Trial* is implausible.

George Steiner, *No Passion Spent*

Ye use to look so sadly when ye mean merrily, that many times men doubt whether ye speak in sport, when ye mean good earnest.

Thomas More, *Works*

Max Brod recounts in his biography of Kafka that when the author read out loud the first chapter of *The Trial* to a group of friends, the atmosphere was anything but solemn. Despite the obvious seriousness of the theme and the almost goetic intensity of its rendering, we learn that the assembled company could not prevent itself from laughing and that Kafka "himself laughed so much that there were moments when he couldn't read any further." It is evident there is a dimension to this novel which the enormous critical sobriety its interpreters have brought to bear upon it has failed to consider; that Orson Welles in his dull, monochromatic film neglected to his prohibitive cost; and that the common reader, intimidated by generations of intellectual prostration, cannot trust himself to respond to without fear of irreverence.

The book certainly merits to be treated in *usum delphini*; but it also displays the broad lines of the cartoon, the characteristics of plain, not existential, absurdity. In the ebb and flow of its tidal style, one sentence nullifying another, the novel recapitulates, on a higher level perhaps, the structure of the Jewish joke with its tongue-in-cheek eloquence, attempting an earnest analysis of the problem of authenticity and guilt in the spirit of high self-mockery. (This does not preclude the simultaneous presence of what Milan Kundera in his essay on Kafka in *The Art of the Novel* styptically defines as "the horror of the comic.")

We must keep in mind that the novel was written by a man who refused to commit suicide because "staying alive would interrupt my writing less than death," a man who considered the moment of awakening in the morning as the "riskiest" moment of the day – as if to say that since being born is the most hazardous act in life, those who wish to live long should prudently avoid it. We should remember that the hunger artist confesses that his disciplined fasting originates not in principle or conviction but in lack of appetite; that Josephine the mouse-singer is celebrated for her *lack* of talent, for her representative mediocrity; that Kafka writes a long, agonizing, confessional letter to his father which is never delivered; and that he instructs his literary executor to destroy his manuscripts, which prepares the piquant scenario of that executor going on to become the curator of the Kafka museum. This is the same man who leaves behind as his most enduring monument a novel the order of whose chapters is still a source of dispute and which is manifestly unfinished: in short, a man for whom life was a fugue of contradictory intentions and for whom fiction was like the Old Commandant's blueprints for the torture machine, "a labyrinth of lines crossing and recrossing each other."

This is not to imply that *The Trial* is not a serious work deserving of our utmost respect and attention. We know that the subject of guilt and suffering is one of the most prominent concerns of the twentieth century and that Kafka's treatment of the theme is grounded both in the experience of his life and of his people, and has as well philosophical antecedents in Schopenhauer and Nietzsche. We acknowledge that his analysis of guilt is masterly and of seminal importance, that is, the notion that guilt is not a function of an act (it is not to be conceived in legal terms). Nor is it a function of mere feeling (it is not to be treated as a psychological concept – Joseph K. does not feel guilty, if he feels anything it is his ineluctable innocence) but must be construed as a *condition of being*, as an ontological category, as a function of the anatomy of the soul. To be born is to be born guilty, and not, as in orthodox Christian theology, as the result of some primordial sin transmitted mysteriously from parent to child ad infinitum, but rather (as in original Gnosticism and its derivative, the Hebrew Kabbalah), as the consequence of a flaw in the creation of the universe itself. We may also give this subject a more personal inflection by applying the idea of "existential guilt," which Martin Buber defines as the guilt that accrues "when someone injures an order of the human world whose foundations he knows and recognizes as those of his own existence." Thus we may pronounce Joseph K. guilty of a remoteness from the source of life that is both affective and epistemic, guilty, in other words, of regarding his life as no more than the sum of his actions and therefore living inauthentically. In the relation between the protagonist and the world, the damage is reciprocal. Joseph K., like Georg Bendemann, insists on turning his existence into a professional, routinely ordered, conventionally acceptable one and excluding any part of himself that might lead to introspection, self-knowledge, and genuine reciprocal relationships with other people. One can describe K. simply as a man who does not know himself and who has no friends. He is personally "guilty" on two counts: of injuring both himself and the world in which he lives. This argument is developed by the majority of commentators on *The Trial*, perhaps most eloquently by Maurice Friedman in his *Problematic Rebel*.

But we must also remember that Kafka is a Jew, and a Jew is one who chronically tastes the bitterness in what is sweet, the sweetness in what is bitter. Kafka's life and work are driven by an acute consciousness of antinomies, and his profound melodies are almost always counterpointed by ironic figurations. This is just another way of saying that his passionate sense of commitment to his subject goes hand in hand with an equally powerful sense of its futility, and the joke is that what he has devoted his life to accumulating he would cancel by one stroke of the pen in his last testament, a joke that is itself partially cancelled insofar as he must have known that Max Brod would have been the least likely of all people to carry out his final request. One of the great difficulties in life as well as literature is how at the same time to be serious and unpretentious, how to achieve the "profound" while avoiding the lugubrious, how to express feeling without being sentimental; or, in the Jewish idiom, how to suffer without redundance. Kafka's method may be described as remedial deflation, the rearing of an immense structure, almost gothic in the imposingness of its design, upon an acre of purest quicksand.

This is merely one form of a literary strategy we may define as psychic prophylaxis. When an author treats a subject he instinctively recognizes as dangerous to his own equilibrium, he devises ways of protecting himself. Entering the flames, he must employ a style of asbestos; plunging to the "depths," a bathysphere to resist the pressures. One thinks of Conrad, writing in a language twice removed from his native tongue, interposing narrators between himself and his theme, relying on the distancing factor of a Socratic irony (and despite all these mediating screens suffering a severe mental collapse). Kafka's mode of psychic prophylaxis is intentional absurdity, the cancelling of pretensions, the raising up and bringing down, the meticulous style compulsively applied to the description of the preposterous – the very technique of the Jewish joke.

The legend of the doorkeeper, originally a parable Kafka later incorporated into the text of *The Trial* (complete with hermeneutics), is generally considered to be the semantic heart of the novel. No interpretation of *The Trial* may regard itself as authoritative unless it takes the legend into account. Ingeborg Henel, for example, argues that the purpose of the legend is to show K. his error concerning the court, which consists first in his belief that he can win his case through influence and bribery, and secondly that he can shift the responsibility for his predicament from himself unto the officials who are revealed to be corrupt. But this is certainly making too much of the poor rustic's picayune gifts, as well as of his confused but well-intentioned surrender to the doorkeeper. Henel's proposition that the legend demonstrates that the law is not universal but derives its validity precisely from the unconditional claim it makes upon the individual is more to the point. This argument recalls the tenets of the Lurianic Kabbalah respecting the Torah; as Gershom Scholem writes in *On the Kabbalah and Its Symbolism*, "every word has six hundred thousand faces ... layers of meaning or entrances, one for each of the children of Israel who stood at the foot of Mount Sinai. Each face is turned toward only one of them; he alone can see it and decipher it. Each man has his own unique access to Revelation." This hypothesis, of seventeenth-century provenance, has a curiously modern ring and might even be labelled proleptically "existential." But while such an interpretation of the legend is no doubt sound, it is far from exhaustive. The door opens inwards, obviously; the law that applies to the single individual has its origins in the dictates of the unconscious mind and requires that the individual penetrate into the furthest regions of his own psyche. *But what of the battery of exegesis that accompanies the legend and distinguishes it from its pristine state in the parables?* This distinction cannot be accidental, and one is strongly tempted to see in these accretions the fundamental reason for the tale's inclusion in the text.

The accretions consist chiefly in the priest's interpretations, or more exactly, in the priest's recital of the various interpretations that have collected around the legend. One school of suppositious critics apparently considers that the doorkeeper is diligent and compassionate and is not, as K. would have it, to be faulted in the exercise of his duties or in his humanity. This postulate is developed persuasively and at length. Another school, however, speculates that the doorkeeper is in fact inferior to the postulant, in some way even contemptible. Now this assumption is impressively supported. It is almost as if the door with which Joseph K. is engaged is a revolving one, for his interpretation of the tale is repeatedly influenced by the priest's rhetorical brilliance. Finally, a third school is adduced which reverses the opinion of the second, and once again the doorkeeper, as a scion of the law, is ably defended. K. is so bewildered by the multitude of conflicting expositions he can only lament that lying is made into a universal principle. Of all that he is given to say in the novel, these are the words that seem most disconsolately heartfelt.

What is the reader to make of this paramythic flux: you cannot step into the same legend twice! Is Kafka perhaps not presenting us with a kind of burlesque of both his intentions as novelist and ours as critical readers? Is he not undercutting his philosophical gravity, offering us a vaudeville performance in the first degree? Does not the doorkeeper resemble the obscure, faintly ridiculous, and yet creditably rigorous novelist?[1] The man from the country: the "innocent" reader who wishes to penetrate the labyrinthine depths of the novel but quails before the formidable doorkeeper? The adroit and learned priest: the erudite scholar? And Joseph K.: the baffled student who so much approximates the original "innocent" reader? Is not the tale as we have it in the text a semiotic model of the text itself, unfinished, frustrating, and insolubly perplexing?

The parable of the doorkeeper does to the novel exactly what the Jewish joke does to the religious meaning of Jewish election and precisely what Kafka's laughter does to the first chapter of *The Trial*. It heightens it while at the same time deflating it, placing the incommensurable in a human perspective, and establishes the only marriage a man like Kafka was capable of solemnizing,[2] the search for significance with the recognition of its complete futility, a kind of nuptial agitation for which rest is the ultimate insomnia. To rephrase the famous proverb of Solomon: since the heart is sad and never sleeps, the mouth curls up in the bed of its smile.

Framing Layton

Expose thyself, thou covered nest
  Of passions, and be seen;
Stir up thy brood, that in unrest
  Are ever piping keen.
Ah! what a motley multitude,
  Magnanimous and mean.

Charles Heavysege, "Open, My Heart ..."

For such a one everything that is imagined exists or can exist, whereas that which does not enter within the net of imagination is in his opinion non-existent and incapable of existing.

Moses Maimonides, *The Guide of the Perplexed*

PANEL I

So much has by now been written about, against, around, on behalf of, in reaction to, in gratitude for, and in displacement from the doyen of Canadian poetry that anyone starting to write an article on Irving Layton must quickly approach a state of prepositional collapse. Doubting that much remains to be said, I almost regret having undertaken to add yet another affidavit to the towering stack of analysis, reminiscence, and obfuscation that constitutes the Canadian mini-industry of Layton scholarship. All I can do, I'm afraid, is hazard a small, tentative, perspectival account, a personal footnote to the Britannica as an apophradic tribute to the man who stands to me and to so many other younger poets as friend, mentor, benefactor, example, and, at times, as monumental Bloomian impediment. For any writer who has been influenced *in any way* by Layton must recognize the accursed precursor-ephebe dialectic that accounts for the peculiar mix of resentment and gratitude one feels for the greatest of our poets. I should confess at the outset that what I feel is mainly gratitude, though honesty compels me to acknowledge those disturbing moments when I could wish that Layton's shadow were not quite so long and so encompassing.

The problem remains. To write about Layton means initiating a series of endlessly deferred beginnings (a bit like Hesiod who has to crank up three separate starts before getting into the *Theogony*), since no end, no final understanding or definitive summation is possible. The analysis of the poems has been long undertaken by a host of perceptive critics. The novel has been written (Aviva Layton's *Nobody's Daughter*). The biography, skewed and controversial, has generated the predictable flap – for three transgressions and for four, there's little point in pummelling Elspeth Cameron any further, and Layton's autobiography, *Waiting for the Messiah*, compensates more than adequately while contributing to the memorial parallax that bedevils the "Life" of any great writer, turning it into a sequence of perpetual adjustments. The Encyclopedia has accomplished its work of canonization. Nobel nominations have added to the reputation. An arsenal of revisionary estimates will be massively deployed in the coming years as time performs its work of editorial sifting, disengaging the core of truly remarkable work from the forty to fifty volumes of Layton's prolific output. And the analyses, critiques, and recapitulations will begin all over again, with the inevitable result of replacing one legend with another, presumably more authoritative, more considered, more definitive, yet I suspect no less a collective fiction, the signal of greatness. (Will we ever find out who really issued the challenge to the famous handball game?) When little remains to be said while the commentaries continue to ramify and proliferate, we know we are in the company of genius, which, being not so much a "life" as a crowd of assumed identities, explains the analogy of plenitude between the creative source and the expository apparatus.

Take three: let me begin anecdotally. I first heard of Irving Layton when I was fourteen, chugging on Lac de Sable (in my hometown of Ste Agathe) in Henry Moscovitch's three-horsepower chaloupe. Henry, a precocious and talented protégé of Layton's, used to spend his summer vacations in the Laurentians. At this time he was preparing his first slim volume of bourgeois-bashing poetry (*The Serpent Ink*), and would regularly putter me out to the middle of the lake, turn off the motor, and read interminably from a blackbound portfolio of terse vituperations that he called poems – he had Layton's crisp accents down pat. Occasionally he interspersed these pieces with resonating verse proclamations of his sexual exploits, testimony to the power of the poetic imagination and to his fidelity as Layton's amanuensis.

I must admit that my complicity was motivated by other concerns, namely the hope that Henry, the scion of a wealthy bourgeois family, might from time to time relent, swing the megapower inboard out of the boathouse, and take me water skiing. But I paid exorbitantly for these brief episodes of genuine fun by a summerful of becalmed, lacustrine recitations which constituted my first exposure to the muse. I discovered that poets were privileged beings, feared by society, honoured by posterity, anointed by God, indefatigably potent, and overwhelmed by the adulterous ministrations of bored, lascivious, middle-class wives. It was at that point that I first began meditating a career as a poet, learning at second hand from Henry what he assured me he had absorbed from the master himself. As further corroboration he quoted prodigiously from the sybilline texts Layton had regularly schlepped into class, the works of the Romantic triumvirate who justified the splendour and necessity of imaginative commitment – Blake, Nietzsche, and Lawrence, none of whom, as a country-school hooky player, I had ever heard of. But the gap in my education was amply filled by Henry's motorboat tutorials and the loan of Layton's early books. And in fact the very first poem I ever committed *voluntarily* to memory was Layton's "The Cold Green Element" which, as Henry's captive if not entirely captivated audience, sweating under the hot sun in the middle of the lake while my tormentor read endlessly from his bulging folder, wanting nothing more than to dive into the water, I would recite inwardly to myself, especially the conclusion:

And misled by the cries of young boys
    I am again
A breathless swimmer in that cold green element.

Four years later, as a student living in Montreal, I attended one of Layton's night classes at Sir George Williams University. I was no longer the country neophyte inhabiting that ambiguous region between awe and boredom into which poetry had inducted me, but a practising poetaster in my own right, bristling with convictions and a sense of adolescent infallibility. Moreover, as a student of Louis Dudek, I had become aware of the hothouse conflict between Dudek and Layton which divided the aspirant community of young poets into roving partisan bands doing battle in the cloakroom of Redpath Library and in the pages of the *McGill Daily*. I was at the time a loyal Dudekin, arrogant with sceptical modesty, heaping scorn and animadversion on the company of mad Laytonians who were immediately conspicuous by the fact that they all affected Layton's clipped, oddly British pronunciation, were "Fanatic in belief some rival / Mode of metaphor lacks wit and style," chewed garlic and onions with revolutionary ardour, and slathered their conversation with the names of Blake, Nietzsche, and Lawrence. I decided it was high time to check out the fire-breathing Moloch who devoured young poets for breakfast or turned them into diminutive clones of his own fulminating presence.

What I encountered was totally unexpected. There, holding forth at the head of the class, short, built like a wedge, resembling a boxer, strode a veritable pedagogic titan. A lordly, megaphonic rhetoric with the "wonderful claiming power" of Sara Jeannette Duncan's Dr Drummond carried across the entire room, so that, sitting in the back row, I felt catapulted to the front, vulnerable, stripped of saving anonymity. But it was the *subtlety*, the fine distinctions he so adroitly manipulated within the protagonistic delivery, that extorted unwilling respect and admiration. The poem under discussion was Randall Jarrell's "The Death of the Ball-Turret Gunner," which I had read with much appreciation and little understanding. Layton proceeded to analyse the poem with such delicacy of insight, probing carefully and lovingly to its metaphoric core (which had escaped me entirely), that I had the uncanny feeling of listening in to the author's own thought processes, as if I were present at the act of composition itself. This was not criticism but telepathy, a transferring of the self into the privacy of another mind, which only the very greatest of teachers is capable of performing. And I was aware even then of the irony tacit in the performance, considering the notoriety of Layton's robust, basilican, and narcissistic poetic ego. I had (and have) seldom observed so gracious and productive a deference of self to the work of another. I learned many things in that class. I learned more about the complex operations of metaphor in an hour than I had in years of reading – I continue to bring Jarrell's poem as an illustration of the metaphoric principle to the attention of my own students to this day.[1] But perhaps most importantly, I learned that love of life-and-literature has many forms and is by no means cancelled or compromised by the driving, aggressive, flamboyant manifestation of self associated with the poetic ego in need of confirmation. Not that Layton's really needed it. Jarrell has said that if a poet is struck by lightning six times, he is a genius. Layton has been *charred* by lightning innumerable times – even a dubious Elspeth Cameron gives him fifteen "world-class poems," and an ambivalent George Woodcock thirty-five "first-rate poems" – so that he bears a metaphorical resemblance to the tree in "The Cold Green Element" "for whom the lightning was too much / and grew a brilliant / hunchback with a crown of leaves." (However, all this notwithstanding, I did not return for the second part of the class, sensing the danger inherent in prolonged exposure to so powerful and *vortical* a personality.)

I finally got around to meeting this strange, promethean hybrid, this nemesis/benefactor, quite by accident some three or four years later, halfway around the world. I had rented a villa for the summer on the island of Mallorca, in a tiny hamlet called Fornalutx tucked away in the mountains to the northeast. Now in my early twenties, I had come to the conclusion that one could do nothing great in Canada (forgetting Layton's example), and that for an aspiring young Canadian writer, expatriation was the only solution to citizenship. After six weeks or so, I reluctantly admitted to myself that not only was I doing nothing great, I was doing nothing at all, with the result that I spent most of my time sitting outside the village café drinking brandy and coffee and at least feeling like a writer if not being one. It was during one of these daily, unproductive sessions that I noticed a taxi pull up across the street and disgorge three uncomfortable passengers, one of whom I seemed to recognize: a short, bullish man addressing everyone in his immediate vicinity in a huge, oratorical voice, pounding away like a Mobilfacta compressor on an Ikea display platform, commenting on the heat, the dust, the glazed enamel of the sky, the remoteness of the village, and didn't Robert Graves live around here, a fine poet and mythographer but somewhat lacking as a novelist, and where was the house he had been promised, why was there nobody to meet him, could that be construed as neglect?[2] "Let's ask *him*," said Bill Goodwin, Layton's nephew, pointing in my direction, and Aviva Layton inquired as to the condition of my English.

My first encounter with Layton and his party did not begin auspiciously. I could not help him immediately locate the house which had been put at his disposal, and Bill considered that they should perhaps backtrack to Soller, the nearest large town. How far was Soller from here, Bill wanted to know. About six miles as the crow flies, I replied. "Well, we don't intend to fly," Bill remarked witheringly, and Layton grunted in approval.

Smarting under the rebuke, feeling more and more like a Canadian and less and less like a writer, intimidated by the proximity of greatness, I left the table and scampered around the village like Carroll's unicorn, asking everyone I met about a mysterious empty house awaiting visitors. This, I realized, was a crucial moment in my development as a poet, once again, as if "to the clanging tunes of appetite and chance," implicated with Layton's charismatic presence, and if I were to fail in my quest – the phrase "triumph of accommodation" ran through my head – I might as well turn in my ambitions and become rich. Fate intervened in the guise of the local blacksmith, who had been informed by the owner of the house and was able to give me precise directions. And so it was that I led the great poet in a triumph of accommodation to the door of his sanctum, receiving in return the benediction of his "good work" and a remark about the appropriateness of the blacksmith – Blake's Urthona, Joyce's forging Dedalus – as a metaphor of the poet. (Layton's comment in his poem "Fornalutx" was untypically laconic: "The house, of course, was decent enough." The town, however, he situated in one of Dante's bituminous circles.)

Later in the afternoon we gathered at the reservoir for a swim. This concrete rectangle, filled with weedy, brackish water, sat in a kind of coulee or arroyo about a kilometre out of town in the direction of Deya where Robert Graves held court. I had heard that Graves was throwing a party that evening for friends and members of the local intelligentsia, but neither Layton nor I had been invited. "One must be magnanimous," Layton observed. "He probably doesn't know I'm here." This led to a discussion of Graves and his work – "a considerable poet," Layton conceded. Across the valley from the reservoir rose the grey mass of the highest mountain in the northern chain, which Layton speculated was the source of one of Graves's most celebrated poems, "Rocky Acres," a meticulously descriptive work, a piece of mood-painting. I suggested rather timorously that the descriptive aspect of the poem was entirely pretextual, that the mountain could only be regarded as inadvertent, and that what Graves was actually providing was a detailed mindscape, a pictorial representation of the spiritual dimension in which he lived, somewhat like Hopkins's sonnet, "No worst, there is none ..." (To credit Katherine Snipes's account in her *Robert Graves*, we were both wrong. The poem is, apparently, a "stark description of the Welsh countryside.") I went on at some length, recalling Layton's own exegesis of Jarrell, and was gratified and relieved by his willingness to listen and his approval of my hermeneutic efforts. I have never forgotten that day in Fornalutx, partly because it was the day on which I first began to feel a preliminary sense of confirmation in that elusive adequacy of self which underlies all the madness and ostentation of the persona. I was never a student, a disciple, or a protégé of Layton's, but I benefited enormously from the mere generosity of his presence – despite the evident dangers. The inveterate talker was also the most stringent and encouraging of listeners – if, that is, you had something to say.

Ten years elapsed before I saw Layton again, this time in another small village on another remote island, as if our encounters had somehow been ordained to be fleeting and insular, intersections, really, rather than meetings. Layton was spending the summer of 1973 in

Molibos (not an island, as Elspeth Cameron assumes, but a village) on the island of Lesbos where I had also rented a house, about five kilometres outside the town in a gaggle of dwellings dignified by the name of Eftalou (Seven Hills). To add to the strangeness of the time, Bill and Aviva were also there, so that the summer we spent in one another's company had a weird, orchestrated air, like something scripted, revised, and polished by an unknown hand. I can't explain how these peculiar things happen except to suggest that certain places tend obscurely to attract certain writers at certain moments in their careers by a kind of coordinate magnetism. In the short time I spent on Lesbos (actually, in Eftalou), I met the Greek novelist Nasos Theophilos, was introduced to the Danish poet Henrik Nordtbrand, entertained Andy Wainwright on my front porch, drank with Harry Sarr and crossed paths if not swords with Peter Green. In the serendipitous light of these occasions, the fact that Layton and I should have found ourselves once more within hailing distance in faraway places should have been entirely predictable.

I do not have the space or leisure here to provide even a digest of a summer's worth of discussion, argument, and speculation, except to say that with Layton life is never dull. Admittedly, I would sometimes try to avoid meeting him on my shopping expeditions into town if only to preserve a sense of beleaguered equanimity, for Layton was always either on the verge of knocking off another masterpiece or had already completed several between breakfast and late-morning coffee. "David, my boy," he would call from his café table, when I had not succeeded in dodging into the nearest lane or arcade, "I've caught two fish already, one big, one small," leaving me to ponder the fate of the minnow I had struggled with all morning, thrumps of groupers shoaling massively by the mind's eye. Sometimes I might be invited for a cup of coffee, and if I demurred, I was immediately assured the coffee was *at his expense*: there could be, in other words, no compelling reason for refusal. (Much later, when reading *Waiting for the Messiah*, I couldn't help but smile over the passage in which Layton writes that he felt "privileged to pay for" Jack Stern's coffee.) Nor could I explain that my reluctance derived from the need to protect what Coleridge called the "initiative," the first slender hint and impulse of a poetic phrase or rhythm, from Layton's philharmonic obliterations. How many poems I have lost to Layton's generous invitations I cannot afford to calculate.

But even though the "relationship" had changed over the years and I no longer felt myself to be the eternally grateful catechumen, I was still to some extent an apprentice and could profit immeasurably from his example. The form of insecurity that troubled me at this time had nothing to do with the vocational doubt of the earlier years and everything to do with whether I was practising my craft in the right contemporary way. I was not only partial to rhyme and enamoured of stanzaic intricacies but I also counted syllables on an internal abacus and would sometimes tell beats and accents on a set of worry beads I kept for the purpose. Could anything be more misguided and preposterous? The poets of my generation spoke of open-ended lines, semantically charged energy fields, and projective verse à la Olson, of the curse of the definite article à la Rostrover Hamilton, of the fragmentation of the modern sensibility reflected in paratactic utterance à la Fenellosa, and of subtle euphonies and wispy internal rhymes à la just about everybody, whereas I seemed to be concerned mainly with the staid, orthodox three Rs of the discipline: Reading, Riting, and Rhythmitic. I brazened on impenitently, but much of my apparent conviction and indifference was merely protective camouflage.

One afternoon Layton, Bill, and Aviva arrived in Eftalou for a visit which, as the day careened on in typical Greek fashion, turned into a multi-course meal punctuated by frequent trips to the retsina barrel. After a couple of hours I noticed that Layton was absent – or rather, I noticed that I no longer noticed him, an unlikely event in itself. Somewhat apprehensive, I set off in search, recalling an acquaintance who had fallen from the cliffs further up the road and spent six weeks recuperating in the Mytilini hospital. I need not have worried. There was Layton sitting cross-legged on the beach, a notepad open beside him, and a pencil in one hand; the other hand served as a timekeeper, fingers toting up the syllables. Then the tip of his pencil began tapping faintly against a pebble, like a fairy tuning fork lightly striking the rim of a martini glass. Layton was counting his syllables, he was measuring out iambs and anapests, he was calling his words to order, he was tallying stress and accent like clusters of his own red chokecherries for the sake of "perfection of form." Here was the Layton whom many, naive readers or detractors – having in a failure of accommodation bought the *enfant terrible* persona wholesale – refused to acknowledge or acclaim: the strict, responsible *maker* or *poiitis* who crafted the nifty Hudibrastics of "Prologue to the Long Pea Shooter," or the deft, ergonomic stanzas of sonnets like "When It Came to Santayana's Turn," "Icarus," "A Strange Turn," and "The Antipodeans," or the honey-tight perfection of "Early Morning in Mithymna," the poet (as Brian Trehearne in the fine introduction to Layton's most recent volume, *Fornalutx*, correctly remarks) whose "striking casualness of tone ... disguises the meticulousness of rhythmic expression." And as I watched from the shade of a plane tree, I was once again confirmed in my congenial practice. From that point on in our relationship, the intimidating Layton became the avuncular Irving, one of the selves in the repertoire I have been most privileged to know.

HINGE

It is almost twenty years since that summer in Lesbos, and Irving Layton, with his plumb-line and basket of fruit, is now my neighbour. Predictably, this means we practically never see each other except for an occasional beer or fitness swimming at the YMCA pool, a distant relative of the Fornalutx reservoir. I find after all this time that I know a fair amount about the work but almost nothing about the man, despite the proliferation of biographical material. What *do* I know? I surmise that Irving Layton is now eighty, since I have attended his seventy-fifth birthday celebration for five consecutive years. I know that he is as passionate, vigorous, eloquent, engaging, and rancorous in his dislikes as ever. I recognize that the creative artist in him, both wise and splenetic, shares something with the playful and destructive temperament of the child, refusing the desiccations of a merely prudential maturity – tending, as Carlos Fuentes enjoins, "the savage ocean he bears within because it's the only thing left to him from two overlapping creations: that of the world and that of the child." (The desideratum, Fuentes says, is "not to dry out.") I know that he is immortal. But I'm not sure where to locate the source of that Lupercalian vitality that swells and quickens his poetry and is responsible for a stanchless productivity that sometimes leads to dilution, crambo, and repetitiveness, to a grainy, low-budget feel, but which makes the best of the poems almost self-memorizing. What is it about the *quality* of the essential work that renders it unique in the history of our literature? Other Canadian poets have written exceptional lines and remarkable poems, at a lower incidence of frequency, perhaps; even so, some crucial attribute is too often missing in the latter. Is it the property of paradoxical candour one finds in lines like "and when I write my lying poems know I am using / an anodyne from which the fastidious man recoils"? Is it the sheer *magnitude* of the oeuvre, of the work and the presence – which differentiates it from that of our "North American Poet[s]" easing "self-contempt by writing verse" – miming the burly confidence of an old-time luxobarge in a swarming traffic of econocars? Is it the pathos, the compassion, of "I want to climb the highest rooftop / in the village / and announce to all / that no one in it will ever die"? The quotable lines remain inexhaustible, so that in writing about Layton one is always in danger of behaving like an anthology.

I suspect that the quality I am looking for has something to do with what Jacques Derrida, borrowing a term from plainsong, calls the *neume*, that species of vocalization that whiffles "between cry and speech, animal and man," a language that, in Derrida's phrase, is "uncontaminated by supplementarity," retaining in its momentum and inevitability a trace of some original plenitude that constantly recedes, eluding the critic and the imitator. It is a language that takes its origin not in contract or agreement, in the prose of our quotidian transactions (as does the bulk of contemporary poetry) but in the irruption of the sense of festival, the "pure presence" of joy, rage, and celebration, the plunge into the conjugal amalgam of the Creation. Thus it is, paradoxically, not a fully finished language in the sense of a medium hospitable to logical discriminations, a mere disruptive accuracy, but a language that is constantly *being born*, a pure vocalization which, as Derrida claims, "is inspired in us by God and may address only Him," uncorrupted by interval and discontinuity. This may account for the feeling one often has in the presence of great poetry, as in the best of Layton's work, that one is not listening or reading directly: *one is eavesdropping*. And this is why, too, before the talismanic power of the word, there is, finally, little to be said that is neither performative nor anecdotal: emulation, repeating out loud what one has heard, indulging in the higher gossip.

The voice of the neume, diffracted into the myriad articulations of grim lament and pure doxology, is the language of restoration, of the discovery and recovery of all that suffers the attrition of an increasingly worried, mundane, and banausic age. As a young poet at least marginally influenced by Layton's vision and practice, I once dedicated to him a humble quatrain with the disproportionate title "Coda to the Twentieth Century":

The minotaur gorges on human pork;
the blood of Theseus sweetens the dish.
Impaled on Poseidon's practical fork
Odysseus goes to feed the fish.

Layton's central awareness is that we are living in a thin, demythologized time that lacks, for all its technological aplomb and its conquest of the natural world, a sense of mythic grandeur, sustaining heroism, and epical vitality ("Runts are the problem, / runts who long for the stride and stature / of giants"). It is precisely these deficits that Layton's muse has determined to remedy and supply. Blake, Nietzsche, and Lawrence are his immediate progenitors, but the lineage he honours and redeems goes back to Theseus who confronts the monstrosities of human corruption, and to Odysseus who resists the envious and reductive temper of the age in which he navigates. Somewhere between Poseidon and the Minotaur, the afflicting and representative god on the one hand and the brutal deformities of the contemporary self on the other, the neumic language of genuine poetry sings and curses in its festival of revival. This is Layton's gift and calling, the source of his authority as a poet, accounting for the tone of carnival exuberance that animates his work as it alienates a progressively empirical audience. And if one objects to the Theseus-and-Odysseus citation as archaic and inappropriate, perhaps one can take Layton at his own word as a mischievous and resuscitated "Dionysus in Hampstead" who looks about him at the diminished spectacle of modernity and observes:

The wise and the just are too solemn
under their long shadows they do not dance
at the weddings I hear in the grass
at the mock funerals I hear in the leaves of trees.

Or as the proleptic mystic of many other poems, the one who asks where

are gone the grizzled ecstatic
faces
    of the vehement crazy men
who dreamed and prayed?

And if the reader should dismiss my reference to Derrida's concept of the neume to characterize Layton's "wild peculiar joy" as improbable, I would direct him or her to Roland Barthes's complementary notion of the "grain of the voice," that elusive yet unmistakable "something which is ... in the cantor's body, brought to your ears ... from deep down in the cavities, the muscles, the membranes, the cartilages ... The grain is ... the materiality of the body speaking its mother tongue." Although Barthes alludes to the actual voice raised in song and not to the written word per se, his distinctions strike me as eminently applicable to the rich carnality of the poetic line, heard in the mind's ear as one reads or compelling one to reproduce the texture of the composing voice itself, to revel in "the voluptuousness of its sound-signifiers" as in the syllables of a beloved name (which, in Layton's words, "ignite each other / ... to let music and flame / astonish the whole world"). The "grain" is that which denies reductive codification and holds in check precisely what "average culture" wants: prosaic, acceptable, and merely decent articulation. What Layton gives us, on the contrary, is the neumic recrudescence of creative ardour in a language that hovers between cry and speech, or alternatively, in Barthes's formulation, the quality of the grain which is "the body in the voice as it sings, the hand as it writes, the limb as it performs." Perhaps it all comes down in the end to the archetypal yet increasingly rare sense of creative gratitude we find in Bede's Caedmon who sings Creation, praising the "Work of the world-warden, wonder of wonders." Or in Layton's "Elephant," who has learned "the necessary art / of converting irritation into pleasure" and whose "ecstasy rotundity / and gratuitous weight / make proportionate to his itch," generating his "rapturous blare."

PANEL 2

In the first part of this essay I spoke of my episodic meetings or intersections with Layton in order to counter one of the most persistent clichés that circulate around his name. Many people find Layton, both in his verse and *in propria persona*, too loud, pushy, orgulous, and self-referential for comfort (as if he embodied his own description of Norman Bethune in *Waiting for the Messiah*: "Here was a man who seemed to be devoured by an idea, an obsession. He did not seem a man with whom one could be comfortable. Some people found him attractive, others, for the same reasons, were repelled"). They object to what they read as an unmediated exhibition of the self, a priapic rhetoric lacking measure or discretion, a display of biblical postures and invectives that are either needlessly abrasive or embarrassingly inappropriate. Detractors will often recall Eliot's strictures against the intervention of the biographical self (Layton, of course, cannot abide Eliot, "at best, a single hair / from the beard of Dostoevsky") or Wallace Stevens writing in "Adagia," *Opus Posthumous*, "The poet confers his identity on the reader. But he cannot do this if he intrudes personally." Layton, after all, just about out-Mailers Mailer in his advertisements for himself, and those fortunate enough to have received the occasional letter from the master may recall Layton's face stencilled on the envelope, somewhat larger than the Queen's stamped beside it. I too must confess to random moments of disbelief at the spectacle of what might appear as an unmitigated hubris, times when I grew convinced I was confronting a certifiable Romaniac. And sometimes I was hard put to detect evidence of that "exigent and censorious taste" (in Lionel Trilling's lapidary phrase) in the man who claimed to have discovered sex for his fellow Canadians and flaunted his luck "to be loved / by the one girl / in this Presbyterian country / who knows how to give / a man pleasure" (hyperbole notwithstanding); who in an act of unprecedented humility conceded "No, I'll never / be greater than William Shakespeare"; whose famous profession of poetic modesty with regard to nature's divided things – "I am their mouth; as a mouth I serve" – sounds a little less apostolic than derivative (poetry, said Rilke, is "a mouth which else Nature would lack"); and whose striving for effect will often betray a surprising inability to gauge or adjust means to ends, leading to the bathos of overkill:

> I want you to feel as if I had slammed
>   your child's head against a spike;
> And cut off your member and stuck it in your
>   wife's mouth to smoke like a cigar.

(George Woodcock reacts with "puzzled wonder that so good a poet could write ... such wretched verse," and invokes the Peter-and-Petrushka principle, the poet as Saturnalian clown-king, to explain the conundrum.) All this is true, I'm afraid, but also false – in the sense that it leaves out *at least* as much as it purports to cover. For a proper, balanced appreciation of Irving Layton requires that the serious reader *frame the name* with quotation marks, despite what friends, critics, title pages, and telephone directories may claim. *There is, in fact, no such person as Irving Layton.* The self has fused into the persona whose full, authoritative, and final name is "Irving Layton," the last in a series of pseudonyms, the name of a neo-Whitmanian fiction who is large, who contains multitudes, and who may contradict himself with epistemic impunity. This is why it is inadvisable to condemn "Layton" for surface infelicities, lapses of taste, or sudden changes of thematic direction: one risks making a fool of oneself. The writer who doubts that he will ever transcend Shakespeare remains fully aware of the absurdity of the concession, incorporating both the manifest bombast and the underlying subtlety as elements constituting the persona ("Damn that unscalable pinnacle / of excellence mocking our inevitable / inferiority and failure"), as if the only effective way of escaping obliteration is via humour. Or, perhaps, apotheosis, Matthew Arnold's strategy, for whom

Shakespeare makes the "Heaven of Heavens his dwelling-place." "Layton's" title directs us back to Arnold's tame capitulation on which the later poem must be read in part as a playful and rambunctious commentary.)

Yet the poet who is notorious for the tympany of self-election is the same poet who writes the compassionate and immortal "For Keine Lazarovitch" or the unforgettable "O Jerusalem" which concludes with the central question of our duplicitous humanity:

And how may we walk upon this earth
with forceful human stir
unless we adore you and betray?

How can the same poet write with the inevitable precision of feeling and form, the verbal etiquette we find in "An Old Niçoise Whore" and then produce a few poems later in the same volume the thumb-in-the-soup piece called "Westminster Abbey" unless it is attempted *in some sense* deliberately or with informed awareness, the mask embracing the whole of our paragon-of-animals to quintessence-of-dust humanity, all the glory, jest, and riddle of it – by choice? The poet is shrewdly conscious of what he is about, as he himself confesses in a letter to Milton Wilson of 9 June 1963, in which he affirms the necessity of donning an outrageous mask in so featureless a culture as ours.[3]

The entire panoramic sweep of Blakean contraries extends before us in the work of this extraordinary poet, from the "five neat graves in a semicircle" spawned by Pere Loisel in "Cotes des Neiges Cemetery" to the "five glorious cherubs / [a]float in the waves" in "The Sweet Light Strikes My Eyes," from the linnet *under* rock in "Still Life" to the butterfly *on* rock in the poem of that name – each visionary bracket making up that "exciting composition" of contraries, complementary oppositions, frailties, and strengths, smallnesses and catholicities, that he himself observes in "Sheep":

And I myself at my wife's deathbed
Shall, I know, weep: weep like Othello, be
grief-rent and troubled
Yet note the small cost of some extra flowers or bulbs.

And how can we be sure that the composite, ostensible self, which intrudes so robustly and with such pectoral swagger into one poem after another, like a weightlifter in a locker room, is neither more nor less than an intentional *effect*, a contrived and intricate prosthetic device, an expression not of the muscular bully of the personal self *but of a personally intrusive, self-aggrandizing persona*, merely one more feature of the protagonistic fiction which can no longer be distinguished from the reality? *And* which, even in its most steroidal forms, carries the same "value" or validity as the subtle, wise, and empathic recorder of the human pageant, the transcendant scribe mentioned by Ezekiel who, clothed with linen and with an inkhorn at his side, accompanies the group of men with slaughter weapons in their hands. (It is, after all, the scribe who is commanded to go in between the wheels of the cherubim and fill his hands with coals of fire. As "Layton" writes in "Esthetique," "poems that love the truth tell / All things have value being combustible.") Thus, in responding as readers to the composite and contradictory, specular illusion of "Irving Layton" (the bearer of a Negative Capability which, as Keats attested, may include even the "unpoetical") with sufficient passion and engagement, whether gratitude, approval, respect, dislike, revulsion, or even a sort of styptic ambivalence, we hypostatize the fiction, confer reality upon the name which now represents a collective hallucination from which neither reader nor writer may disengage. It is almost as if, in repudiation of Lampman's facile conclusion to "The Clearer Self," "Layton" understood that the isomorphic phrases "the clearer self, the grander me" simply don't work for him as conceptual appositions, and are in fact more likely to be mutually inhospitable than reinforcing. Rather, the source of that immense vitality, of "the grander me," lies in a kind of pluralistic *élan*, like his own "Artist-God who shapes and plays with ... infinite variety" and with the "joyous impermanency" of the innumerable forms of existence, incorporated into the poetic ego.

For "Layton" has been possessed, in a Bloomian sense, by a pleroma of archontic selves: the loving father ("Poem for My Daughter"), the bitter satirist ("From Colony to Nation"), the tender and compassionate lover ("Berry Picking"), the erotic imperialist ("Nausicaa"), the quintessential poet ("The Birth of Tragedy"). A throng of lesser or commonplace selves is also present, part of the unedited "humanity" to which the work bears theatrical and often strident witness. With "Layton," it's the whole bloody bird, or bard. Chauvinist, bully, mythographer, elegist, worshipper, tyrant, and servant, ultimately he transcends possession and becomes – *veritably becomes* – that daemonic succession of voices, characters, phases, phrases, and multiple nictitating selves (like an updated version of Rameau's Nephew) collected in his nearly fifty volumes, so that the category of the "real" blends and coalesces with that of the imagination, the "imaginary-imaginative." One could quite plausibly interpret "Layton" as the objectification of the Lacanian ego which – as Lacan writes – "is absolutely impossible to distinguish from the imaginary captures which constitute it."[4]

Abrogating the distinction between text and life, "Layton" must finally be approached as a poetic event or phenomenon, a powerful and consistently inconsistent self-improvisation whose impact on others (whether as readers or interlocutors) is never merely benign and necessarily entails consequences. Thus it is futile and irrelevant to object to "Layton," as so many have done, on pragmatic or narrowly ethical grounds, for one must understand him as the Compleat Man (or Mangler) in the most radical sense of the term, a thesaurus of synonymous contraries self-defined in various poems as a "cringing semite" with a "hot Hebrew heart," as a "quiet madman never far from tears" smugly and with vicarious bluster paging Mr Superman. This is not a "life" with a psychological centre in the ordinary sense: this is rhetoric incarnate, a *dramatis personae* of both effective and embarrassing roles and masks, "today Bluebeard, tomorrow / Babbitt," to quote James Merrill, an abstraction blooded by belief in immaculate beginnings, a "cold-eyed artist" who in his own words "finds enjoyment in contemplating the infinite theatrical shapes life so lavishly creates," and who attains in the fullness of his career to the status of the Daemoniacal Sublime.

For it is precisely the fourth of Harold Bloom's revisionary ratios that comes closest to explaining the phenomenon of "Irving Layton." I refer once again to the category of daemonization, which Bloom defines as "a mythification of the father ... purchased by withdrawal from the self, at the high price of dehumanization." "Layton" has incorporated and rewritten the seminal or initiating texts that go by the name of Blake, Nietzsche, and Lawrence, setting up as Counter-Sublime a self-constructed, legendary presence: the sonorous, oratorical voice, the clear, unCanadian elocution, the studied magnanimity of gaze and gesture clouded suddenly with prophetic fury and denunciation, the grandeur of phrase doubly conspicuous in common circumstance, the familiar citations from the illustrious dead,[5] the calorific greeting and valedictory rodomontade, and the sense of apodictic assurance, of absolute lexical confidence, all of which go to make up his aura. And of such poets who share the antithetical burden of greatness, a Shelley, a Blake, a Yeats, a Layton, (to use the names straight) one can merely say that the most "human" quality they possess, perhaps the only "human" thing about them, is their death – the one power that escapes recruitment and is therefore a match for the daemonization of the ego, which in turn is rendered all the more human for its poignant fragility.

As for the question of the managerial self, the gerundive essence, which moulds and manipulates the mask and is responsible for the *trompe l'oeil* of an impersonating presence, this is something that cannot be addressed, for the epistemological recession is endless, red-shifted out of reach. "[B]efore all my arrogant poems," writes Whitman, "the real Me stands yet untouch'd," a remark whose meaning resides not only in explicit content but also in the piety of nostalgia or regret. The fact remains, as with most of the poets we honour with the sobriquet "great," we have to frame the name with inverted commas as we do the titles of the poems that cluster round that name, since in the last analysis they behave like identical, interchangeable fictions, orbiting one another like satellites around an invisible centre. As for the "real Me," it either does not exist, or exists but cannot be addressed, which amounts to the same thing.

It thus becomes almost beside the point to quibble over an objectionable "Layton,"[6] to restrict him from our personal libraries or our imaginations, while extending the favour of our conventional regard to the laundered, acceptable, innocuous "great" whom an F.R. Leavis might have duly vetted into the tradition. Moreover, his many on-again, off-again selves consort synergetically with his typical writing practices, for "Layton" composes like a magpie, with a pica-like appetite for materials that other writers would undoubtedly reject as indigestible gristle, the "charred bones" and predatory "smiles of fair-haired humans" that make up his "lyric." The word and the event in all their multiplicity have coincided and merged to become one and the same thing, which is, when you come to think of it, the meaning of the Hebrew term *davar*, a term whose appositeness in context is self-evident. Word and event, work and life struggle to encompass the entire body of the world while there is still time, to produce the "saint, madman, fool" of one poem, the "seer, sensualist, or fake ambassador" of another, wishing to become "all one, / existence seamless." In the last analysis "Layton" is not so much a person as a force, a kind of verbal hurricane whose "rapturous eye" evades detection but in whose radial sweep can be found all the treasure and debris that make up his Collected Works, the poems as well as the selves – the "daimons," he tells us in *The Gucci Bag*, that he is "impatient to greet."

Troubling as his manifold, declamatory presence may sometimes appear to us, whether as legislator or seeker, as gadfly to the critics, self-appointed conscience to Canadians, or Covering Cherub to his younger competitors, I think our final response should be one of gratitude for the fact that he is among us. For what other Canadian poet has given us such sensual and ironic poems as these, poems to discomfit "the pragmatic vegetables in their stands" – poems, that is, which pack a *political* wallop, attacking both our consensual anonymity and the arrogance of ignorance, poems that have probed to the Schikelgruber depths of all of us, victor and victim alike? That have so candidly and unsparingly confessed "the anodyne from which fastidious men recoil" and at the same time blessed the "sweet light" in poetical hosannas for the transfigurations of joy it confers upon us. Poems dying down into love without "disquiet or passion" only to be re-ignited by "genital electricity," testifying to the antinomies that both disrupt and glorify even the meanest of lives. It is probably clear to us by this time that without "Layton" to revile and esteem, to condemn and praise, to dismiss as a raving narcissist or exalt as one of our Promethean benefactors, without that *summa* of many conflicting selves, gentle and abrasive, blessed and damned, this country would be all the poorer, all the more devitalized,

like an unoccupied chair in the park
like brown grass without water
or trees without birds.

Pronominal Debris

A Brief Analysis of Erin Mouré's "Pronouns on the Main"
(for my students)

My bucolic visions
Turn grey from these field trips.

Claude Peloquin, "Vision"

Not to be dignified or green again
But sinking, sinking always
Into your pallium of dynamic grey.

John Glassco, "Montreal"

NOTE

This essay was prompted in part by my horror at the spectacle of innumerable, alien pronouns thronging the most interesting street of my favourite city, making it unsafe for the casual, the distracted, and the elderly to go about their daily business. Montreal – where as A.M. Klein wrote in his poem of that name,

English vocable and roll Ecossic
Mollified by the parle of French
Bilinguefact your air!

and which may not, as John McAuley writes in his poem of the same title, remain "always majestic above the labial shore" – has enough language problems at present not to be threatened by a new wave of glossematic speculation.

As a teacher of a course in poetry appreciation, focusing on methodology and technique as well as on poetic language, I have found it useful to introduce from time to time an undeniably bad poem into class discussion. Notorious screamers, such as Erasmus Darwin's "Eliza" or Rod McKuen's "Thoughts on Capital Punishment" (or indeed anything by Rod McKuen), are excellent pedagogical devices for teaching students how to discriminate merit from mediocrity by providing clear examples of infringement and omission. Questions such as "What is wrong with this poem?" or "What is missing in this poem?" force novice readers into examining their preconceptions about the nature of poetry (or about the nature of the analytical moves they tend to make in evaluating a poem), if only because the *via negativa* comes as a kind of shock or makes an unexpected "cut" into the subject. Assessing howlers like the ones mentioned above, for example, students quickly discover the principle features bad poems have in common, such as: cliché (the verbal reflex of sentimentality or laziness) or flat, prosaic, hydrogenated, forgettable language; inconsistency in the development of idea or image; willful or needless obscurity (obscuring its own obscurity as rare insight); banalization (in terms of both attitude and subject); an *haut gout* of arch self-consciousness or self-infatuation; and derivativeness.

Having come across Erin Mouré's "Pronouns on the Main" in *Books in Canada*, and being startled by the appalling badness of the sequence, I decided to bring the thing into class as a kind of experiment, a litmus test, to help me determine whether my reactions were merely private and eccentric or at least "intersubjectively" valid. Now this particular class was one whose collective acumen had impressed me from the start, one which took its subject seriously, did its homework, was not afraid of research, and thrived on controversy – and which, as I ruefully yet delightedly learned, was by no means intimidated by its professor. It seemed to me reasonable to test my own findings against the analytic competence of a group of readers whose responses struck me as informed and mature. Moreover, as I did not wish in the nature of the case to influence the class by indicating my preferences and dislikes in advance (so far as this was possible), I gave my students no initial hints or pointers and tried my best to keep a neutral expression on my face and a matter-of-fact tone in my voice. I merely asked them to read the poem with a view to subsequent analysis and to consider into which of our two simplified categories it would most plausibly fit. A week's preparation and a three-hour discussion produced a general consensus, an almost total agreement on the uniform and unrelieved "deadness" (to quote one student, punning weakly on the French infinitive) of the piece under consideration (not, I assure affronted Mouréans, under attack – at least, not initially).

To begin with, very few of my students, including the more sophisticated readers among them, were able to understand clearly what was going on in this poem. They could find little that approximated a cohesive theme or content or, for that matter, a detectable narrative. When

I suggested that perhaps such questions were not the right ones to ask, a number of my respondents insisted on their status as naive readers – a poem, however recondite, elusive or allusive, still had to be *about* something (Stephan Mallarmé, Susan Sontag and Frederic Jameson notwithstanding) – while others, willing to concede the point, were still visibly dissatisfied. Even if beagling for subjects was no longer in season, the poem still struck them as uncompromisingly trivial, although they could not indicate precisely why. Possibly what they took or mistook for banality at first reading may have been a function of what they perceived as obscurity or thematic aimlessness.

I then suggested a vaguely discernible plot line. Someone, a woman, is walking along the Main observing people engaged in various activities: buying groceries, writing novels on the backs of cigarette packs, carrying bicycles to the hospital, getting haircuts, contemplating suicide, talking pronominally to one another or to themselves. Could we take it from there? Regrettably, no one was particularly interested as yet in pursuing this line of inquiry; certainly no one could fathom the purpose of the exercise. I began to suspect that the boredom these students were displaying with the poet whose poem they were instructed to read was exceeded only by the resentment they felt against their teacher for assigning it in the first place.

Nevertheless we persisted. Inconsistency turned out to be a non-issue, primarily because the binary category, consistency/inconsistency, seemed not to apply. No one could decide what there was in the text that could be fruitfully described as either one or the other. When I inquired about the rhythm of the piece, assuming that poetry is still in some sense to be read as musical, sonorous, or incantatory speech different from the "pure" colloquial measure of street or marketplace, I was met with a baffled silence. Finally someone hazarded the assertion that the poem was rather "jerky or bumpy" and another student said that the poem seemed "out of breath." This corresponded to my own impression that the piece exhibited a cadence desperately in need of a respirator, that it consisted of a long list of paratactic fragments or, as in much of her book *Furious*, a series of verbal units requiring the reader to hyperventilate through to an at times vertiginous conclusion. Such did not appear to me, however, as a failure of rhythmic competence so much as a faltering of "visionary afflatus," of the internal élan or conception (or "initiative," as Coleridge put it in the *Biographia*) that can carry a poetic passage through several enjambments to a "natural" temporary closure.[1] Unless, of course, the poem conforms to a controlling paradigm such as the litany or the list itself, which generates the anaphoric structure – though the principle of mimetic form must always be very carefully managed. (In writing about boredom, so to speak, one must still be interesting.)[2]

Students had more to say about the language of the poem, which could perhaps be most charitably described as basically *unmemorizable*. A few weeks earlier we had read Auden's "Lullaby." *No one* had trouble recalling the first two lines of the poem, one student committed all four stanzas to memory, and several others were able to recite sizeable chunks of the first or fourth stanza without much labour or effort. A week later no one could recall a single line of the Mouré poem. As one student said, this was "loose writing," and another dismissed it as "jottings," diary entries – and why should anyone bother to commit someone's notebook graffiti to memory merely because he or she had been styled a "poet" and had won the Governor General's Award? (It's perfectly conceivable, of course, that from this random accumulation of notes, with enough time and energy, a genuine poem might gradually emerge. But it would require both the humility to recognize that what is there on the page is a collection of scribblings *and* the discipline to work at these notes – selecting, cancelling, elaborating, revising – until something resembling a poem, a unified structure of significant ideas and feelings in sprightly, powerful, sonorous, or memorable language, begins to take shape.)[3]

More to the point, Auden's poem, by virtue of its charged, tensile, economic use of language, its cunning rhyme scheme and its strict metrical/syllabic count, tends almost to memorize itself or at least does half the job for you. Because it draws on the full resources of the craft, it will not allow itself to be disregarded or easily forgotten, presents itself immediately as *authoritative*, demands acknowledgment. Mouré's piece, on the other hand, induces instant amnesia or, if it is remembered – not retained – that is because it rides on the local reputation of its author, as the cover of the magazine ensures. It is difficult to tell whether the poem stumbles because the language is inert, the rhythm on the flaccid side, because the ideas are undistinguished, the minimal units of narrative it stitches together lacking in intrinsic interest, or all these things at once. What is one to make of

> But, then, some of us have been
> old already, & have grown up elsewhere.

(Shades of Bob Dylan's "But I was so much older then / I'm younger than that now.") And why, for that matter, the ubiquitous ampersand, a gadget dear to the hearts of contemporary poets? Technological chic? Stenographic egalitarianism? A way of saving time? (But what's the hurry? "With these pronouns his novel is shorter!" Mouré writes, this text soon to be retranscribed, no doubt, on the inside of a match booklet.) Or how are we to respond to the potential suicide shuffling along with

her jacket & bag of Saturday groceries,
of pears & carrots, of 2 bananas & a piece
of requin, sliced from the belly ...

Even the leguminous or gustatory muse of Robert Kroetsch (an alimentary "intertext")[4] or the guest appearance of Yannis Ritsos a couple of lines down the page cannot persuade us to accept what is essentially a shopping list as an instance of demotic or proletarian verse. Well, I counter, might it not help to regard the poem as a sort of inventory, a poetic taxonomy or what the eighteenth century called a *videnda* – people, places, items that are to be seen in one's travels, in this case along the ethnically inflected Main between Sherbrooke Street and Duluth in Montreal? Might not all the fragments of perception we are given constitute the materials from which a history is pieced together, a communicative circuit patiently established, a vision of life assembled with needlepoint fidelity to detail, so that at the end we are presented with a relevant, user-friendly poem? After all, here is the social-revolutionary poet Yannis Ritsos, and there is a man writing a novel – itself a revolutionary or perhaps integrative act. Or may not this poem, like Hughes's "The Thought-Fox," be about itself, miming its own creation, constructing a reified sensibility in a world unfavourable to the pursuit of meaning or intelligibility – "(today is cold)"? Possibly, a student replies, but "The Thought-Fox" is an interesting poem, neat, cohesive, tightly laced up, with high verbal modulus. And besides, someone else wants to know, why are all these pronouns jogging up and down the Main in their Reeboks *with their laces untied*?

At this juncture it is hard to resist an instructive comparison with Quebecois "street poetry" – the difference in achieved sensibility and poetic competence to be found, for example, in Sylvain Garneau's sidewalk-and-cigarette poem, "Au printemps," in which the poet as sensitive flaneur cruises, observes, and records:

With just a packet of tobacco,

I swear to you, a man can go far.
So many frontages there are
And fine shop windows here below.

And so we leave to flirt in snatches
With every movie queen we know
With just a packet of tobacco
And our paper and our matches. (trans. Fred Cogswell)

Or in Jacques Godbout's "Les pavés secs" with its complement of snoring motorcycles, hatless ladies, "packed restaurants / and empty dishes," dream gardens, astonished moons, and cries to the Lord rising out of "fictitious hells." In both poems the inventory is determined by a genuine seeking for coherence and a desire for *substantive* experience, reflected in the masterly control of the versification. Similarly, in Robert Melançon's "Montreal," the dispersal or fragmentation to which the poet paradoxically *belongs*, deriving a sense of unity from pedestrian diffusion, involves real people in an actual city

rebuilt, demolished, restored, charged
with more memory than European cities.

Yet – what is most important – all these streets and cities form part of an interior dimension held together and controlled by *style*, an architectonic that does not reflect or reproduce discontinuity but sublimates, transmits, or evokes it with a minimum of self-conscious interference or "noise." And when it comes to the mapping, both literally and figuratively, of the streets of Montreal, one cannot do better than consult the "Rue Saint-Denis" of Jacques Brault, in which the "thing" that waits "at the end of the street," beneath the sullen, ringing bells, beyond

The jaundiced grass on the lawns the splash of
        shit on the sidewalk
The damp stale cigarette the six o'clock sun on the
        shoulder

brings its sinister intent to bear on real living people, not on parts of speech or pronominal debris.

And indeed these questions concerning the radical dispersal of the self, all these jogging or strolling pronouns, I cannot answer even in my intermittent role as devil's advocate, although I do make a feeble effort. Pronouns have become extremely popular these days, I explain, especially since Emile Benveniste's *Problems in General Linguistics*, which makes a great fuss about the first and second persons as prime deictics and regards the first person pronoun as representationally problematic. This, taken in conjunction with Luce Irigaray's pluralizing of the feminine voice, may explain the emphasis in Mouré's poem on "her," "elle," and "she" and their multiples rather than on "I." And Jacques Lacan (as well as Mikhail Bakhtin) has written copiously about the self as a kind of echo chamber inhabited by alien discourses. Moreover, Barbara Johnson in her recent *A World of Difference* devotes considerable space to Adrienne Rich, whose "To a Poet" sets "aside both the I and the you – the pronouns Benveniste associates with personhood [but doesn't everyone associate these pronouns with personhood, by definition?] and reaches instead toward a 'she' which belongs in the category of 'nonperson' ... The poem is trying to include what is by its own grammar excluded from it, to animate through language the nonperson, the 'other woman.'"[5]

Then the poem, one student submits, is not about creating any old self from the disparate elements of experience, or the self of a human being who just happens to be a woman, but about constructing a *specifically feminine* self. Very likely, I agree, conscious both of the narrow, polemical nature of the process and of the fact that Adrienne Rich did the job a lot more convincingly (this latter by relying, at least in part, on *form*, which in "At a Bach Concert" she defines as "the ultimate gift that love can offer – / The vital union of necessity / With all that we desire ...").

Someone interjects (a female student) that the feminine self is already in place in the poem, as the first person pronoun is paradoxically in evidence in both its nominative and accusative forms. Another student (Deborah K., a close reader on whom I can usually rely for pertinent insights) counters by pointing out that only the feminine pronouns, and exclusively those in the third person, are set off in inverted commas, as if in our culture the woman's existence depended on its quotability. The feminine, in other words, is a mere *virtual* phenomenon, excerpted from a subtext or metro-text extraterritorial (to apply Steiner's notion) to the "surface world," the nexus of social and political relationships in which its (her) existence is always problematic.

Citation works in another, yet related, manner, I suggest; namely, as a form of implicit disavowal, as when we put in quotation marks a word or phrase which is not part of a legitimate vocabulary, one from which we wish to dissociate ourselves or which we recognize as somehow foreign, other, solecistic. Perhaps this explains, Deborah continues, the peculiar emphasis in the poem on groceries, clothes, shelter (bar and hospital, the latter picked up in the last line by the word "cure") as well as the analogous stress on modes of transport – walking, "I cannot walk yet," and the dysfunctional bicycle on the stretcher. The embryonic woman, not part of the "legitimate" social text or glossary, struggles toward a long-deferred realization and requires nourishment and protection.

Someone else proposes that the poem may have something to do with women as they are portrayed or represented in literature – the man writing a novel in which the "she" figures in the second and third chapters. If the poem does have a subject, it is the stereotyped reflection of women in that vast, pervasive, pseudo-literary text to which we all contribute, a novel on which we are all collaborating in order to domesticate and subdue the feminine reality and which we must unwrite or dewrite if men and women may one day meet on the "definite sidewalk." Makes sense, Deborah replies, yet she is troubled despite her advocacy by the indiscriminate use of the pronouns, the congeries of "she"s which do not seem to be properly distinguished from one another. There is already a considerable number of "she"s in the novel (given its shortness), yet the novelist "waits for her" and when "she" finally arrives, the novelist has left the café. Which "she" is in the novel and which "she" ultimately arrives, but too late? Which is the fictive "she" and which the authentic or possible "she"? Do the citational "she"s form part of a common feminine substratum or are they to be discriminated – not against, but from? (Or, though I do not obtrude the notion, are they merely a thronging company of shifters, in Fredric Jameson's sense (in *The Political Unconscious*) of "empty pronominal slots in which transitory subjects can lodge in succession" – which would clearly lead, if taken seriously, to thematic expropriation and the end of the discussion.) And why the sudden leap or plunge into French – "elle"? To assert and reinforce difference? To establish identity, a common cause? To bring in the French fact, since the pronouns meet, converse, and separate on Boulevard St Laurent? And how many categorial "she"s are we permitted to count? Two or three: the fictional or surface "she" whose function is to suppress the real or potential "she"; the "she" which remains virtual, since it "cannot be cured"; and/or the small vanguard of free, hypostatized, authentic "she"s who "walk by" (they *can* walk, whereas the speaker "cannot walk yet") and "turn to each other," presumably in the joy of mutual recognition and contact?

At this point I can't help wondering aloud about the early, prototypical status of Shakespeares's Sonnet 130 (that wonderful parodic debunking of Thomas Watson's Seventh Passion from his *Ekatompathia*, in which the literary, fictional, and *constructed* "she" of the Renaissance florilegia is bluntly and humorously subverted:

And yet by heaven I think my love as rare
As any she belied by false compare.

The Watsonian "she" is of course still with us, but the process of dismantling, of *Abbau*, had already began in the 1580s in a witty, playful, coherent, and linguistically charged poem which, as a sonnet, might conceivably be inscribed on the back of "a cigaret package."

The student to whom Deborah had earlier responded reverts to her original argument: all these "she"s founder grammatically on the shoals of "I" and "me." Who, after all, is speaking here? The first person *must already* to some degree subsume the insurgent and disaffected third person, which is thus undercut, stripped of its textual credentials, rendered inoperative in context since it is by implication *already authorial* and at least morphologically established. This is certainly true but, after all, I suggest, one is nevertheless constrained to use language in which the first person, dubious fiction that it might be, refuses exile, and besides, the antinomy enjoys a rich philosophical pedigree. For example, Kierkegaard's paradox of "repetition" which is productive of the self, yet possible only in virtue of the self – the problem of the hermeneutic circle, which Heidegger also grappled with.

Heidegger Schmeidegger, mutters one of the best and most pestiferous students in the class (a young man with the Hessian name of Demian, a jewel flaring in the wing of his nostril – Eliot's "young man carbuncular" or one of Milton's "men of a sensitive nostril"? – and an immense stock of erudition of which he is inordinately proud). The central issue, it seems to him, has nothing to do with pronouns as such, Kierkegaardian paradoxes, radical feminism, or the lexical ribs from which the new woman is to be resuscitated, but with "arrant derivativeness." None of this is *new*, none of it is original or particularly illuminating. The linguistic ground on which the poem is raised has long been churned to rubble and marl, the reverse of Frost's "The Road Not Taken" in which the paths were equally untrodden. In this case, just about everybody has been over the terrain by now: Benveniste, Lacan, Barbara Johnson, Adrienne Rich, and a host (or hostess) of feminist writers whose works are being assiduously studied in colleges and universities across several continents.

The poem is boring not only because its language is flat and gormless and its organization arbitrary but because it is old hat, merely *fashionable* and consequently disingenuous. It is mainly engaged in passing itself off as radical or unprecedented, as "Amazonian," but in fact it only *seems* new. He then proceeds to direct our attention to another "poem" in the photocopied handout called "Loony Tune Music" (shades of Steve Luxton), which I had not assigned and had scarcely looked over myself, and inquires into the status of certain lines and passages such as:

> The image of that not presence or self but
> absence
> perfectly replicated.

"That's just Derrida warmed over," he declares. "As I was saying, it's all derivative stuff."[6] There is little doubt that Demian has a valid argument. Studying the piece more closely, and disregarding its manifest triviality – "After we fell in love and the café became a success" or "I never thought I'd write a line about the woman's curls" – we collide with Paul de Man in the shape of "the questioning of the poem leads to infinite fragmentation & the loss of the lyric whole," and are flattened by another blast of Derridean rhetoric, "the throat fails to mask the trace of the individual voice" (though the *sentiment* is not Derridean). Demian is right; none of this is new, it's just trendy, increasingly commonplace, linguistico-feminist jargon served up in the approximate shape of a poem or prose-poem in language that sags and droops down the page like – the simile need not be completed.

This is really a poetry entirely without distinction, animated by a "vision" which *seems* savvy and irreverent, decenteredly postmodern, but which in its infatuation with ego and its aeonian crooning over the beloved remains mawkish and self-indulgent, the confections of a praline sensibility. The verse is not only discontinuous, rattling its lexical fragments for improbable effect, but is almost wholly incomprehensible as well. ("I don't know what it means," said one of Mouré's supporters, a well-known poet in her own right, "but I know that it's important.") It is also a dangerous form of rhetorical practice because, by virtue of its clamorous subject matter and its conspicuous technical aliasing (in computer graphics the effect is known as the jaggies), it lobbies for a presumably disenfranchised vanguard that soon finds itself massively funded by granting agencies and vigorously defended in the so-called avant-garde journals. It thus ends up polluting the language of our poetry by attracting a dedicated following that perpetuates its verbal brittleness, thematic destitution, and covert sentimentality – Gresham's Law all over again.

And I'm not sure (thinking things over a little while later) what disturbs me more, the *general* "deconstructive" matrix in which these poems so glibly insert themselves or the apparent specific imitation of the Benveniste-inspired Johnson analysis of Adrienne Rich. I realize the problematic nature of distinguishing between apparent plagiarism, evident influence, and lucky accident, but it seems to me that what we may likely be observing is a reversal of the relation that often holds between an academic term paper and the poem which it is presumably studying – the relation of paraphrasis.[7] Here the Mouré poem seems to comment on, partly reproduce and partly paraphrase a prose analysis which has preceded it, working up a series of critical insights and aperçus into ostensibly poetic form. In addition, the narrative introduction of feminine gaiety, the female speaker kissing or not kissing, falling in love with, waking up in bed with other women (as if taking literally and adapting the famous conclusion of Sontag's essay "Against Interpretation," replacing hermeneutics by erotics) tends to distract the reader from more germane considerations. One is either titillated, scandalized, or given to programmatic approval, depending on one's persuasions.[8] But if these events were to be reported in so bland and journalistic a manner in a poem written by a male poet to his *donna angelicata*, it would be dismissed out of hand as merely picayune. What counts, it should be obvious, is not the event but the language, the infusion of poetic vitality, the rich deployment of imagery, and (as Jonathan Culler rightly says) the rule of metaphorical coherence. But the Mouré poem, as is the case in so much contemporary and especially "feminist" verse, relies on the double novelty of ostensibly daring linguistic speculation and arch lesbian erotics to disguise its lack of poetic distinction. Nor should this come as a surprise, since a decline in poetic power inevitably follows whenever poetry becomes a displaced form of politics or of any sort of partisan agitation.

There is a curious sense in which both the language and the ideology of this species of poem rhyme with its subject or nominal subject: literary lesbianism is at least as old as Sappho and the relative prominence accorded to it, whether here or in *Furious*, should not by itself provoke the reader's interest or merit attention. For some readers, apparently, the subject is shocking or liberating, justified by its unexpectedness, but as my student said, it only *seems* new, as do the pronominal veligers swarming on the Main or the deconstructive traces and absences; as does the prose manifesto in *Furious* ("The Acts") in which Mouré remobilizes the creaking siege engine of the trade once again and proposes "to move the force in language from the [obviously patriarchal] noun/verb centre. To de/centralize the force inside the utterance, to the [obviously feminist] preposition." All this, mind you, in language absolutely *centred* in the noun/verb dyad with the preposition still in its usual oppressed, subsidiary, and securely aproned condition.[9] But Mouré makes all the right pseudo-lexical moves, from "synecdoche" in the first entry of "The Acts" to "metonymy" in "South West, or Altadore" in the photocopy I distributed to my students, from phrases like "the lyric finally an *erasure* of the *excess*" (italics mine) to all the other dreary predictables, "de/centralize," "referentiality," "re/presents," etc. Yet beneath these lexical sequins a drab and frowsty language remains in sartorial evidence, for Mouré, unlike Wordsworth, takes her own advice seriously: "just use the ordinary words in their street clothes" ("The Acts").[10]

And the ordinary letter is there all right, but the extraordinary spirit is missing, a Joycean gnomon. I recall somewhat nostalgically Gottfried von Strassburg's wonderful invocation, "the glowing crucible of Camenian inspiration," which still gleams, however faintly, in Brian McCarthy's implement of vanadium steel or Seamus Heaney's meal-bin. But when the retort is replaced by the shopping bag, when the poet as alchemist yields to the poet as bag lady, the haunted intermediary to the complacent linguistician, poetic power is inescapably subverted and banalized, reduced to the level of bathos or unintentional self-parody. In this particular case, if we consider the poet's crucial three R's, the reading appears to have been done, but not the riting or the rhythmitic. As Bakhtin puts it in *The Dialogic Imagination*, although the poetic word continually encounters the heteroglot and stratified languages of contemporary usage, "the records of the passage remain in the slag of the creative process, *which is then cleared away* ... so that the finished work may rise as unitary speech."[11] But in this contemporary "verse," it is precisely these social, critical, and psychologically fragmented heteroglossia that have been canonized, at the expense of an authentic, incontestable, and memorable language.

And this is precisely the trouble. Studding derivative ideas with a precious but *fenced* critical vocabulary and sewing them into a fabric[12] of insipid or commonplace language does not produce good or memorable poetry – in fact, it does not produce poetry at all, in any meaningful sense of the term. It generates rhetoric, shoptalk, manifestos, jottings, fey esoterica, but as for poetry, as a student joked at the end of our class, that has become the new P-word, a lexemic "absence" remembered monumentally by an initial letter, a fragment, the rest having gone underground.

Intoxicated Words: Language in Shakespeare's Late Romances

> The movement of signification adds something which results in the fact that there is always more, but this addition is a floating one because it comes to perform a various function, to supplement a lack on the part of the signified.
>
> Jacques Derrida, *Writing and Difference*

> I will a round unvarnished tale deliver
> Of my whole course of love – what drugs, what charms,
> What conjuration, and what mighty magic ...
>
> *Othello*, 1.3

In the opening scene of *Cymbeline* the king in an access of rage and frustration condemns his daughter to a slow death:

> Nay, let her languish
> A drop of blood a day, and being aged
> Die of this folly!

The sentiment echoes ironically at the end of the play when it is revealed that the queen had prepared a "mortal mineral" which "Should by the minute feed on life and, ling'ring, / By inches waste you" (an equally languishing decline, and one echoed in the *The Tempest* by Caliban, who wishes "inch-meal" infections upon Prospero). Iachimo, insidiously trying Imogen's chastity, misreports Posthumus as a mocker of all fidelity who cannot understand how it is that a lover will gratuitously "languish for / Assured bondage." Cornelius, presenting a box of drugs to the queen, asks her what she intends to do with "those most poisonous compounds, / Which are the movers of a languishing death."

The carriers of these languishing poisons are not primroses and cowslips but words and metaphors. Language is pressed, doctored, recombined; and its acids, extracted and honeyed o'er ("a wonderful sweet air with admirable rich words to it"), are administered to the unwary. The intention behind the manipulator's efforts is not necessarily the death of his victim but some form of personal aggrandizement: to possess a throne or a woman, to extort obedience, to enjoy revenge, to acquire real or imagined goods. The instrument employed in the pursuit of such degenerate ambitions is invariably language, but language deflected from its apparent office of communication and disclosure. The effect of this degraded language is to intoxicate, to blur distinctions, induce forgetfulness, distort awareness, and cause honour and commitment to languish beyond the hope of restoration. But language is equally poisoned by its debased and ulterior purposes and must flee for its survival into the complementary realms of invincible naivety or delphic complexity. Outside the pastoral or the oracular modes of discourse it can only suffer and languish in a sort of semantic viscosity, the expression of perverted will.

What we may be dealing with is a drunken homonym: language "under the influence," language perverted, debased in its function, reeling off its deictic centre, "language" slurred into "languish." In this view we have to consider language as poisoned at its source, suffering from cirrhosis of original intention; its purpose is subverted: no longer does it name things directly and speak of the innocence of the heart, but it deceives, abuses, infects. The pastoral worlds evoked in the late romances are in essence prelapsarian, although we observe them at the pivotal moment in which the serpent of reality effects its entry: Cloten appearing before the cave of Belarius, Autolycus shearing the shepherds, Sebastian and Antonio on the point of shedding blood. When Eden is breached and Nature shudders, language is immediately corrupted. Even ordinary communication tends to work at cross-purposes.

As the queen's bouquet in *Cymbeline* is to be transmuted into poison, so words may be pressed into the service of illicit desire. Language staggers and falls into the world of postlapsarian defilements; like Noah, it has become drunk with too much experience, and it condemns the innocent who inadvertently witnesses its declension. Iachimo uses language in the service of deceit; Belarius is traduced by jealous courtiers and driven into exile. Cymbeline is deluded by his wicked queen, who persuades him to seek war with Rome; Cloten speaks the language of brutality and "penetration." Imogen, the spirit of pastoral candour, utters her first word in the play – "Dissembling" – a precocious intuition of the world's obliquity, of language's axial tilt.

In the world of fear and desire, of Blake's "experience," language may be contaminated in two related ways: it may be brutalized, turned into the blunt instrument brandished by rage – Calibanized ("I know how to curse"), Clotenized; or it is rendered elliptical and malignantly subtle, infused by the genius of misrepresentation. (Imogen is tested by *two* false suitors, the bestial Cloten and the supersubtle Iachimo.) Thus it is no longer innocent, the language of yea and nay; neither is it deuterogenetic, naming that which God has created and so re-creating it in its locus of human significance, making it recognizable. The pastoral tradition invokes the golden age of meaning when signifier and signified lived in wedded harmony, when things were what they seemed and words were denotatively faithful to their spousal objects. But if language is the child of love, it is also the victim of time; and the brave new world of Shakespearean pastoral – with its lovely and incorruptible heroines attacked by the emissaries of a fallen world, by lust (Caliban), resentment (Iachimo), or authority (Polixenes) – is given as the reflex of an incurable nostalgia. The world as we know it represents the victory of history over eclogue, and the truth – for the communication of which language was ostensibly invented – finds a congenial refuge in the cryptic and protective maze of the oracle. It is probably no accident that the soothsayer in Cymbeline is also preoccupied with etymologies, digging down to the roots of words, and ironically coming up with a false derivation.

In *A Natural Perspective* Northrop Frye suggests that the conclusion of *The Winter's Tale* – and by extension, no doubt, of any of the romances – is "not an object of belief so much as an imaginative model of desire": the rediscovering of that primal realm or *pratum felicitatis* in which language is still in its ruddy-complexioned youth and Nature is all the dictionary it needs. Thus Perdita, the votaress of "great creating Nature," rejects all hybrid flowers for their unnatural "piedness," as she deplores makeup for its deceptiveness – in this showing herself less sophisticated than her precocious brother, Mamillius. Ironically (in act 4) Perdita is forced by circumstance to assume a disguise and "disliken / the truth of [her] own seeming." The irony is further compounded by the fact that what she takes to be her true identity as a Bohemian shepherdess is really an element in still another masquerade, of which she is unaware.

Even the young Mamillius recognizes in his facetious wordplay with the serving women the need for cosmetic heightening, for a second, remedial, *inscribed* creation: the brow should be made up "so that there be not / Too much hair there, but in a semicircle, / Or a half-moon made with a pen." Artifice may serve as an enhancing medium but shortly afterwards the prince is "infected" (one of the keywords in the play) by the corruption brewing in the court and, as Leontes remarks, misconstruing the true cause of the infirmity, "He straight declin'd ... / And downright languish'd." The sad tale of the man who dwelt by a churchyard, meant to while away the time pleasantly and casually, is translated by the perverted will of Leontes into reality and becomes the substance of the first half of *The Winter's Tale*. The imaginary replaces the imaginative.

"There is a sickness," Camillo informs Polixenes, "which puts some of us in distemper, but / I cannot name the disease." The disease is that "ling'ring dram" which Camillo has mentioned before, and which Leontes – with his distorted thought and infected will, as expressed in the syntactic lurch of his early speeches – administers to those around him. Hermione, bewildered and vulnerable, is intuitively aware of the canting vertigo that has attacked her husband: "You speak a language that I understand not." It is Paulina, approaching (unsuccessfully at first) with "words as medicinal as true," who revives Hermione and serves as the agent of eventual reconciliation. The lapsed pastoral is restored by faith and candour. The reader, however, may be tempted to speculate on an unwritten sequel: Leontes composing another script, an even wintrier tale, as the wrinkled Hermione and the crusty Polixenes leave Paulina's house arm in arm to renew their innocent friendship.

Are we permitted to read a contrapuntal message here regarding the viability of the pastoral world, desirable as it may be? It is a world that now survives only intravenously, dependent for its tenuous existence on the serums of the imagination, on myth, dream, poetry, and the fleeting moment in the rose garden when the improbable suddenly blossoms. But the time must come when such privileged moments can no longer be expected – merely remembered or imagined.

Albert Camus has remarked that the tragedy of the human condition is owing partly to the fact that love and lust are both tied to the body: their physical expression is identical. As a result duplicity is unavoidable. In the same way language discloses an inescapable duplicity – or, perhaps, triplicity. There is the nostalgic language of pan-pipe candour, of yea and nay in which things are presumably played "exactly as they are."[1] (There is also, of course, the language of silence, which as Paulina gravely informs us, "often of pure innocence / Persuades when speaking fails"; but this golden silence is clearly an Arcadian dialect.) There is its complement and obverse, the language of deceit, illusion, evasion, destruction, dedicated to the utterance of the thing which is not – the compensatory language of mortality in its negative and deprived condition.

Allied to this corrupted tongue is the language of imagination and wit that seeks not to indemnify our bankrupt state by the exercise of power in the service of egotism and *ressentiment* but to create a second, plenary world to replace or augment the one that is fallen and deficient. This is the language associated with Autolycus, the purveyor of ballads and colourful exaggerations. In fact Autolycus behaves very much like the playwright's imaginative projection of himself into his own play, a Jacobean Hitchcock strolling through acts 4 and 5 of the *Tale* with his bag of rhetorical tricks ("he hath ... more points than all the lawyers in Bohemia can learnedly handle"), his songs of which it is said that "No milliner can so fit his customers with gloves" (Shakespeare's father is thought to have been a glover), and his thespian affirmation that "I can bear my part; you must know 'tis my occupation." The mercurial language he deploys in speech or song, cozenage or revelation, is ultimately a redemptive one, for "the red blood reigns in the winter's pale."

Although the world that is ransomed in the end is indeed the pastoral or romance world – or, more accurately, a fugitive image of it – it is ransomed only by means of a poetic munificence, the rich and commutative language of art. It may operate perilously close to deceit, may infringe on the norms of decency and expectation, but bootleggers have been known to endow universities.

This is also a compensatory language but with a positive acceptation, working in the interests of an imaginative heterocosm, the language of art or, as George Steiner puts it in *After Babel*, of "counter-factuality" and "alternity." Language, Steiner claims, "is centrally fictive because the enemy is reality"; it is unlikely that man "would have survived without the fictive, counter-factual, anti-determinant means of language ... to articulate possibilities beyond the treadmill of organic decay and death." (Steiner also quotes Nietzsche, who declares that we "need lies in order to live," and Ibsen, who tells us that man lives by virtue of "the Life-Lie." In this sense it is language as such, and not any special form or mode of it, that is understood as a deflecting medium, a complex system of lexical brattices to divert attention from reality. The point I am making, however, is that language is by no means a unitary phenomenon as the above argument claims; if it were, we would have an insoluble paradox on our hands, since the essentially fictive nature of language would effectively prevent such arguments from being formulated. The Steinerian thesis articulates a general "metaphysical" truth that allows for a sufficient number of instrumental exceptions to call its absolute deposition into question. Moreover, even were the argument entirely valid, here would still exist a number of different ways in which the "Life-Lie" could be applied, a variety of modalities and specifications: to communicate directly, to deceive or oppress, or to exalt, order, renovate, or reconstruct.)

That which makes it necessary – as well as provides us with the means – to defraud, ensnare, and cajole is at the same time that which makes it possible – as well as provides us with the impetus – to construct, imagine, and redeem. There is a familiar set of bivalent words that evince this connotative duality, words like *design*, *conjure*, *artifice*, *fabrication*, which are applicable to both the creative and deceitful spheres of activity, predicated as these are on a condition of temporal permadebt. And the two languages that arise from our insufficiency are constantly crossing a mutual border that remains as shifting and protean as the vision of plenitude to which they are equally committed. Hence some of Shakespeare's great villains are in their own way consummate artists, poets, rhetoricians; and similarly the pastoral world of frankness and probity is ultimately untenable. The Iachimos our protagonists encounter are the illegitimate children, the vindictive Ishmaels, of an imaginative potency that attempts to ensure its succession in the desert it is willy-nilly condemned to inhabit. And Iachimo-speech, wherever we may find it haunting the abode of a lost beatitude, is speech devoted to the befuddlement of spiritual legitimacy – of knowledge, integrity, and love.

Thus we live in a country in which three languages are spoken; the nostalgic, the hedonic,[2] and the commutative; but the first is almost untranslatable, and the last is seldom mastered.[3] The second, our lingua franca, bespeaks a fallen world in which "language" becomes "langrage" – a type of shot used in naval engagements to damage sails and rigging; in its toxic state of glottal distortion, we hear the syllabic meld of "languish," indicating the suppression of that lucid sobriety in which things are seen, felt, and said as what they are. But the ambiguity in the word *intoxication*, in which the *toxic* component is neutralized and the sense of joy (euphoria or exaltation) is stressed, implies that language, irremediably compromised, is the only guarantee of recollected unity, the only preserver of an impossible future. The crowning irony is that without a language grounded in the (threefold) capacity to lie (to misrepresent, omit, and exaggerate), Arcadia would cease to exist – would languish without hope of revival.

Dukes and Duchesses: A Minority View of "My Last Duchess"

> What can I give thee back, O liberal
> And princely giver, who has brought the gold
> And purple of thine heart, unstrained, untold,
> And laid them on the outside of the wall
> For such as I to take or leave withal,
> In unexpected largesse? Am I cold,
> Ungrateful, that for these most manifold
> High gifts I render nothing back at all?
>
> *Sonnets from the Portuguese* (8)

> "Tut, tut, child," said the Duchess. "Everything's got a moral, if only you can find it."
>
> *Alice's Adventures in Wonderland*

Browning's "My Last Duchess" is one of those poems that has assumed a doubly canonical status in our literature. It not only occupies a firm place in anthology and classroom as one of the most frequently read and taught of English poems but hangs in the portrait gallery, so to speak, of the "public mind," transferred from the Renaissance palazzo of the Academy to the municipal museum of everyday awareness. Not so famous, perhaps, as Elizabeth's forty-third sonnet or Gray's "Elegy," but close. My father, who was anything but "literary" and whose own education ended, quite decisively, with high school, adopted "My Last Duchess" as a homiletic text which he expounded with tractarian vigour throughout his life. His constatation, unlike that which resounds in the Academy, was irrevocably ducal, and he regarded the poem as the last word in the battle of the sexes. Women were untrustworthy, fallible, undiscriminating, flighty and genetically unfaithful creatures. Men, systematically abused and deceived, could not do better than emulate the duke, arise in justifiable anger, and exterminate what St Chrysostom once called a "desirable calamity."

My father's interpretation of the poem need hardly be taken seriously and is certainly discountenanced by the powerful and authoritative reading the University has accorded it. The poem, in fact, has now become a scholarly institution in its own right and the only controversy it generates has to do not with alternative perceptions of the duke's character but with competitive attempts to out-vilify him. The staple, monocotyledonous reading understands the duke as that from which women have been struggling to free themselves for centuries – as if the duke were a "semic" category waiting to be valourized in *personal* existence, a textual prefiguration of Elizabeth's father, Edward Moulton Barrett, "the worst kind of Victorian tyrant, bending his family to his will," in the words of Dorothy Porter. (Although the Victorian homology, as we shall soon see, does not work on the level of *historical* transposition.) Insecure, psychologically disadvantaged, brutal, and avaricious, a sort of twisted Duke Nukem demolishing obstacles with screenal indifference, he can compensate for his fractional and dependent existence only by exercising a ruthless domination over whatever threatens his precarious identity. Thus his obsession with ownership and control, his transforming the world in which he functions into an *object* deprived of all possibility of response and therefore of resistance or challenge to his hegemony. Like Fowles's Frederick Clegg, he is a *collector* – not only of paintings and sculptures but of women, the greatest threat to his masculine integrity. The murder of his wife, whose behaviour he finds insulting, successfully changes her from a responsive (read: capricious) being into a silent and manageable object memorialized in a painting and posthumously "lessoned" in a piece of sculpture. Transfixed in paint she can no longer unsettle; she is both present and absent at once (a presence disarmed, underwritten, and *spoken for* by the ward or guarantor of absence and silence). Her fate is at the same time *justified* by the sculpture of Neptune taming a sea-horse; the duke, who chooses never to stoop, domesticates the undomesticable in the only way the apparent logic of the situation permits – by rendering it (an)aesthetic. As an animal is tamed only by deforming its essential nature, by rendering it no longer an animal but a controllable mechanism, so the only way in which a woman may be tamed is to remove or deaden the nerve of her peculiar entelechy – infidelity – and reduce her to the status of an object.

On this view, of course, her death need not be taken literally (though it almost always is); reduction to the condition of slave, echo, or household appliance amounts metaphorically to the same thing. By the same token, her infidelity need have nothing to do with sexual waywardness, but may be glossed or inflected as indifference, inattention, preoccupation with anything other than the mutely clamouring child-groom. No serious reader would contend any longer that the duchess had succumbed to the painter's seductive blandishments – except, of course, my father, and the pop singer Chris de Burgh (cf. "The Painter," on his *Spanish Train* album).

A slight modification of the standard reading of the duke is that which deems him the Renaissance prototype of the adventure-capitalist, the man who has swept the diaphanous lady of the sonnets (as symbol of pure spirituality and hardly attainable grace) from the pedestal of ascension to the gross, dumb, mycelial earth. The desacralized madonna is no longer an avatar of the Holy Mother but a diminished and humiliated exemplar of Mother Nature. The "new man" refuses to accept his Adamic office as the steward of a trust, as a fostering and gerundive agent, but instead usurps the privilege and authority of the Master and like the gnostic pseudo-deity replaces him on the throne. The earth and all its productions, symbolized by the woman, must now be "possessed," "conquered," "had" – the masculine euphemisms for rape – a captivity or colonializing represented by the accumulation of lifeless objects[1] (the more valuable the better) and sublimated in the Luciferian abstraction of money: no just pretence of mine for dowry will be disallowed.

A second permutation of the normative reading, one that strikes me as merely procedural, is to read the poem as a temporal analogue in reverse or as a sort of commutative fable. This readjusted focus would appraise the duke as the Renaissance correlate of the Victorian autocrat, and the poem would now be reperceived in the context of nineteenth century England. The historical distancing functions as an ironic or protective device enabling the author to pursue his real aim unimpeded, a guerrilla attack on the sexual mores of a complacent, hypocritical, and tyrannical epoch – his own. But this technique of subtle infiltration by means of historical deflection would very likely come to grief on the score of poor logistics: the lines of communication are overextended. Or to put it another way, the Renaissance mood or setting is too vividly and authentically realized, too deeply installed, to allow for easy transposition of periods. The duke as Renaissance magnifico neutralizes the duke as Victorian despot and paterfamilias: the point of the whole exercise is lost. In any case, in considering these two subsets of the standard approach, it is obvious that the duke as Renaissance protocapitalist or as Victorian demiurgos is merely a specification of the duke as male chauvinist pig, the archetypal masculine. (The local and topical embellishments do not prevent a correspondence between the particular and the general (or history and ideology) as they inhibit the equation between two particulars (or two historical periods): in the first instance the terms are asynchronous, saved by disjunction; in the second they are unitemporal, cancelled by apposition.)

The evidence for the majority reading is now so deeply entrenched that a mere skimming recapitulation will suffice here. The duke is transacting for the hand of the Count of Tyrol's daughter and in the process of negotiation gives the count's nuncio a guided tour of the Castello Estense. The tour is calculated to impress the delegate with the duke's wealth, status, dignity, and exquisite taste. The one-sided conversation on which we are permitted to eavesdrop serves the basic function of acquainting the visitor with the duke's expectations: an ample dowry along with a submissive wife. Hence on the one hand the emphasis on the duke's possessions: a painting by the celebrated Fra Pandolf ("I said Fra Pandolf by design"), a sculpture by the renowned Claus of Innsbruck, a nine-hundred-year-old name (a moniker not to be trifled with, available only for a price); on the other, the desideratum of absolute spousal loyalty tantamount to complete subservience, and the disclosure of an authority, an imperiousness, that will not shrink from inflicting the ultimate penalty if disappointed. When the duke judges that the lesson has been properly taken, the curtain of the portrait is drawn shut, as is the invisible curtain that frames the psychodrama just enacted. The duke then performs three strategic moves in close succession: the articulation of his real purpose (the dowry), qualified by a false and polite disclaimer ("his daughter's fair self ... is my object") – but phrased in the language of power and domination so different from the apparently meditative rhetoric that precedes it; a disingenuously humble gesture in deference to the nuncio ("Nay, we'll go together down, sir"); and a concluding – and conclusive – three-pronged allusion to his aesthetic taste, his wealth, and his rigorous expectations (the sculpture, evidently valuable, representing an act of supreme domestication).

Yet, in a proleptically Derridean manner, the staple reaction which the poem has elicited since its publication mimes the duchess's blithe misapprehension of the deeply affronted duke. The duke's misprision by his wife, who refuses or neglects to read him correctly, corresponds on another level to Browning's being resolutely misconstrued by most of his devoted readers. The perseverant misapprehension of the poem, all the hermeneutic "noise" that has washed out its "message," attests to a lack of discrimination – precisely the transgression of which the duchess is accused.[2]

The minority reading of the text recognizes and accepts all the evidence normally cited by the majority consensus that discredits the duke and privileges the duchess. The basic situation remains the same – the duke of Ferrara in the midst of matrimonial negotiations treats the anonymous delegate to a tour of his palazzo. But from that point on readers are required to revise their habitual parallax and rearrange the events they record, the items of perception that constitute their view of the scene, in a different semiotic configuration. Duke and envoy halt before a portrait set off from the others in the gallery because it is curtained. Immediately the painting calls attention to itself, which is rather curious since it represents a wife who has been confessedly murdered. The duke, for reasons not yet clear, chooses from time to time to draw the curtains and to discourse unreservedly on the portrait which is revealed.[3] This is often explained as the psychological consequence of guilt obsession – an explanation that obviously works against the familiar hypothesis of the duke as the cool, rational, and shrewd arch-manipulator. To make matters worse, the duke patently dismisses the one extenuation that would justify his actions in the eyes of an observer: sexual infidelity (Guido's claim in *The Ring and the Book*). The unbecoming – yet very becoming – blush on the duchess's cheek, which provokes the sceptical or astonished reaction of whoever happens to remark it, does *not* testify to an illicit liaison with the portraitist ("It's the painter," blurts Chris de Burgh), but as the duke patiently makes clear, was "called" up by a series of innocuous compliments, the inventory of the courtly stock in trade. "I said *Fra* Pandolf by design" – a friar or monk, one who has sworn a vow of celibacy, and is moreover employed by a presumably jealous and possessive patron (plainly not one to qualify for Rossini's *pappatacci*), a *patrone* who would not likely have taken any chances on this score. (One may presume that Fra Pandolf was no Robert Redford for looks or Iachimo for subtlety.) If the duke is engaged in contriving a lucrative, dynastic alliance, it is surely a tactical error of the first magnitude not only to project himself as a wife-slayer (whose proclivities may verge on the chronic) but to casually or deliberately annul the one mitigating factor without which these sensitive negotiations must surely be jeopardized. What is the likelihood of the Count of Tyrol dispatching his daughter together with a handsome dowry to a self-avowed wife-killer with marked pathological tendencies? Either one must give up the conventional reading of the duke's character and reconsider him as a gross incompetent, an archetypal klutz, the incarnation of brute stupidity, or an out-and-out madman. After all, an astute and wily protocapitalist or a man used to having his own way and ensuring his tenure of domination by *any* means whatsoever does not cheerfully self-destruct just because he happens to be in a confessional mood. (Nor for that matter can the confession continue to be regarded as a strategic manoeuver since in any real, comparable situation it must instantly cancel its clandestine purpose.) *Or* one must set about recalibrating the traditional hermeneutic automatism preventing an unbiased reading of the poem.

We might begin with a brief situational analysis and note that the duke presents a very different case from other well-known lovers in the Browning gallery. To cite just a few examples: He does not murder his Porphyria in an act of charity intended to help her preserve the passionate fidelity she is too weak to maintain on her own. Nor on the other hand does he indulge his wayward Lucrezia in the meditative wisdom of resignation or, as it may be, in the attempt to win a moral victory by deliberate self-abasement. (Or is it merely self deception?) At any rate, for the duke as well as for Andrea, there is to be no contented sitting by the window, "Both of one mind, as married people use" (and no sense, as with Elizabeth in Sonnet 31, of the utter unimagineableness of inner severance, "that we two / Should for a moment stand unministered / By a mutual presence"). But unlike the Florentine painter, he cannot tolerate disaffection. Nor should the Duke of Ferrara be assimilated to the young duke in "The Flight of the Duchess," whose vanity and artificiality would have plainly led to the emotional asphyxiation of his wife had she not fled into the gypsy ozone. The temptation to connect these two poems (a result not only of their titular and "inverse" similarities but of the strong focus on the Andromeda figure) produces a kind of interpretive astigmatism, as in William C. DeVane's lamenting the absence of a Perseus "to come to the rescue of outraged innocence" (*Yale Review* 37). Nor does Fra Lippo Lippi's famous remark,

> we're made so that we love
> First when we see them painted, things we have passed
> Perhaps a hundred times nor cared to see

apply to the duke's absorption in the portrait. The duke makes it abundantly clear, in contradistinction to Fra Lippo Lippi, that he did indeed "care to see" – he is nothing if not observant – as he cared in turn to be seen.

To leave the canon for a moment, the temptation to apply Mrs Sullen's lines from *The Beaux' Stratagem* to "My Last Duchess" would merely fudge the issue. "Women are like pictures, of no value in the hands of a fool, till he hears men of sense bid high for the purchase." To begin with, the duke is speaking to an underling; moreover, the initial effect of the painting is to elicit suspicion in the viewer – the inclination, that is, to make a low bid. One can also anticipate the tendency to derive the poem in part from Byron's *Parisina*, which opens another sordid chapter from the annals of the ill-fated house of Este (as does *Sordello*). The temptation here is to identify Browning's duke with Byron's Azo: they bear the same noble name, are proud, authoritarian figures, and of course execute their wives. But the similarities stop there. Azo is taciturn, while the duke is loquacious; the former is elderly, the latter appears to be in the vigour of manhood, closer in age to the young Hugo; Azo judges infidelity and incest (decapitating a son into the bargain) which, while complicating family life, simplifies the story line, and provides Byron with the opportunity of extending a closing moral to the length of an epic simile. Browning, working in a very different mode, remains enigmatic, elusive, indirect, ironic, complex, cutting a poem whose flip side may turn out to be the hit. As Richard D. Altick comments in his analysis of "A Grammarian's Funeral" in *Studies in English Literature*, vol. 3: "the device of the dramatic mask enables Browning, as we learn from fresh intensive study of his best monologues, to indulge his ambivalences by talking out of both sides of his mouth." These ambivalences, "which so often find reflection in his presentation of character," should make us wary of accepting "unreservedly the traditional reading of a poem."

To return to the Browning text: it would be a serious mistake to read the duke as an early sketch for the nefarious Guido Franceschini in *The Ring and the Book*. It is evident that the two poems share a broadly similar narrative design, but this would appear to attest not so much to a preoccupation with a particular theme – the themes of the two poems are very different – as to a structural predilection, the Andromeda paradigm that governs Browning's imagination. This paradigm may be multiply inflected; or to put it another way, the characters who simultaneously reveal and conceal themselves in their dramatic contexts may be understood, in Greimas's phrase, as actantial functions, structural "operators," the surface embodiments of deep "semic" transformations. These characters and the actions in which they are involved bear a surface resemblance to one another that serves to obscure their "actantial" or functional significance as expressions of distinct underlying ideas. What we are observing is not the familiar "variations on a theme" principle but variations on a structure – a structure, moreover, both stable and flexible enough to permit the expansion of discrete figurations. Pompilia "contains" or unfolds an idea, a conceptual "kernel" (to use Barthes's word) different from that associated with the duchess.[4] If we can imagine performing a simple commutation test, a sleight of textual garfinkling, replacing the duchess with the more energetic and perceptive Pompilia (that is, with a character who *develops* in this direction), the entire situation which "My Last Duchess" enacts would be radically altered. In fact, we would have a different poem altogether. As for the duke, he is neither Guido nor Caponsacchi but, in a sense, a curious amalgam of the two. He would no doubt have been bored or disenchanted with the untried Pompilia, yet the Pompilia who has suffered and matured might conceivably make an excellent wife to him. But the question of the duke's conjugal happiness, as well as the gravamen of the case he is making, is almost always curtained by the reader's habitual prejudice.

Naturally the bias hardens to institutional status the moment the unwary reader realizes that the duke has foully murdered the duchess. One cannot condone murder under any circumstances and especially not when the victim is as innocent, fresh, good-natured, spontaneous, and generally delightful a person as the young duchess manifestly is. Who could argue with this reaction? But it may be useful to recall that a historical event underlies the poem and that Browning, though writing in the nineteenth century, remains largely faithful to Renaissance – perhaps more to the point – *Italian* attitudes and preconceptions. This by no means justifies murder or acquits the duke, yet we must beware of anachronistically projecting judgments and assumptions upon people (or characters) who did not enjoy the benefits of the Enlightenment or who came too soon to participate in the liberal ethos of progressive democratic societies. While we may deplore indiscriminate violence in any form, it is, for example, surely short-sighted and absurd to dismiss out of hand the inhabitants of the Old Testament or of the Greek epics as mere barbarians, Bronze-Age swaggerers, oversized dunces, and insane prophets who liked nothing better of a morning than dunking in rivers of blood. Renaissance Italy is not *categorically* different in this respect from Testament or epic, in that it demands to be historically *placed*.

The democratic and enlightened reader who cannot *see past* the murder of the duchess should perhaps consider that if the narrative of the poem were in fact located *in the present* (and in another country), the duke would have found no need to "give commands"; he would merely have picked up the telephone and dialled his lawyer. In other words, the murder of the duchess, a plausible rendition of the events surrounding the disappearance of the daughter of Cosimo I de'Medici, *is not the central fact in this poem.*[5] Rather it is to be regarded as relative, extraneous or subsidiary to the principal subject, which treats of the complex nature of the relationship that holds between lovers or spouses – the choosing of the beloved over the world or in some way acknowledging his or her unique status in the world, a form of election of which Browning himself in his married life was to become a privileged recipient.[6] It should be understood that this contextualizing of the duke's actions *vis à vis* his wife does not amount to a recommendation or an exculpation; at the same time the ethical verdict of a century and a half, the remanding of the duke to endless proceedings culminating in the inevitable resounding mono-judgment, smacks of the sanctimonious rather than the discerning, of *Schadenfreude* rather than insight. The reader must labour to transcend the *res judicado* state of mind, to *decathect* a fixation every bit as intense as the one which he attributes to the protagonist of the poem. Neither the reader nor the poet (nor the fictional duke himself, as I am arguing) is interested in sanctioning uxoricide. The unfortunate event is both historically indicated and logically necessary: other options were not readily or always available to a mid-sixteenth century Italian nobleman.[7] The internal dynamic of the story recounted in the poem, demanding that the husband reject, separate from, disown the wife, can scarcely issue in any other conclusion more palatable to the ethical norms by which we live and which we take for granted. The real and perennial moral dilemma the poem deals with has been regularly scanted and occluded by an ethical or judicial fervour which distracts the reader from what may be the central event of Browning's imagination: the relation between "men and women," the actions and desires of the "dramatis personae" of this world. The killing is regrettable, unfortunate, despicable – but as an element in the sub-narrative of the poem, it is entirely contingent and adventitious. At the same time, as a component of the theoretical and dramatic *structure* of the poem, it is logically inescapable, almost, one might say, preordained.

Of the remaining passages that have regularly served to stigmatize the duke, his preoccupation with his nine-hundred-year-old name is a typical bit of adverse testimony. The duke is commonly cited for pride, arrogance, ostentation, haughty affectation, and what have you by commentators who conveniently forget that the Renaissance attitude to the family name is not qualitatively different from the Roman conception of the cognomen or, for that matter, the Hebrew estimation of the importance of the first name. The name defines the individual and establishes his relation to the cosmos, and is thus perceived as performing something like an entelechial function. Furthermore, the individual as a member of a privileged or aristocratic caste is understood to bear a certain responsibility to the name and what it represents, the essence or "genius" of the family into which he was born and which it is his solemn duty to preserve, defend, and advance. Hence the rigorous taboo against female infidelity, which can lead to either pollution or divagation, a weakening of or deflection from the mystical line which unites the generations – and of which "blood" is either a reified metaphor or regarded as the substance that carries the sacred essence. (Some of Shakespeare's most pathologically jealous characters, for example, such as Othello or Leontes, would not have registered for a playgoer of the time as especially freakish, certainly not as insanely morbid and gloomily obsessive as we habitually see them today.) All this is not to say that the duke suspects his wife of sexual incontinence but rather to suggest that the inordinate value he ascribes to his name is perfectly reasonable *in context* and that the disaffection in which he holds his wife for not sufficiently honouring it would have been immediately seconded by his interlocutor. A millenarian name is not to be trifled with under any circumstances, not to be ranked on a level with sunsets, cherry boughs, white mules, or whatever else induces the approving speech or blush.

In this connection, we should read "Who'd stoop to blame this sort of trifling?" as a complex locution, in part rhetorical and in part genuinely interrogative. On one level, the answer is "not me" – since the duke as he informs us chooses never to stoop; on another, no answer is foreseen or even possible, as the question is in fact a declarative crowding on the vetative: "One must never stoop." "Trifling" is also ambivalent. Cherry boughs and white mules are indeed trifles, bagatelles, sensuous or aesthetic truffles, ephemeralities in comparison with the grave and ritualistic import of the name. At the same time – something which has escaped nobody's attention – the duke is practising a rather mordant brand of irony. But the common tendency is to read the ironic thrust as directed against the memory of the duchess or to affirm the dukes's own plutocratic contempt for these conjugal irritations – it is easier to kill than to educate. What is left out of such neat pedagogical equations is that the duke has hung the portrait in the gallery despite his disenchantment. Had he felt only patrician disdain for a woman he regarded as vulgar or obtuse, why is it there? And why does he keep it curtained? Certainly it would be far more emotionally efficient, more in keeping with his scornful and ironic nature, if not to destroy it altogether, at least to banish it to the attic with the rest of the bric-a-brac that piles up in an Italian palazzo. The duke is drawn to the portrait yet cannot bear to confront it – hence the curtain. He is driven to speak of the wife he has executed, yet he works against his own material advantage by exonerating her of the one offence that would justify her death and would thus not be expected to alienate the father of his prospective bride.

There is no doubt that the duke is obsessed, but there is no evidence in the poem that he is obsessed with guilt. His confession to the deputy is a model of lucidity and candour: the real transgression is scrupulously (yet inopportunely) anatomized. May not the irony which he so adroitly wields be directed against himself, as a species of self-defence, a way of *appearing in control* at precisely the moment when he is in imminent danger of losing it – a typical function of self-ridicule? "Even had you skill in speech – which I have not ..." False humility? A cynical gesture of democratic bonhomie to butter up his interlocutor, as when he refuses the deputy's obeisance and offers to descend the stairs "together"? Surely an unaccustomed humility would be painfully transparent and an egalitarian gesture entirely unnecessary. May not the duke be speaking his heart, cruelly mocking his own prodigious eloquence – *his* as well as Browning's – a limpid rhetoricity that not only enables him to reveal the clear, unflattering truth but to keep his own shaken spirit from unseemly collapse? Irony withstands: it has iron in it. May not, in other words, the duke have loved his wife as he continues to love her still, even as we find him in the midst of a skilled and lapidary disquisition, practising, however inconsistently, the art of negotiation? (That is, the rhetoric is brilliant, but the negotiating is flawed.)

Another passage that would appear to provide enough damning testimony to satisfy the most avid prosecutor is the one in which the rapacious duke shuts off the hot confessional tap and briskly turns on the cold water faucet of *realpolitik*. "I repeat, the Count your master's known munificence is ample warrant that no just pretense of mine for dowry will be disallowed." I write it out to italicize the cool prosaic nature of the sequence – the rhythm giving no indications of line breaks – in contradistinction to the reflective and lyric euphony of the revelation that precedes. This is generally taken as an involuntary disclosure of the duke's "true character," his "real motives," the practical business for which the melancholy avowal that comes before serves as mere preliminary massage. The duke's haste and greed prevent him managing the transition delicately, and thus he stands revealed in the pure diabolism of his nature. (Although the devil would hardly be so maladroit, one imagines, and would not so clumsily have let his victim off the hook had he desired to further his own purposes.) But the evidence needs to be examined with a little more attention.

In discussing how the narrative function of magic has been rationalized and secularized in the bourgeois world, Fredric Jameson writes (in *The Political Unconscious*): "the 'higher' and 'lower' worlds of white and black magic have been rewritten as two independent and irreconcilable psychological 'instances': on the one hand a realm of spontaneity and sensibility, the place of the erotic ... on the other a source of vanity and ambition, hypocrisy and calculation, the locus of all those ego activities which ... find their fulfillment in commerce and in the obsession with status." Now the two distinct idioms the duke commands, variants of the aureate and the inkhorn, would appear to corroborate both Jameson's thesis and the reductive argument of those who see the duke as a protocapitalist wheeler-and-dealer, a kind of historical, affective, and linguistic battlefield in which the forces of reification or objectification are inexorably driving out the increasingly archaic consciousness associated with feeling, love, loyalty, passion – that is, the realm of both *eros* and *caritas*. In this reading the duke is understood as a sort of world-historical figure who foreshadows an inevitable future, a man who finds his "fulfillment in commerce and in the obsession with status" (his nine-hundred-year-old name) and who seeks his justification, like Robinson Crusoe, in possession and rampant accumulation. (Just as marriage has no significance apart from its dynastic and contractual status, so art is reduced to the level of commodity-value and prestige-function: notice my Picassos, a Pandolf on the wall and a Claus by the staircase.)[8]

There is, however, another and I believe equally persuasive way of *reading* the two languages the duke mobilizes in the text, which reverses the accepted relation of displacement. Instead of regarding the first or confessional language as manipulative and insincere and the second as the undoubted expression of his underlying sentiments and motives, it is on the minority reading equally plausible to interpret the first language as authentic, a genuine revelation, a disburdening, and the second as apotropaic speech, an attempt to turn away from or suppress what is too painful to acknowledge for any length of time – what we now call "changing the subject," disguising pain and weakness by the sudden reversion to an original topic or the businesslike introduction of a new one, a way of recovering equilibrium by the adoption of a brusque, efficient, and "hard" demeanour. That is, the fiscal dialect into which the duke lapses performs exactly the same function as the rhetorical irony we considered before. It is not so much a question of prestige as of prestidigitation: now you see it, now you don't, a manoeuver with which anyone who has disclosed too much of himself and become uncomfortably vulnerable should be immediately familiar.

Jameson quotes as a prime exhibit a passage from Stendhal's *Le Rouge et le noir*: "Grace is perfect when it is natural and unconscious: Julien, who had distinct ideas about feminine beauty, would have sworn at that moment that she was only twenty years old. All of a sudden the wild idea occurred to him of kissing her hand. At first he was afraid of his own idea: an instant later he said to himself: It will be cowardice on my part not to carry out a scheme that may be useful to me, and cut down this fine lady's contempt for a laborer just liberated from his sawmill." The correlation between Julien's and the duke's congenial forms of doubletalk, "the mutual interference of these two systems and the mechanisms by which they short-circuit each other," would appear to be convincing. But it is also possible, as I have argued, that the ostensible correlation is skewed and illegitimate.

On the minority thesis, the duke continues to love his duchess – genuinely. But this does not exempt him entirely from the charge of disingenuousness: "though his daughter's fair self, as I avowed at starting, is my object." The duke requires a wife, is presumably interested in fathering a male succession to carry on the family name, and is by no means immune to the advantages of dynastic speculation. As a good Renaissance nobleman, what are his alternatives? Yet the surface lie conceals a profound emotional truth, his continuing attachment to and passionate involvement with the wife he has had to *renounce*. (Not murder. It is the renunciation that occupies the *thematic* centre of the poem.) Thus the brisk alacrity of this passage, the peculiar and insincere *stegography* meant to suppress, to cover over, a disruptive content. It is very far indeed from what Jameson would call commodity language, but is rather a kind of thermometric speech that provides an exact measure, if one learns how to read it, of the duke's feverish condition.

A final, abrupt transition, a sudden pause. The duke halts and calls the envoy's attention to the bronze, a rarity, of which he is ostensibly proud ("cast ... for me!") – although, as suggested earlier, it may not be so much the statue *per se* as its subject to which he alludes.[9] A god taming a sea-horse is a completely different kettle of fish from one human being taming another. The reader usually succumbs to the temptation of serenely identifying the duke with the omnipotent god (that is how the duke sees himself) and the duchess with the sea-horse, the beast of burden (that is what the duke has made, or rather unsuccessfully attempted to make of her). Thus the equation is once again tidily satisfied and all the loose ends accounted for. Everything computes and we have solved not a riddle or mystery but a kind of mathematical allegory. But the content of the sculpture would seem to imply otherwise. A beast cannot be tamed unless it is driven from its nature, "broken," compelled, rendered less and more than itself at once. Such is its "function' in the human world in which it is forced to participate. A god, however, requiring obedience and worship in order to fulfil *his* nature,[10] is absolved, so to speak, from all due process, indeed is exempted from the sphere of ethical claim and dispensation altogether. The god can bend to the material creation in order to satisfy his demands and to work his will without suffering either diminution of self or moral ignominy, because he is wholly free from all but internal constraint, ontologically disengaged, entirely other. But the duke chooses never to stoop (not even to conquer) not because he is a god or – what such a refusal would now logically entail – more than a god, but because no human being ever chooses willingly to stoop, to expose need and weakness unless some form of power or salvation is at stake.[11] (Martyrdom is a good example, or political manoeuvering such as Henry Bolingbroke's [in *Richard II*] who is ready, prior to assuming kingship, "my stooping duty tenderly to show.") In the older sense of the word, stooping – plummeting like a falcon to its prey – is precisely what the duke abjures, for the duchess is not his prey or victim.[12] (For "murder," read "divorce," as suggested earlier.)

What, then, does the duke desire in his consort? Precisely that which he is accused of destroying as a threat to his self-sufficient masculinity: *independence*, but an independence wedded to perception, intelligence, and responsibility. The duchess is no doubt a glorious young lady, a flower child, an ingenue (but, let us recall, of spousal age), whom all regard with warmth and affection and who replies in kind, a votaress of the Lord's Creation in which levels and hierarchies need not be distinguished: a compliment, a cherry bough, and a sunset are on a par, equivalent to a Duke of Ferrara. Who could quarrel with so innocent, joyful, and pantheistic a sensibility? The answer is: every last one of us.

For the duchess blithely refuses to discriminate, in fact, does not even seem to be conscious of the need to make distinctions – a need that human love absolutely insists upon. As much as we may appreciate the duchess and deprecate her husband, I suspect few of us indeed would settle for a lover or spouse who habitually placed us on a level with ice-cream cones, Ford Mustangs, and exhilarating panoramas – even if that level were dizzyingly high (and even if we were unable to trace our names beyond the third generation; but the point is that, like Sterne's Yorick, we all have nine-hundred-year-old names). For to be exalted *equally* along with everything else that is precious in the Creation is no different from being catastrophically reduced in our sense of dignity and worth, as Pope playfully yet ruefully suggested in his portrait of Belinda who, like the duchess, "Favors to none, to all she smiles extends" and whose eyes "like the sun ... shine on all alike." And as Freud wrote towards the end of his life, "A love that does not discriminate seems to me to forfeit a part of its own value, by doing an injustice to its object."

Naturally, in our familiar domestic relations[13] we are all aware of the need for compromise, for political trade-offs and mutual education. Marriage, we have learned, is work, and is guaranteed by neither love nor compatibility taken solely in themselves. Compromise – "stooping" in the modern acceptation of the word – is the foundation on which all enduring relationships are predicated. Yet, in an ideal world, the substance of our happiest and most redemptive dreams, compromise yields to reciprocal transparency, and partners respond to one another on their own initiative, never needing to be taught, trained, cajoled, "lessoned so." But in a real world polluted by clichés, husbands shape their wives' personalities to conform in greater or lesser degree with their own most pressing requirements, and wives scold, manipulate, or tactfully remodel their husbands' natures to accommodate *their* essential needs. The duke is obviously to some extent an idealist, one who discerns and feels the pain of finite hearts that yearn, yet not an idealist entirely, for what he demands of his partner is authenticity: insight, dedication, and the higher fidelity that is an expression of genuine caring, what we usually call "love." A democratic passion that subsumes the lover, and that *reduces by equating*, is nothing less than a form of homicide, an obliterating of the value and distinctiveness of the other. An ironic reversal is inescapable: in terms of the *inner relation* between husband and wife (not with respect to the theatrical paraphernalia of the poem), *it is the duchess who has murdered the duke.*

It should be clear by now that, irrespective of which character we prosecute, the real charge is not murder but a kind of conjugal violence that is the *symbolic equivalent* of murder. The duchess, in her innocent yet systematic practice of neglect and reduction, has negated the personality of her husband. She has not learned to *pay attention* and refuses to cross the *pons asinorum* of reciprocal obligation, thus remaining on the yonder shore of marriage in a state of oblivion whose inevitable result is domestic estrangement – all the more "deadly" for being unconscious. The duke, like any man (or woman) in a similar position, feels himself obliterated, discounted, forgotten, effaced – symbolically speaking, "murdered."

Why, once again, does the duke refuse to stoop? Because compromise, necessary and hygienic as it may be, leaves a disquieting aftertaste. Is the renovated behaviour of the other or the newly manifested response which has been so carefully and diligently teased into existence a sign of authentic love, of independent choosing, of the autonomy of selective desire and elective loyalty? Are we not all more or less in the same bereft or precarious condition as Frost's eremite in "The Most of It" who would "cry out on life that what it wants is counter-speech, original response" rather than an answer which is "but the mocking echo" of his own voice? This is exactly why the duke refuses to "educate" his duchess. It is always the lingering misgiving that what we receive from our partners may be tainted or alloyed with inauthenticity, that "original response" has in fact been shaped, provoked, influenced, urged, monitored, which leaves us edgy and dissatisfied. I suspect that in our essential selves (if the hypostasis be permitted) we bear a much closer resemblance to the duke in his painful dignity than, for example, to Lewis Carroll's Mock Turtle singing about soup and inquiring, "Who for such dainties would not stoop?" Or that we find Molière's Alceste, despite his repellant severity and righteousness, as he delivers the principle by which he regulates his life –

> I spurn the easy tribute of a heart
> Which will not set the worthy man apart ...
>
> I choose, Sir, to be chosen; and in fine
> The friend of mankind is no friend of mine.
>
> (trans. Richard Wilbur)

– ultimately more sympathetic than, say, another (reversely obstreperous) duchess, Gilbert and Sullivan's Duchess of Plaza-Toro who concludes her frolicsome aria,

> So with double-shotted guns and colours nailed to the mast

I tamed your insignificant progenitor – at last!

And so as an individual reader for whom "My Last Duchess" remains one of the great poems in the language, I come full circle to my father's original position, reinstating the duke and extraditing the duchess, but for reasons that have nothing to do with dogmatic misogyny. As the duke wishes to be singled out in his wife's affections, to be made to feel special, so the duchess *in the context of the poem* has been elevated and honoured by the bestowal of a ducal name and the austere responsibility that accompanies it. *Mutatis mutandis*, making allowances for social and cultural differences, for a changing historical contextuality, a similar reciprocal privileging holds for all intimate or spiritual relationships. In the private sphere every man is a duke and every woman a duchess. An abiding recognition of the high obligation of mutual election should dispense with the need for dynastic mediation through the agency of either nuncio or attorney, legate or lawyer. As John Gay writes in his noble but unjustly neglected *Trivia*:

Beneath his eye declining art revives,
The wall with animated picture lives.

Joyces's Choices

So when Amphion did the lute command,
Which the god gave him, with his gentle hand,
The rougher stones, unto his measure hewed,
Danced up in order from the quarries rude;
This took a lower, that an higher place,
As he to the treble altered, or the bass:
No note he struck, but a new story laid,
And the great work ascended while he played.

Andrew Marvell, *The Government Under O.C.*

After Joculator Basiliensis' grand accomplishment, the Game rapidly evolved into what it is today: the quintessence of intellectuality and art, the sublime cult, the *unio mystica* of all separate members of the *Universitas Litterarum.*

Hermann Hesse, *Magister Ludi*

Source-hunting in literature is an ambiguous exercise, as compelling as it is deceptive. Occasionally, when it provides historical information that better enables us to appreciate a work of art, it is not only justifiable but necessary. When, however, it encroaches on the sphere of the genetic, the result is often embarrassment: for the author if he or she is alive, and for the reader who may feel that authors' gropings, influences, and researches are exclusively their own affair, like their taste in clothes or their sexual proclivities. But so long as the line between the historical and the genetic remains shifting and obscure, source-hunting will continue to flourish and the critic to manoeuvre in that troubled region between the datum and the scandal.

The problem is especially acute when it comes to Joyce scholarship. The great author's fetishistic preoccupation with Nora's panties is surely something that neither clarifies nor enriches our understanding of Leopold Bloom. Nor, I would suggest, does Gerhart Hauptmann's prior accumulation of demotic epiphanies shed much light on one of Joyce's congenial techniques in *Dubliners*. But readers who have sampled Swift's "little language" in the *Journal to Stella*, deciphered Win Jenkins's letters in *Humphrey Clinker*, and meditated on Humpty Dumpty's lexicological exegeses in *Alice through the Looking-Glass* may find themselves in a better position to unpack Joyce's portmanteaus in *Finnegans Wake*, like highly trained customs inspectors who enjoy their job. Similarly, some familiarity with *A Tale of a Tub* and *Tristram Shandy* prepares us for Joyce's typographical hijinks and his suspension of narrative continuity by establishing a literary context in which such creative liberties are seen as hereditary and legitimate – and Irish.

In his fascinating study *The Stoic Comedians*, Hugh Kenner refers to Joyce as the comedian of the inventory, as a writer obsessed with lists and compendia, maps, directories, documents, newspapers, compilations of all kinds, and all of these as exhaustive as possible. Partly, Joyce is driven by his passion for realistic detail, for strict verisimilitude; but he is equally compelled by his insatiable need to contain reality within the limits of the printed book – ultimately, one suspects, within the circular and echoing universe of the single ur-word. His inventory is encyclopedic, yet theoretically finite: "on this is based the endlessly diverting joy of recognizing what we have seen before," as facts, images, persons, and events infallibly reappear in the serenely static motion of the universal carousel. It is as if Joyce is tacitly relying on something we might designate as the Second Law of Thermo-composition which governs a closed linguistic system in a state of perfect equilibrium.

Kenner traces the encyclopedic compulsion back to Flaubert, in particular to *Bouvard and Pecuchet* and the *Encyclopedia of Received Ideas*, and plots its psychic trajectory through Joyce and into the work of Samuel Beckett. Here the source-hunting is interesting at the very least and possibly remunerative as well: a knowledge of Flaubert enhances our reading of Joyce just as, by a kind of back-formation, does our knowledge of Beckett contribute to a richer and more complex response to *Ulysses* and the *Wake*. One might be further tempted to bring Rabelais into the equation at precisely this point and emphasize the nature of *his* inventory, the incessant listing of practically everything which the world he knew had to offer – library catalogues, fish dishes, names of plants and herbs, tympanic curses, descriptive epithets, and so on.[1]

Gabriel Josipovici in his provocative *The World and the Book* sees the indefatigable piling up of names, lists, words, and phrases in Rabelais as an attempt to draw attention to the description and not to the objects which correspond to it. "Language becomes a form of action rather than a mirror of pre-established reality," since the natural order has been drained of divine significance and the private self is without authority. All that is left is the act of description which itself becomes the true object of our attention: "Dindenault really asks us to admire his rhetoric and not his sheep."

Curiously, Josipovici does not consider Joyce in his discussion of modernism, and given his central thesis, it is easy to explain the omission. The modern novelist can no longer resist the pressure of reality, he argues; rather than perform the desperate manoeuvre of presenting his fiction as veridical, he calls attention to its fictiveness. "In this way the act of reading becomes the subject of the novel," and the reader is shocked "into the recognition of the difference between the imagination and the world." As Roland Barthes deposes in his influential article "To Write: An Intransitive Verb?" the contemporary writer attempts "to substitute the instance of discourse for the instance or reality," which means that henceforth, "the field of the writer is nothing but writing itself." Or in Josipovici's words, "the modern novel is an anti-novel, because it lulls the reader into a false sense of security and then, by pointing to its own premises, *pitches him into reality*" (italics mine). This makes us "realize that we are dealing not with the world but with [a book], one more object in the world." Here we are once again on the ironically familiar ground of the Brechtian *Verfremdungseffekt*. We are no longer intended to conceive of the work of art "as an image of the real world," which is, Josipovici assures us, to fall into the trap of solipsism. The modern – or should we say postmodern – book provides us with the "negative of reality."

And this is precisely why Joyce is conspicuously absent from Josipovici's honour roll. For from the perspective to be taken up here, Joyce has more in common with the traditional novelist than with the professional (post)modern alienator. His *oeuvre* does indeed intend, at least in part, to present us with "an image of the real world," and even further, to attract the "real world" into its gravitational orbit, ultimately to incorporate it wholesale. Thus Joyce could demand a lifelong fidelity from his ideal reader without, presumably, considering that such devotion might be excessive or pathological, an aberration or betrayal of reality. And Joyce's last book was, finally, *better* than the world because it would make sense, because it was elegant, consistent, harmonious, potentially exhaustive, ouroboric, and cross-referenceable. With Joyce, imagination and world do not conflict or repel one another: they converge and are unified. Displacement yields to absorption by means of such devices as the list, the resonating etymology, and the literary bill of lading replete with factual details. The book gradually becomes the world's muniment room. (One thinks analogically of

Proust's cork-lined writing room as well as Joyce's cork-framed picture of Cork.)

At any rate, the impulse to perpetual tabulation is one of the aspects of Joyce's literary technique that repays further examination in that it tells us something about both the problematic enterprise of fiction and the peculiar anxiety of the literary mind. It is in this connection that the reader may profitably consider the relation between *Robinson Crusoe* and *Ulysses*. Both books appear at the beginning of their respective novelistic traditions (though neither may be regarded as the exclusive *fons et origo*). But *Robinson Crusoe* with its low mimetic hero and apparent plausibility, its loving and minute description of homely detail, its canonization of *fact*, bears a privileged association with realistic fiction we habitually accord to no other individual book. In the same way, while acknowledging the work of Dorothy Richardson, Virginia Woolf, and Gertrude Stein, we customarily think of *Ulysses* as standing in a unique and even gerundive relation to that psychomimetic technique which, borrowing from William James, we have learned to call stream of consciousness. What has changed is the descriptive focus and method: Defoe and his congeners (including Richardson) describe by presenting; Joyce and the moderns (*pace* Dujardin) describe not only by presenting but by re-enacting. In the one case the emphasis falls on the external world (of which psychological operations form a kind of semi-detachable unit), in the other, on response, the internal, perceptual, and reflective world. Both techniques, it is important to note, by virtue of being *techniques*, are objective (conscious and deliberate); what the moderns discerned is that subjectivity can be more accurately rendered by psychological mimesis, that is, by placing Stendhal's mirror inside the observer. Both techniques are equally "realistic," equally conventional; and Defoe and Joyce are to be regarded as equally original in their exploration of the "universe" of realistic fiction.[2]

One of the most remarkable features of Defoe's protagonist is his inordinate need to compile lists. Not only does he docket his salvage in scrupulous detail (down to the number of Dutch cheeses he manages to make off with), itemize the contents of his shelves, present us with a dated journal covering much of the ground previously traversed in the narrative, and open his financial books to the reader's inspection, he devises a casualty list that uncannily prefigures the body counts the Vietnam war made familiar to us and enumerates the remnants of a cannibal feast – so many hands, so many feet – with a methodicalness that can only strike one as neurotic. The reader begins to suspect that for Crusoe nothing is real unless it can be counted, that quantifiability is the guarantee of meaning and substantive existence. The divine imperative, Be ye fruitful and multiply, takes on a parodic and insidious significance as Crusoe, perpetually adding to his stores and resources, emerges from his captivity in a condition of plutocratic splendour. The enisled mariner is saved, like Noah; the solitary sufferer is enriched, like Job.

In his study *Defoe and the Novel*, Everett Zimmerman (identifying Defoe and his protagonist) regards Crusoe's avidity for collecting and quantifying as an expression of the radical fear of de-materialization: "Crusoe's possessions and fortress, Defoe's lists and amplifications – all serve as self-protective psychic diversions." Crusoe-Defoe, according to this theory, is driven by a kind of *horror vacuus*, the anxiety of the inchoate and formless self which lives in imminent danger of what contemporary analysts call "implosion." In order to stave off collapse, the imperilled self attempts to subdue the disorderly and burgeoning world of nature (human and otherwise) by, among other things, the power of tabulation. Thus the individual "attempts to organize everything external as part of himself" (Zimmermann) and gives himself over to rampant accumulation – collecting, naming, recording, counting, checking and double-checking – as if stacking up furniture against a door which some nameless, invisible antagonist were threatening to break down. The obverse or psychic reflex of this desire to accumulate and label, this pica-like appetite for facts and lists, is of course the "ubiquitous fear of being devoured." Crusoe's entire career can be seen as a flight from the potential devourer: from the lions of Africa to the wolves of Languedoc, from the lower middle-class whose virtues and benefits his father extols so extravagantly to the actual cannibals of the Caribbean littoral to the domesticities of an advantageous marriage in retirement. It is emptiness, nothingness, chaos that terrifies and obsesses our hero, and this accounts for the "masses of material" with which he surrounds himself and which he ultimately digests, having himself become a sort of cannibal in his need to dominate other people. The irony here, as J.M. Coetzee in *Foe* and Michel Tournier in *Friday* suggest, is that it is not Crusoe but Friday who is spiritually devoured by his anthropophagous master.

It is at least possible that Joyce's instinct for "literary" accumulation, so evident in the pages of *Ulysses*, is of the same order as Defoe's – or on another level, that Bloom's fingering the potato talisman in his pocket performs the same apotropaic function as Crusoe's consoling handling of material objects. With respect to Joyce's method of composition: the index card tames the disorderly profusion of an endlessly multiplying world. Whatever can be named can be tamed; what can be cross-referenced can no longer wait in ambush; what is countable is no longer insurmountable. A book may theoretically become a depot in which all the sprawling materials of the Creation may be hoarded and disciplined – in a word, *contained*. The self is always at a loss in its confrontation with existence: the external world threatens to overwhelm it with its idiot prolixity and complication; the fragile internal world is always in danger of collapse before the suspicion of its own nonentity, the devouring vacuum at the core of its existence. For the writer who is consciously or unconsciously actuated by such feelings, the writing of a book in which the world is absorbed and *held* is perhaps the only survival tactic that works – if only provisionally.

There are no doubt historical periods in which this sense of aimlessness and dispersion is more pronounced than at others, but in itself, whether intensified or reduced, it remains a psychic constant, the coefficient of our behaviour. Certain individuals are probably more susceptible to its menace than others, but all must choose among a limited number of alternative procedures: sensuous anaesthesia or other forms of deliberate amnesia, political ideology, religious fanaticism, a Camus-like heroic lucidity (perhaps itself a delusion) – and artistic creation, which is at its root the construction of a second world, a heterocosm,[3] elegant and consistent as raw experience is not, vital and lexically exuberant to repair what Conrad called "the penalty of dailiness" and Stevens "the malady of the quotidian," the muddle and opacity and muteness of the given. (Consider how in the Circe episode Joyce confers the gift of speech upon the inanimate). With James Joyce we are in the presence of the ultimate verbivore, the artist who solves the problem of existence by *writing it into his book*, by including it as Odysseus tried to contain the winds in a little bag or as Erysichthon, cursed by Demeter, attempted to devour the entire inedible world, ending with himself.

The more one studies Joyce, the more one gets the eerie impression that he designed his later work to expand significantly with time, to provide for the emigration of history within its growing and hospitable borders. Nothing that happens in the world is unimportant or seems unintentional. Even the briefest consideration of names seems to rule out the operation of irony or accident. The Vico road in Dublin had to be there; the reader should not be surprised to learn that the new Bloomusalem echoes the title of a popular American song, "Kafoozalem," written circa 1866 by a certain F. Blume, a fact of which Joyce was likely unaware, or that the song "The Low-Backed Car" was written by Samuel *Lover*, or that the man who exalted Penelope should be subsidized by a woman named Weaver, or that many of Joyce's manuscript papers should come to harbour in the Cornell library at Ithaca. One suspects that eventually everything in the world will find a place already prepared for it in *Ulysses* or *Finnegans Wake*, that what we are tempted to ascribe to a kind of historical irony or coincidence is in the last analysis *willed*.

The imagination, meant to illumine and vivify the world we experience, turns about and engulfs the very mind from which it springs – the Frankenstein syndrome, the hypertrophy of creative enfranchisement to which the Romantic poets tended to succumb (and for which the only antidotes were, apparently, early death or subsidized mediocrity). As every artist in moments of sober lucidity knows, the imagination confers an ambiguous blessing upon its possessor. (We recall the French word for injury, "blessure," and the double sense of the Latin "sacer.") In his lecture on Blake delivered in Trieste in 1912, Joyce honoured the poet who "by minimizing space and time and denying the existence of memory and the senses ... tried to paint his works on the void of the divine bosom." *Finnegans Wake*, comments Anthony Burgess (in *Here Comes Everybody*), is very much this kind of book, and to a lesser extent so is *Ulysses*. But neither Joyce nor Burgess seems willing to recognize the enormous danger, the gigantism inherent in what since the Romantics has come to be glorified under the rubric "the creative process." It is no accident and scarcely a paradox that poets who write most movingly and tenderly about their children are generally the worst fathers. (Anne Yeats, the subject of one of the most magnificent poems in the Yeats canon, remarks that her father failed to notice her until she was seventeen.) This dialectic of praise/neglect, of extravagant worship coupled with persistent betrayal is, in a sense, the occupational hazard of the creative temperament, raised exponentially above the shabby inevitabilities of common life itself.

It is plainly unfashionable in our literary post-Romantic climate to denigrate the operations of the creative imagination or to express any suspicion about the presumably unmitigated spiritual benefits that flow from its transactions with the world. But the motif of the son-devouring father is part of our mythological inheritance. The "paternal" imagination is the source of vital, passionate, effulgent life, but it is also totalitarian and relentless, betraying a titanic disregard for its own immediate progeny, the radiant and privileged self.[4] This is merely another way of saying that the poetic imagination, which begins by illuminating life, will often end by obscuring it altogether, if its predatory impulses are not monitored and resisted.

In one essential aspect the artist may be regarded as the most insecure of human beings, driven to imaginative creation as a form of compensation for the nagging awareness of both personal inadequacy and the general futility of all things. The work is the justification; in it is consummated a vision of a world which, for sense, meaning, and consistency, not only rivals but surpasses the Creation. The "blessed rage for order" is the reflex of an insupportable anxiety which the artist with "that weird thing called genius" transmutes into cosmogonic splendour. But the creation of a universe exacts a tremendous price from its creator – the sacrifice of that very life it was intended to secure and enhance. The Word absorbs the deed into its nebular convolutions and the mind disappears into its primordial text, a *deus in machina*.

It is natural in seeking documentation for this (let us say) gastronomic process to turn to the Lestrygonian episode in *Ulysses*. There we follow Bloom through the intestinal loops and coils of an anthropophagous city in the act of digesting its inhabitants. Dublin is going to lunch, masticating, spitting, swallowing, regurgitating. A dog pukes in the road. Bloom visits the urinal and afterwards passes a plumber's display of close stools. On a vaster and slower scale of peristalsis, Time is laboriously disgorging and excreting monuments, walls, stones, towers, cities; on a higher level still, the universe is spinning its gasballs about in the "same old [cosmic] dingdong." We are in what Lawrence Durrell (in *Monsieur*) called "this munching universe," a cosmos predicated on the digestive tract, whose eternal, visceral cycle Joyce described in an appropriate "tripology" as "Gas, then solid, then world, then cold, then dead shell drifting around, frozen rock like that pineapple rock" (with which the episode opens). Well may Bloom feel "as if I had been eaten and spewed"; readers, too, by this time may feel as if they have been broken down and *rendered* in that great, Viconian, gastric abattoir presided over by a butcher God.

Yet Joyce's vision has been understood ultimately as a resounding affirmation of life, of that cyclic process in which death is the condition of renewal, dissolution merely one face of the inevitable *ricorso* or met-him-pike-hoses. It is certainly true that *Ulysses* and probably *Finnegans Wake* constitute a great hymn to the Creation. At the same time, as we grow increasingly saturated with the graphic realism and vivid, enteric detail of the Lestrygonian chapter, we recognize that pervasive Crusonian anxiety that expresses itself in the irrational horror of being devoured. At the root of this infirmity, to which the creative temperament is acutely prone, is the abiding suspicion of one's "ineluctable" nonentity, the intuitive awareness of hollowness or insubstantiality whose only remedy is a tremendous infusion of fact, detail, taxonomic stuffing, verbal ballast – the psychological equivalent of putting on weight to prevent oneself from being blown away by the wind of time and process, or what amounts to the same thing, from being devoured. Meditating on the ravenous seagulls he feeds with crumbs, Bloom is led to an (erroneous) consideration of Crusoe's diet, "all seabirds, gulls, seagoose. Swans from Anna Liffey swim down here sometimes to preen themselves. No accounting for tastes. Wonder what kind is swanmeat. Robinson Crusoe had to live on them." But what we live on is finally what lives on us, and the strategy of containment always backfires; by incorporating what threatens to swallow us whole, we find that we are being inexorably eaten, nibbled at from the inside.

One becomes aware of correspondences. Both *Robinson Crusoe* and *Ulysses* represent in part attempts to come to terms with, to domesticate and control a refractory and hostile world, the great Cannibal itself. Each of the protagonists is terrified of being devoured, and each recruits a complementary ally, a Friday, a Stephen, to deflect the menacing sense of personal nullity and vulnerability – resembling in this way the father and the son in Lucian's *True History* who manage to survive in the belly of a monstrous whale, which is also, proleptically, Crusoe's "Island of Despair" and Bloom's universal Dublin. And both Defoe and Joyce, like Rabelais before them, appear engaged in the bulimic effort to subdue the disorderly and blastular world of nature by virtue of the power of tabulation and incorporation, the making of encyclopedic lists, inventorial inclusiveness; that is, by *bookkeeping* in the various acceptations of the word. What we are observing, in Arnold Kettle's apt phrase, is a kind of "cosmic pedantry" at work.

In our critical dealings with books of this nature, we are continually prone to the temptation of biographical indiscretion. In order to "explain" *Ulysses* and *Finnegans Wake* as fully as possible, to do justice to their referential intricacy, the critic must go to the facts of Joyce's life just as Stephen in his explication of *Hamlet* has recourse to the biographical scraps and fragments of Shakespeare's (or as Joyce, as William Schutte makes clear in his *Joyce and Shakespeare*, relied heavily on Lee and Brandes for the details that give Stephen's argument a semblance of plausibility). I am not suggesting with the New Critics that biography is an exegetical irrelevance; rather, that when it becomes indispensable for understanding of a work of art, we find ourselves in the presence of an amoebean structure whose outlines are constantly wavering, a proliferating Tunc page, a "Tiberiast duplex" (to cite from the *Wake*). This is another way in which "life" succumbs to textual osmosis, consumed not only in the act of creation but, at least vicariously, in that of explication as well. The relation between experience and art has become teeteringly unbalanced, and the life begins to exist for the sake of the work which ends by devouring it entirely. A thorough examination of the work thus entails, as in Bloom's psychologue, the introduction of something green, a mess of biographical spinach: "Then with those Roentgen rays searchlight you could."

So the writer in his study comes to resemble Bloom in his bathtub, or Bloom reclining by the sea, his relation to the world a genetic aberration rich in memory and fantasy but ultimately sterile in transitive experience. The nonbegetting father generates the unbegotten son of his text, teased and supported by theological manipulations. What we have here is a bizarre, culminating irony. In *Ulysses* Joyce attempted to incorporate the world – the world of a particular place and time, but by analogy the significant whole of his experience. Yet as we know from history, conquest has a way of being undone by assimilation. In *Finnegans Wake*, which may be regarded as one immense, resonating word arbitrarily divided into typographical segments, the author finally disappears into the body of the text, his signature on the title page the only indigestible remnant by which we guess at the catastrophe. His effort to contain and master the world ends in his being swallowed by the book. Containment leads paradoxically to encapsulation, as if we were dealing with the mischievous properties of mathematical doughnuts.

Dedicated readers run some risk of succumbing to a like process, equipping themselves with bibliomap, dictionary, and gloss as they set off on their voyage of discovery into *verbum incognitum*, possibly never to be heard of again. It is a distressing – and revealing – fact that no one can find a way through the ontophanic corridors of the *Wake* without the assistance of a lexical *cum* biographical apparatus[5] – reminding us to some extent of Eliot's five pages of notes at the back of *The Waste Land*. But Eliot's appendix may have been partially the result of a literary joke – a sheaf of blank pages needing to be filled – and Eliot was not called "Possum" for nothing, a brainy and (in a sense) irreverent Pogo threading his way through the Okefenokee of the modern world. Moreover, the reader may be expected to survive four hundred lines of tangled, polyglottal allusiveness. *Finnegans Wake* bears a closer resemblance to Pound's *Cantos* in its encyclopedic scope, literary idiosyncrasy, didactic thrust, and biographical underpinnings, and we must not be surprised that these works (we must include *Ulysses* as well) have spawned huge exegetical industries supported by and supporting those with the proper entrepreneurial credentials. But the *Wake* constitutes a special case, a vast, echoing, man-made Logos shot through with humour and erudition, yet in the last analysis compelling awe, worship, surrender, and reader-encystment. The price exacted by a work of this nature, for both writer and reader, is affectively extortionate: nothing less than the body of experience itself cast sacrificially into its foundations, that is, the ultimate stasis or freeze-framing of common life without which the mythological impulse, the literary élan, and the exegetical passion are devoid of any real substance.[6]

To avoid misunderstanding I should emphasize that in *Finnegans Wake* as a whole and *Ulysses* in part, it is not the presumed unintelligibility to which I am objecting. This so-called unintelligibility turns out as often as not to be merely apparent; time, education, and repeated exegesis dispel the swaddling clouds in which such works appear. It is, rather, the urge to inclusive totality which these works betray, their tendency to swallow and absorb "reality," to contain proliferation, to encircle the foe, that I find psychologically and emotionally perilous. Such books always have something of the *tour de force* about them:[7] they are impressive, astonishing, unforgettable, but they are conceived not only in creative joy but, I suspect, in creative paranoia as well. The type of this kind of artist is Melville's Captain Ahab, "fixed by infatuation or fidelity, or fate," whose struggle with the leviathan results in his eventual foundering as a person, his disappearance into the vortex of his obsession – or as Joyce might have said, into the *vortext*.

For myself I read *Ulysses* and the *Wake* with mixed emotions, whose somatic effects sometime resemble those of indigestion, sometime of vertigo. Delight and amusement yield inevitably to bafflement and irritation crossed by involuntary spasms of fury. This book, one says, may be wonderful, unprecedented, unsurpassable, but this book is dangerous. Disturbing images arise: a gigantic octopus flexing and undulating through an oscillating medium of words, hunting for prey (the two-headed octopus of the end of the world?); the peristaltic flux of a digestive organ, having assimilated the author, preparing to engorge the critics and commentators who approach unwarily;[8] Lewis Carroll's carpenter leading a file of succulent little oysters to their caecal destiny; those haunting stories and legends of men who enter paintings and are discovered after long searching, tiny and immobile, within the confining frame. For the peculiar fate of the great creative artist is that he not only lives in his work, he also dies in it – unless he is shrewd enough to know exactly when to break his staff and drown his book deeper than did ever plummet sound.

Swift and Sartorism

But we must now distinguish not only between what is potential and what is actual but also different senses in which things can be said to be potential or actual.

Aristotle, *De Anima*

In order to construct fictional systems accounting for the difficult ontological situations in which we find ourselves, we do not need to opt for maximizing incompleteness or indeterminacy.

Thomas G. Pavel, *Fictional Worlds*

MEASURING

In *A Letter of Advice to a Young Poet*, Swift recommends that the aspiring poet "should always remember to dress badly while in company." The irony of this statement emerges from the context of the argument in which the novice is urged to "work solely upon his own materials and produce only what he can find within himself (since) he is under no necessity of becoming a good scholar or of troubling himself with philosophy." In other words, the "poet" need not acknowledge the social consensus regarding manners and conduct or the accepted rules and methods of intellectual inquiry. He is *sui generis*, the inspired individual, resembling the self-sufficient spider or the inwardly lit conventicler. His clothes render him ostentatiously conspicuous, setting him off as one who pursues "form" while disregarding "matter." Thus his unkempt appearance is the symbolic equivalent of *haute couture*. But if poetry from the Augustan perspective is, as Ricardo Quintana suggests, "the cultivated statement of the thoughts and perceptions shared by enlightened men of taste,"[1] its sartorial analogue is obviously not ostentatious shabbiness (or actual *haute couture*) but the kind of habiliment we would describe as presentable or distinguished, part of the wardrobe of the social body.

The preponderance of sartorial imagery in Swift has been noted by many readers and critics, especially with regard to the *Tale of a Tub* where it figures prominently as part of the inside-outside dialectic, and to the divan of "scandalous" poems in which Swift seems intent on stripping off the fashionable or deceptive exterior to reveal the corruption that lies beneath. Nigel Dennis, for example, remarks in passing the extent to which "cloth, scissors and thread"[2] are invoked throughout *Gulliver's Travels*: the tailors in Lilliput, the carnival garments of the Laputan sages, the tanned and cured Yahoo skins Gulliver does not shrink from using. He notes that the sequence of defiant letters against Wood's halfpence was written by a "Drapier," makes the obligatory allusion to the *Tale of a Tub*, and refers to the "scandalous" poems in which glitter and filth are juxtaposed, elegant dress masking ordure and decay. We might recall as well that mordant touch in the *Modest Proposal* in which it is suggested that the skins of the delectable infants could be profitably marketed in the form of gloves and boots.

But we misunderstand the pervasive sense of Swift's sartorial metaphor if we concentrate on the vehicle at the expense of the tenor, or enucleate one of the terms of that metaphor while neglecting its complement. If the body, as the Hack in the *Tale* confidently informs us, is "the inward Cloathing" – nakedness or undress as merely one more article in our metaphysical or symbolic chiffonnier – then it is plainly impossible for a human being to strip down to the naked essence. We are always dressed. The only detectable difference between us is one of appearance, of the cut and quality of our manifested selves.

Moreover, in reminding us of Celia's internal plumbing or of Diana's "vapours and streams," Swift is not (or at least, not entirely) expressing that horror of the flesh and its unsavoury operations for which so many readers have censured him. On the contrary, it is the horror of affectation, pride, and vanity that oppresses him. The organic crudities he is so prolifically and compulsively given to mention, especially in his poems, must be understood as a metaphorical reflex. The strength of his aversion to bodily unpleasantness is really the measure of his contempt for personal ostentation. His insistence on the filth and sordidness beneath the fashionable drapery and titivating niceties of a degenerate society should be seen as a form of rhetorical displacement: it is by dwelling on the former that he most decisively condemns the latter. The horror of the flesh turns out to be a sort of code in which he expresses his hatred of something very different – which is, quite simply, *lying*.[3]

There are, it would seem, basically three ways of lying: by fabrication or misrepresentation (saying other than what is), by exaggeration (saying more than what is), and by omission (saying less than what is). The Houyhnhnm definition of the lie as saying the thing which is not (or as we might be inclined to add, implying that which is not) covers at least the first two modes of falsification – which may explain why the Houyhnhnm master is capable of concealing certain truths about Gulliver from the equine community without the slightest pang of conscience or awareness of contradiction. The form of lying that Swift appears to object to most acrimoniously is exaggeration: pretence, affectation, the passing oneself off as "more," better, prettier, nobler, holier, smarter than one really is or can be. By stripping the creature of its brilliant *coquillage* and revealing the unprepossessing snail beneath leaving its trail of slime, Swift exposes not the truth but the lie – or rather, in disclosing the truth, the underlying reality, he points up the lie, the superficial camouflage. It was the all-too-human passion for display, for meretricious lustre, which he understood as the real distortion. As he rhymed it in his "Verses on the Death of Dr. Swift":

> He spar'd a Hump, or crooked Nose,
> Whose Owners set not up for Beaux.
> True genuine Dulness mov'd his Pity,
> Unless it offer'd to be witty.[4]

The idiot quoting a verse from Horace is ultimately no different from the lady whose various effluvia are collected in the "Ivory Table Book."

Swift's vision, then, is not so much excremental as it is unsentimental or desentimentalizing. Since it is not the flesh that is (exclusively or entirely) abhorrent but insincerity and pretentiousness – anatomized as mentioned above through the technique of rhetorical displacement or metaphorical reflex – we might plausibly assume that the body and its attendant functions did not hold any special terror for Swift. The man who dined at Bolingbroke's copious table and went swimming naked in the Thames, and who could write with a refreshing candour about the socially unmentionable, was obviously no prude or example of neurotic repression. Certainly there were times when he found the body a hindrance or embarrassment, as who would not; no doubt there were other occasions when he saw the flesh as providing legitimate access to the experience of pleasure and beauty. I would suspect that, more often than not, as he went about his affairs as political essayist, dedicated clergyman, loyal friend, and bitter enemy, the issue that shocked some of his early biographers and later critics was in itself a matter of almost complete indifference to him. Clothes and body, disguise and nakedness were, essentially, metaphorical counterweights, or as we might say today, a kind of binary code for intellectual dandyism and moral affectation, the Peter Principle and the Jack Quackery of his age (which he reviled and exposed through the deployment of his sartorial imagery) on the one hand; and on the other, the reality, the substratum, that which is to be manifested in the social and intellectual worlds. But the equation is a complicated one, for the body is a polyvalent metaphor: it can, variously, represent crudity, another layer of dress (as in the *Tale*), or the primary material to be shaped.

What Swift is saying in his ridicule of fashionable clothes (or ostentatious tatters) is not simply that the body – the reality – beneath is corrupted and foul (the superficial reading) but that simple decency has been obliterated. The satiric contrast is not between clothes and nakedness but between two sorts of clothes: vain plumage and plain homespun. The latter covers (but also discloses certain moral qualities), the former falsifies. Given the obtrusive physicality of the body, as well as the reality of our natural sentiments, there are two ways of dealing with the "body": wearing modest apparel (of which good manners is one more article), neither denying our condition nor flagrantly exposing it; or sartorial ostentation (whether in the form of Peter's bangles or Jack's rags), which either denies it utterly or exposes it crudely in mock abasement as a means of drawing attention to the self.

Swift's sartorial imagery is thus capable of extensive application. As Nigel Dennis explains, "The beau who falsifies the naked truth of his body is the divine who corrupts the Gospels with his fashionable glosses. He is the courtier who prefers the polished lie to the plain statement, the fop who hides his mental defectiveness in a voguish vocabulary ... He is the politician who has learnt how to disguise greed as a service to the nation." The Whinnies, we remember, believe that Europeans wear clothes to hide their deformities – here clothes are equivalent to lying. But the Whinnies are the creatures of Swift's satiric stables, curried, exercised, and led back to their stalls as their author sees fit. For Swift "costume" and "mendacity" are by no means equivalent terms. We might suggest, at the risk of simplifying, that fancy clothes represent lying by exaggeration; shabby dress, lying by omission. In the one case man passes himself off as more than he is; in the other, he is content to seem less. Plain accoutrement is in effect the most attractive form of dress because it expresses humankind's true medial nature, neither bestial nor seraphic. Appropriate clothing does not hide or suppress and therefore does not lie; in fact, it discloses not the body but the state of mind, the soul, *haecceitas*, identity – when, that is, this natal potentiality has not been aborted or perverted.

Canvassing some of Swift's later poetry, we find as one of its most prominent qualities the horror of affectation, of the mode of exaggeration that embodies all that is deceitful and ephemeral, or merely adventitious. In "To Stella, Who Collected and Transcribed His Poems," we read

> Now should my Praises owe their Truth
> To Beauty, Dress, or Paint, or Youth ...
> They could not be ensured an Hour.

And again:

> Your Virtues safely I commend;
> They on no Accidents depend.

In the poems of friendship and commendation written for his former pupil and lifelong confidante, we discern what for Swift comprised the stellar norm of beauty, conduct, and dignity. Stella herself, in the 1721 birthday poem for Swift, paid tribute to her mentor's values and ideals:

> You taught how I might youth prolong,
> By knowing what was right and wrong;
> How from my heart to bring supplies
> Of lustre to my fading eyes;
> How soon a beauteous mind repairs
> The loss of changed or falling hairs;
> How wit and virtue from within
> Send out a smoothness o'er the skin.

These moral and spiritual qualities, which are seen as restorative or preservative, are contrasted with the "tatter'd nets" and the exclusive "endowments [of] a face," an effect of smoke and mirrors whose influence is both deceptive and fleeting. We immediately recognize the informing metaphor of sartorial lamination: the body as the dress of the spirit, and by extension, clothes as a revelation at second remove.

The human reaction to the body has always been ambivalent; enamoured of health and beauty, one soon realizes, as Yeats lamented, that one is "fastened to a dying animal." Delight and disgust, pleasure and nausea are intimately and inexorably linked. Which term of the equation we select for emphasis depends to a large degree on our physical state but also on the moral perspective we take upon the world. Thus the physical side of our nature is susceptible of extensive metaphorical recruitment. There is no doubt that Swift was acutely and luridly conscious of physical corruption, of uncleanness, defilement, ordure; and the body is tailor-made to serve as the most available metaphor of one of the fundamental truths of the human condition. If this, however, were the only truth the body exemplifies, then who would not, like Strephon, steal away,

Oh! Repeating in his amorous Fits,
Celia, Celia, Celia shits.

But without intending any disrespect, one might also remember that the virtuous and inimitable Stella was equally subject to the same intestinal productions. The difference between Stella and Celia is a difference of attitude or, one might say, of spiritual condition. Stella's dressing room, if a Swiftian protagonist had been so bold as to penetrate its sanctities for the sake of a "poetic" inventory, would obviously not have looked like an alchemist's laboratory. Similarly, Stella going to bed, despoiled of artifice and accessory, would bear no resemblance to Corinna in her shorn and destitute state.[5] For the body is also a medium in (or by) which a person can reveal the moral imperative and spiritual dignity of his or her nature. It is not simply a vessel of corruption but the expression of a moral possibility attaining to the status of fact: modesty, reserve, candour, steadfastness may be expressed through carriage, deportment, and dress. This metaphorical congruence of body and mind is clearly assumed by Swift in his 1727 birthday poem for Stella:

Does not the Body thrive and grow
By Food of twenty years ago?
And, is not Virtue in Mankind
The Nutriment that feeds the mind?

And in a 1721 instalment, we are meant to understand the *rapprochement* of body and mind as more than metaphorical, but as causative:

And ev'ry Virtue now Supplyes
The fainting Rays of Stella's Eyes.

Her attractiveness is heightened not by means of Lusitanian dishes and physical contrivances but by "Breeding, Humour, Wit, and Sense." The physical metaphor is first introduced in this piece by relating "Stella's Case" to that of an aging but hospitable inn, under the sign of the Angel:

And though the Painting grows decay'd
The House will never lose its Trade.

The first birthday poem of 1719 had established the metaphorical armature on which the entire annual sequence would be predicated:

So little is thy Form declin'd
Made up so largely in thy Mind,

It is the crucial word, "Form," and its network of implications – physical shape, proper manners, and philosophical principle – that we will now proceed to consider in greater scope and detail.

SEWING AND STITCHING

> *Hylomorphism*: (Gk. *hyle*=matter; *morphe*=form, contour). A theory that all physical things are constituted of two internal principles: the one of which remains the same throughout all change and is the passive basis of continuity and identity in the physical world, called *prime matter*; the other of which is displaced, or removed from actuation of its matter, in every substantial change, called *substantial form*.
>
> Dagobert D. Runes, *Dictionary of Philosophy*

Swift was undoubtedly familiar with the Aristotelian concept of hylomorphism[6], and would have known that for Aristotle *hyle* can never appear in its pure state but only insofar as it had already been informed by the *eidos*, the idea or form. We should not, accordingly, misinterpret Swift as insisting that flesh, matter – the underlying reality – is invariably gross, shocking, or hideous; or as recommending, on the other hand, that the so-called "inner truth" or constituent matter be resolutely and unflinchingly exposed. The *prima materia* must be clothed in order to appear, but the raiment in which it presents itself, or the "form" responsible for its manifestation, must not be falsely exaggerated, unduly sumptuous, or misleading. Swift does not advocate the forcible separation of form and matter in the name of some ultimate verity, as if matter represented "truth" and form stood for "falsity." Rather *certain* aspects of form, or of the morphological representation of the self, are rejected as deceptive, but there is an aspect of form that does not falsify or exaggerate but presents, manifests, *permits* existence.

As A.E. Taylor explains in his discussion of Aristotelian First Philosophy, one can "distinguish two aspects in an individual [substance], its

Matter (*hyle*, *materia*) and its Form (*eidos*, *forma*). The individual is the matter as organised in accord with a determinate principle of structure, the form."[7] Applying this distinction to our analysis of sartorism, we may suggest that for Swift the truly human being is the properly clothed person: both slovenliness and foppishness are forms of ostentation (Jack's tatters and Peter's brocades), in which the individual's nature is distorted, violated, or debased. What holds true, then, of decent apparel is equally true of good manners, correct speech, the religious *via media*, as well as of the rule of law and authority in political life. These are the *forms* of individual and social existence in which the constituent matter of the self finds its appropriate expression and embodiment; otherwise this matter is, quite literally, *deformed*.

The Aristotelian doctrine of hylomorphism may also be brought to bear on the problems of education. Taylor continues: "We may therefore speak [with regard to character] of native disposition as the matter or stuff of which character is made, and the practical problem of education is to devise a system of training which shall impress on this matter precisely the form required if the grown man is to be a good citizen of a good state." The individual attains his true status as a human being, or actualizes his potential self, by developing his social nature according to the principles of political harmony and justice. The concept of "citizenship" is an essential determinant in the definition of "humanity," cognate to "civilization" and opposed to "barbarism." True humanity is not a hyletic given but requires the concomitant of a *formative* education that moulds and prepares the individual for public responsibility, for citizenship, and constitutes the test of his authentic humanity. As nakedness must in part be construed metaphorically in Swift, so we may argue, with Taylor, that matter is not to be confused with body. Rather, "the relatively undetermined factor which receives complete determination by the structural law or Form is Matter, *whether corporeal or not*" (italics mine). Form, then, is "the *last* determination by which the thing acquires its complete character, and the Matter is that which has yet to receive this last determination." In the same way, the individual reaches his destination, *qua* human being, when he has successfully assimilated the last determinations of form, or education in manners, speech, ethics, politics, and religion – that is, when he has become *civilized*. Civilized man is authentic man.

In the Swiftian dialectic (using our Aristotelian terminology), we would have to interpret nakedness not as pure matter or "prime Matter" in all its rawness or undifferentiated crudity, but as *matter only partially formed*. "Dirt is essentially disorder," says the anthropologist

Mary Douglas, and she goes on to quote William James who defined dirt as "matter out of place";[8] in our terminology, we might redefine it as "matter not yet in place" or as "matter relatively unformed" (matter that has either lost or not yet received its last determination), which would explain why nakedness and filth are so resolutely linked with one another. Beauty and decency are (for Swift) interchangeable notions because they imply the proper and complete formation of constituent matter as distinguished from the partial or improper formation of that same matter. Totally unformed matter has no sublunary existence; only the Creator is privileged to inspect the amorphous rudiment of his Creation – or Hudibras's squire, Ralph, once a tailor, who

> had First Matter seen undressed:
> He took her naked all alone,
> Before one rag of Form was on.[9]

As nakedness is matter relatively *unformed*, so foppishness or sartorial extravagance is matter fantastically *deformed*. Excessive ornament and display, the magnificent facade in dress – or its complementary, programmatic dishevelment – is in Swift the metaphorical correlate of pretentiousness in speech, affectation in manners, needless refinement and complication in theological exegesis. Rags and tatters may be as much a form of ostentation as lace and embroidery. We learn in the *Tale* that it is "the Nature of Rags, to bear a kind of mock Resemblance to Finery," the two "not to be distinguished at a Distance," so that Jack is constantly being mistaken for Peter. Dress is an expression of the spirit, or, again, as Butler rhymed it,

> Thus was he gifted and accoutered,
> We mean on th'inside, not the outward.

In the Swiftian context, the real dichotomy is not so much that between nakedness and dress as between ostentation and decency. Ostentation may take the shape of either excessive embellishment or deliberate slovenliness, luxurious adornment or ascetic reduction, opulence or indigence. As stated earlier, the distinction, in its strictly sartorial representation, is not between dress and nakedness, but between two kinds of dress: that which betokens affectation (with its subdivisions into refinement and disarray), and that which signifies modesty and reserve – in short, between the decorative and the decorous.

At the risk of sounding wantonly paradoxical, one might tentatively suggest that there is a sense in which "nakedness" as such does not exist for Swift but is to be understood, metaphorically, as a rudimentary mode of dress. In this case we would inflect our terms somewhat and propose a tripartite distinction between ostentatious dress (embroidered or diminished), vestigial or undeveloped dress (nakedness), and, the middle term in this sequence, modest or decent apparel, in which the individual finds truly human form. *Ultimate* nakedness would correspond to the Aristotelian substratum or "primal Matter," which is accessible neither to the sensorium nor the mind. Contingent nakedness is seen as abortive, larval, barbaric dress (i.e., dress in its unfinished condition), representing humanity undeveloped and brutish, or still largely unmodified. Dandyism or foppishness (or its obverse, *deliberate* undress) represents humanity deformed, self-infatuated and misshapen, in which Form is to Matter as the Procrustean bed is to its disfigured victim. Proportionate dress signifies humanity in its realized and appropriate nature, as having achieved its intended condition, or entelechy. As the historian of philosophy William S. Sahakian phrases it, the principle "whereby each essence within (or ideal form of) the phenomenon realizes itself is *entelechy*, the word used by Aristotle to signify inner purpose, end, or completion."[10]

(Contingent) nakedness, then, equals substance on the way to its goal, but prematurely arrested, prevented from accomplishing its destiny; sartorial ostentation (negative or positive) is substance deflected from its goal toward the grotesque, the vapid, the distorted. Modesty in dress would represent, in the quaint phraseology of Marjorie Grene, the "end-point, the developed individual ... the *being* to which and from which the runner nature moves,"[11] or in other words, the completed process or entelechy.

Aristotle informs us in the fourth chapter of the twelfth book of the *Metaphysics* "that there are three principles [determining substance] – the form, the privation, and the matter," a thesis illustrated with regard to colour as "white, black, and surface." (Most commentators on Aristotle dispense with the concept of "privation" – for simplicity's sake, no doubt). For our purposes we might say that along a continuous scale of sensible change, privation would correspond to what I have called "matter relatively unformed" or nakedness, in which entelechy has been forestalled or thwarted. Here, keeping to our analogy, we discover ourselves on the level of raw, physical life, the undisciplined needs and desires of the body, sensual appetite, as well as physiological decay. Form prospering at the expense of matter – suppressing, distorting, or exploiting it – finds its analogical equivalent in sartorial extravagance (in the double sense of embroidery and self-conscious tawdriness), which in turn suggests the various kinds of dissimulation Swift anatomizes. Form and matter riding in tandem, working reciprocally, in felicitous union not only with one another but with their divinely appointed *telos*, may be translated metaphorically into sartorial modesty. This in its turn betokens for Swift decency in speech and manners, the Anglican compromise between reason and faith,[12] and the principle of "mutual subjection" between the diverse echelons of the political hierarchy. Sartorial restraint and propriety express, on the level of a humble analogy, man's entelechial consummation as a social creature governed by law, fealty, and the sense of mutual obligation. Ideally speaking, we are neither to offend nor to abuse one another but to acknowledge the simple truth of our being as reciprocally dependent creatures whose interrelationships with the larger community are meant not to obscure but preserve the essential dignity of each. Such is the individual substance which is man, properly dressed for the occasion.

ODDS AND ENDS

"Substance" is attained only as the result of the proper conjunction of its constituent principles. Gulliver, for example, as Robert M. Philmus argues, fails to connect "sight and insight, external observation and introspection, superficies and essence. His disjoining of visible appearance from inner being is the source of delusion about human nature."[13] The Brobdingnagian court, and to some extent the people, have presumably attained this level of hylomorphic appropriateness, in which outside and inside have been compatibly wedded. Their clothes, Gulliver reports, "are a very grave decent Habit." Quintana comments, with respect to Brobdingnagian learning, politics, law, and literary taste, that these exemplary people are distinguished by "their dislike of over-refined speculations, their forth-right, practical natures, and their strong moral sense." But Gulliver, as we remember, clothed at first in "the thinnest Silks that could be gotten," emerges from Brobdingnag wearing breeches of mouse skin.

We find this sartorial line of reasoning given special prominence in book 2 of More's *Utopia*, one of the possible sources of *Gulliver's Travels* and specifically of Gulliver's sojourn in Houyhnhnmland. The Utopians, we learn, have only contempt for those "who think themselves better for having finer clothes." Such deluded souls imagine "they are somehow superior, as if they excelled by nature and not by wrong opinion." The same remonstrance applies to those who are "pleased by the useless marks of *outward* respect," as well as to "those who are enamoured of gems and jewelry" (italics mine). The basic contrast on which these reproaches depend is that between external conspicuousness and internal "nature": fine clothes, mere gestures, glittering ornament (which could just as well be counterfeit) on the one hand, and on the other what Hythlodaeus defines as "the essential qualities of anything" which neither custom nor taste can influence.

But it is important to see that More (or Hythlodaeus) is by no means advocating a return to Eden or the condition of pristine nakedness. The Utopians wear "loose-fitting leather clothes, which last as long as seven years." Their outer cloaks, which are replaced every two years, are all of the natural colour of wool. "They like linen cloth to be white and woollen cloth to be clean, but they are indifferent to fineness of texture." Eschewing both haberdashery and crammed closets, they can see "no reason why a person should want more clothes," which would neither protect nor show to genuine advantage. Their consumption is in all respects "moderate." Garments, manners, and customs are expressions of their essential and unperverted human nature, neither mutilated nor over-refined, as they tread the middle path between the extremes of barbarism and sophistication. It is precisely here that we find a prefiguration of Brobdingnagian measure and proportion.

It may be interesting at this juncture to consider the sartorial metaphor in another context entirely. The editors of the Oxford *Classic Fairy Tales*[14] see the same sartorial technique at work but diffracted, as it were, through the prism of the fairy tale: "The magic in the tales (if magic is what it is) lies in its people and creatures being shown to be what they really are." Thus, the "transformation is not an actual transformation but a disenchantment, the breaking of a spell." Cinderella, for example, in the original folk story which Charles Perrault either recorded or altered (or possibly re-invented) was the abandoned daughter of a royal couple; her sartorial transformation at the hands of the fairy godmother does not signify the theme of "rags to riches, or of dreams come true, but of *reality made evident*" (italics mine). If we discount for the moment the glitter and finery as a property theatrically peculiar to the mode of the fairy tale, what we are in fact left with is the *implicit* theme of sartorial appropriateness, of clothes mirroring condition or functioning as the symbolic attribute of the self. Form and matter are once again in conjunction, and reality, no longer obscured or distorted, is made evident. Or, in Aristotelian terms, potentiality is made actual, becomes substance. The self achieves its proper manifestation in conformity with its potential nature.

Fairy-tale heroes and heroines are almost invariably modest creatures (as was the Stella for whom Swift invented his "little language"). The finery in which they are eventually bedecked is meant to signify not ostentation or glamour but the human splendour of the quiet virtues: modesty, courage, loyalty, and patience. The noble title to which they succeed, or which is conferred upon them, is the metaphorical correlate of true, inner nobility or their proper *areté*. It is, in other words, their essential humanity that is expressed in their gorgeous investitures.

If we apply the Aristotelian concept of entelechy, in the sense of "reality made evident," to our fairy-tale protagonists, we find that their essential natures comprise not only a kind of ontological substrate awaiting manifestation but also the propensity towards the accomplishment of heroic deeds *that do not call attention to themselves*. The antagonists in these stories are usually braggarts, *alazons*, who flourish in their reputations, that is, who exalt the name over the deed. The distinction between the deed and the name[15] is a critical one, considered in terms of the traditional dichotomy between reality and appearance – which would correspond, for example, to the disparity between the Word as creative act or scriptural law and the word as textual commentary or exegesis. The name would represent the formal element in an approximate vacuum, divorced from its accompanying matter; the deed is the process or act by which a form is realized in conjunction with matter, that is, the *energeia*. Did Spenser, one might speculate, have this distinction in mind when in *The Faerie Queene* (2.2.17) he introduced Sir Hudibras as "yet not so good of deedes, as great of name," and as one whose possession of reason was "with fool-hardize over ran"? We may also remark that this original Hudibras is dressed to the hilt for the purpose of terrorizing, "all armd in shyning bras," a costume intended to make a definite impression, not to express the inward man in the reciprocal unfolding of essence.

Of course the terms we are working with are susceptible of semantic modulation. The name may also denote essence as underlying identity, and "appearance" may be interpreted dynamically to mean something like the revealing of the inner or hidden truth. But we are relying here on that familiar system of nomenclature in which the name suggests the "uncreating word" with which Pope concludes *The Dunciad* (or the sense of "in name only"), and "appearance" implies deception, illusion, *trompe l'oeil*. Swift makes his attitude toward the superficial or accidental quality of the name pretty clear in his pamphlet *Against Abolishing Christianity*: "Will not Heydukes and Mamalukes, Mandarins, and Potshaws, or any other words formed at Pleasure, serve to distinguish those who are in the Ministry from others?" Tories may just as well be called Margaritians and Whigs Toftians, a suggestion that is satirically heightened when we recall that "whig" originally meant a Scottish Presbyterian outlaw, and "tory" an Irish Catholic bandit. Similarly, Thomas More's Utopians tended to consider what men call "delights" as "only the emptiest of fictions (as if men could change their nature by changing their name)."

We should note, however, that there are ironic intricacies at play here, too. The name plainly corresponds to the mere surface; yet if the surface is not equally attended to, we find ourselves prone to obscurantist declinations, taking refuge from the intellectual labour of making distinctions in the vague and the inchoate, in meretricious *profondeurs*. There may be a sense in which names are essential. If religion is not "an arbitrary matter," then "to substitute another word for the Church is therefore to shift the grounds of the argument and the nature of what is in dispute," says Robert Philmus. While not discounting the importance of this perception, I would suggest that it touches on the present argument only at a tangent. The point is not that the name is inevitably deceptive or empty but that the name (as form) must correspond to the material substrate (as deed, as character, or as "nature") in the proper manifestation of substance or entelechy. But, as it happens, the name frequently exhibits a kind of occupational tendency to obscure or misrepresent or exaggerate rather than to disclose or present.

FITTING

In the year 1530[16] there "appeared" a book whose influence on the concept of *civilité* was to be profound and extensive. It was reprinted over thirty times in the first six years after its publication and eventually went through 131 editions, of which thirteen were issued in the eighteenth century. It was translated from the Latin into French, German, Italian, English (1532), and even into Czech, and began a new subgenre of literary-cum-sociocultural treatise of which the most recent exemplars are serious studies like Levi-Strauss's *The Raw and the Cooked*, and more frivolous manuals of etiquette, such as Emily Post's compendia of behavioural rules and conventions. The book which was to have so pervasive an effect on western civilization was Erasmus's *De civilitate morum puerilium* (*On Civility in Children*).

Erasmus's treatise comprises seven chapters dealing with the "condition of the whole body," "bodily culture," pious manners, banquets, encounters, amusement, and the rites of the bedchamber. It consists principally of rules and maxims governing civilized behaviour in its personal, social, and religious dimensions. A considerable effort is made, for example, to reform the personal appearance and the table manners of Western Europe. Snot must not be wiped away with the sleeve, we are gravely informed, but deposited in a cloth. Spittle should be rubbed underfoot after expectoration. It is permitted to vomit at the table, "for it is not vomiting but holding the vomit in your throat that is foul" – but "ore pleno vel bibere vol loqui, nec honestum, nec tutum" (to eat or drink with a full mouth is neither respectable nor prudent). Nor is it becoming to remove masticated lumps of food from the mouth and place them on one's quadra (plate or slice of bread). The list goes on.

The cultural historian Norbert Elias has devoted an important chapter to this treatise in his masterly *The History of Manners*,[17] in which he stresses the technique of metaphorical displacement employed by Erasmus. Although the treatise, as its author says, is primarily about "outward bodily propriety," Elias shrewdly comments: "Bodily carriage, gestures, dress, facial expressions – this "outward" behaviour with which the treatise concerns itself is *the expression of the inner, the whole man*" (italics mine). Erasmus himself mentions in passing that "this outward bodily propriety proceeds from a well-composed mind." It is this pivotal phrase on which Elias's exposition turns. While Erasmus, he observes, proceeds "to criticize 'rustic,' 'vulgar,' or 'coarse' qualities," he can also see "very exactly the exaggerated, forced nature of many courtly practices," indicating that Erasmus was aware of conspicuous forms of behaviour both in terms of vulgarity and over-refinement, and wrote in the service of a natural courtesy located between the extremes of rudeness and affectation (in Swiftian terms, the extremes of nakedness and exaggeration).

Elias continues: "Clothing, he says in one place, is in a sense the body of the body. *From it we can deduce the attitude of the soul.* And then Erasmus gives examples of what manner of dress corresponds to this or that spiritual condition. This is the beginning of the mode of observation that will at a later stage be termed 'psychological'" (italics mine). *On Civility* is by no means the first book purporting to enumerate a series of rules and principles with respect to civilized conduct; Caxton's *Book of Curtesye*, for example, printed in the late fifteenth century, is such a prescriptive manual:

For thrusteth wel upon your berynge
Men wil you blame or gyve preysynge.

But *On Civility* is the first book to site the social imperative in that broad psychological context in which good behaviour, proper table manners, and *the symbolic nature of clothes* receive subtle and informed consideration. Clothes are understood neither as mere covering, as if they constituted nothing more than an artificial pelt against the weather, nor simply as indices of social rank, but as manifestations of a spiritual condition, signs of the inward man. The idea of modesty and propriety in manners, speech, and dress has, of course, its classical antecedents in the Platonic notion of metriopathy and in the Aristotelian Mean (or *to meson*) as established in the *Nichomachean Ethics*.[18] But now we find it treated not as the sign of oligarchic great-mindedness (*magnanimitas* or *megalopsychia*) but as the expression of a fundamental *humanitas*, theoretically accessible to all, in which the relation between matter and form,[19] spirit and act, inward state and outward dress, are seen as reciprocal and collateral.

Erasmus is acutely conscious of courtesy or civility as a mediating term between excess and deficiency. If on the one hand it is impolite to smack the lips like a rustic, it is at the same time unnatural "to purse the lips ... as if whistling to oneself," an act that "can be left to the great lords when they stroll among the crowd." The point is that the individual, striving to achieve the proper mode of civilized behaviour, must discover and evince the *via media* in all situations ranging over the entire spectrum of social address and comportment: speech, manners (including, of course, table manners), and dress. It is in this way that civilized men and women may express their essential humanity.

ADJUSTMENTS

If the Aristotelian notion of hylomorphism serves as the philosophic context for Swift's sartorial metaphor, it is the Erasmian tradition of cultural advocacy in which that metaphor is historically rooted and from which it receives its effective nourishment. As Erasmus's *Folly* stands behind the sophisticated intricacies of section 9 of *A Tale of a Tub*, so his *Civility* underwrites the sartorial imagery of sections 2 and 3. We should view Swift's sartorism as a metaphorical argument for the "middle way" in manners and behaviour, in religion and politics – ultimately, we might say, life in general. And since *On Civility* converges on the *Nichomachean Ethics*, the application of which it both widens and specifies, we might legitimately posit an Aristotelian-Erasmian nexus as the context for Swift's conservative thesis.

But Swift is nothing if not playful and resourceful, and will turn his metaphors inside out like reversible jackets to get as much wear out of them as possible. The coats that the three brothers in the *Tale* are bequeathed no doubt represent, as the scholiast asserts, "the Doctrine and Faith of Christianity," Christ's seamless garment for which the soldiers diced at the foot of the cross. Peter's titivating, with which he at first leads his brothers astray, stands as we know for needless theological complication; Jack's eventual reducing of his coat to rags in a belated attempt to rid himself of Peter's fashionable additions plays on the paradox that perpetual, feverish mending is little more than constant unravelling, or as Butler put it:

As if religion were intended
For nothing else but to be mended.

Religion becomes the exegetical residue of

A sect whose chief devotion lies
In odd perverse antipathies,
In falling out with that or this,
And finding somewhat still amiss.

Martin, who may represent Lutheranism, as Nigel Dennis seems to think, but more likely the Anglican *via media* between Catholic splendour and Puritan vehemence, attempts to restore his coat, carefully and gradually, to a reasonable approximation of its original condition – that is, to the text, not the hermeneutic.

When the Hack proceeds to cite certain Professors who hold "that Man was an Animal compounded of two Dresses, the Natural and the Celestial Suit, which were the Body and the Soul: that the Soul was the outward, and the Body the inward Cloathing," we are likely to feel puzzled at this apparently wilful paradox, and to remain unconvinced (as we may be intended to) by the absurd reasoning enlisted in support of the hypothesis, except as evidence of madness. But there is a sense in which the formulation is philosophically suitable, for the body as "matter relatively unformed" is the inert and "internal" principle that requires differentiation, and the soul is the active or governing principle that determines what would otherwise remain unconditioned and imperceptible. Form is the *sine qua non* of manifestation, the dynamic factor that takes the inchoate substrate and yeasts it up into visible shape or determinate function, and in this sense it may be regarded as "the outward Dress [which] must needs be the Soul." But, of course, we are now also interpreting the word "form" as roughly equivalent to "shape" or "figure" and not as "*eidos*" with its meaning of "dynamic pattern" or "shaping force." The confusion is partly lexical. But soul or form in its partly misconceived role as transcendental cookie-cutter clearly implies, as the giver of shape, an outward determination. Properly considered, form is no less internal than matter, and it is the conjunction or concurrence of the two that produces the manifested substance.

The sartorial metaphor plainly takes certain liberties with the metaphysical distinctions made by Aristotle. Deformation is form gone mad, overlaying original substance (form and matter in proper union) with the products of its own disordered invention. "Embroidery was Sheer wit; Gold Fringe was agreeable Conversation, Gold Lace was Repartee ... All which required abundance of Finesse and Delicatesse." Here it is "outward Dress" that predominates at the expense of appropriate conformity to the body or "inward Cloathing." Obviously if all we have is clothing, whether outward or inward, soul or body, form or matter, then we are entitled to ask precisely what it is that is being clothed in the first place. The confusion at this point is not so much a question of lexicality as it is of versatility: the sartorial image is being tailored in protean fashion to a number of concurrent measures and patterns. When we are told that "those Beings which the World calls improperly Suits of Cloaths, are in Reality the most refined Species of Animals ... Rational Creatures, or Men," we know the image is being deployed satirically, as if to say "Clothes make the man" or "the world judges by appearances." We have left both Aristotle and Erasmus, classical philosophy and Renaissance humanism, aside for the time being. In fact, we have entered the domain of semiological analysis whose vestimentary dimension has been most recently explored by Roland Barthes in *The Fashion System* where we learn that clothing as a signifier stands for two principle signifieds: the World (Ensemble A) or Fashion itself (Ensemble B). The former is a "naturalistic" system that corresponds to practical need or function; the latter is a "logical" system, an expression of the Law or the Word, generating social and semantic distinctions which may then be deployed for purposes of exclusion, differentiation, or, as in the cases we are considering here, ironic manipulation. Swift's disclosing satire in this context depends upon his subtle mixing and matching of the elements that constitute Barthes's Ensemble B.

Thus, when we learn that the "True Critick is a sort of Mechanick, set up with a Stock and Tools for his Trade, at as little Expense as a Taylor," and that "the Taylor's Hell is the Type of Critick's Common-Place-Book, and his Wit and Learning held for by the Goose," we are to understand that modern learning is all form and no matter, or as the Bee suggests later on, it is all "method and Art" without consideration of "Duration and matter." Once again, form is construed as "outward," as mere superficiality, the Spider's mathematical designs or the tailor-critic's heated iron which impresses its weight on surfaces, while matter is reinterpreted as "substance" in the sense of "solid meaning," or "intellectual content.' Here Swift is ringing lexical changes on the philosophical vocabulary. When he continues the metaphor by affirming in the next sentence "that it requires at least as many of these, to the making up of one Scholar, as of the others to the Composition of a Man," we are meant to realize that a scholar is made up of paper in the same way as a man is stitched together out of rags. What, then, is a genuine scholar, and what is an authentic man? Where is the mind beneath the paper and where is the man beneath the clothes, if mind *is* paper and man is costume? We understand well enough what Swift is getting at, for the genuine scholar and the authentic man both exist, despite the fact that there may be fewer bees than spiders, not as many Martins as Jacks and Peters, one Temple to a tribe of Wottons. But the point I am making is that the sartorial image is inflected or applied in a number of different though related ways. In its present "form," it stipulates that the modern soul is a flimsy and superficial thing indeed.

But the larger context is Aristotelian and Erasmian. Nakedness or undress in one metaphorical system, usually associated with the Romantic turn of thought, may stand for truth, reality, authenticity, or fact,[20] that which subtends one or another sort of camouflage or pretence. In the classical-Renaissance dialectic, however, nakedness or undress represents boorishness, rusticity, unmodified physicality, the "all-too-human" or the "not-quite-human" in the sense of *humanitas*.[21]

At the other end of the spectrum, moving from infra-sartorism to ultra-sartorism, elaborate costume (or *intentionally* diminished costume) signifies affectation, effeminacy, dissembling, or self-infatuation in the realms of conduct, speculation, and worship. The *meson* is symbolized by discretion and restraint in dress, in which clothes and body are in functional conformity with one another: the sartorial expression of the *via media* and the genuinely human. Inflecting the Aristotelian vocabulary, we might depose that these three stages or moments in the process of manifesting substance correspond, on the infra side, to matter relatively unformed; on the ultra side, form elaborating itself at the expense of matter; and in its median and therefore "finished" condition, form and matter in functional harmony, that is, entelechy. In Swift, then, what we recognize as decency in conduct or dress that neither obliterates nor flagrantly exposes the body (and is the symbolic expression of soul or attitude or state of mind), is entelechy in the personal and social dimensions of life. The "Anglican compromise" and the principle of mutual subjection within a lawful and hierarchically organized state is entelechy accomplished in the religious and political spheres.

We might go on to suggest that the political infra or matter relatively unformed in this scheme would correspond to anarchy; the political ultra to autocracy, expressed, for example, in the magnificence and grandeur attaching to the court of Louis XIV, or in the Cromwellian *affectation* of simplicity.[22] Swift's sermon *On Mutual Subjection* (after 1720) would seem to present his settled convictions on the political question, favouring as it does a hierarchical polity based on reciprocal obligation – a kind of ethical oligarchy midway between anarchy and despotism. The religious equivalent of nakedness or undress might be deism or perhaps atheism – man shedding the garment of revelation; religious sartorism is to be found in the idle complications of hermeneutic analysis, connected with Catholic Peter, or the Hudibrastic perversities of a reductive theology undermined by revisionist excess, associated with Puritan Jack. And Martin stands for the middle way in ecclesiastical matters, neither refining or mutilating nor removing his vestments, but restoring them as nearly as possible to their "Primitive State."

IRONING

Swift's tropology, as I have argued, is not fixed but is on the contrary open to considerable modulation. A certain confusion is inevitable, owing principally to the metaphoric versatility of the term "body." In one schematism, usually associated with the "scandalous" poems, the metaphoric scale might look as follows:

nakedness (body)	clothes (proper)	clothes (exaggerated)
corruption	decency	ostentation

which simplifies and to some extent trivializes the analogical relations Swift is playing with. What I have called the "classical-Renaissance dialectic" bypasses the troublesome issue of "corruption" or of the pathological implications which the Excrementalists – Murry and Brown in particular – have seen in Swift's imagery. A more flexible schematism could be diagrammed:

	nakedness (body)	*clothes (proper)*	*clothes (exaggerated)*
Aristotle	matter relatively unformed (privation)	entelechy (form-matter: telos)	matter partially deformed (form, at expense of matter)
Erasmus	deficiency (rudeness)	propriety (via media)	excess } foppery; intentional dishevelment

Inflecting our terms somewhat to correspond with a more "philosophical" set of distinctions, the sequence would read

ultimate nakedness	contingent nakedness	entelechy	deformity
unperceivable (primal matter)	humanity unformed; barbarism	humanity realized; modest dress	humanity deformed; overdressing or underdressing

I do not mean to suggest that the body-corruption nexus and the simple metaphorical scale are entirely inappropriate constructs but merely that, rigorously deduced or applied, they tend to distract the attention from the complex and protean nature of the Swiftean tropology. It is time, perhaps, to discard the "soiled nappy" approach to Swift's deployment of sartorial imagery.

STEPPING OUT

One of the tenets of this essay is that the sartorial schematism is enormously versatile and adaptable. It is not only permuted in a number of ways by Swift himself in his texts but can be flexibly applied by the reader to these same texts as a technique of interpretation.

Considering, for example, the perennially controversial fourth book of *Gulliver's Travels*, readers may find themselves speculating not on the relationship between Gulliver and the Houyhnhnms or Gulliver and the Yahoos but between the Houyhnhnms and the Yahoos in their own violent reciprocity. It may be the real reason for their mutual antipathy is that what we recognize as two distinct species were originally consanguineous, as it were, descending from the two incompatible steeds harnessed to the soul's chariot in Plato's *Phaedrus*. The Houyhnhnm resembles the right-hand, light-coloured horse, "upright and cleanly made ... a lover of honour and modesty and temperance ... guided by word and admonition only." The Yahoo, while more simian than equine in shape, bears a curious resemblance to the left-hand or sinister horse, "a crooked lumbering animal, put together anyhow; [who] has a short thick neck ... is flat-faced and a dark colour ... and blood-red complexion." He is, Socrates tells us, "the mate of insolence and pride ... hardly yielding to whip and spur" – the original of the intractable and rebellious Yahoo. Thus *mutatis mutandis*, one may see the Yahoo within the fiction not simply as man in himself or as man debased, but as *degenerate Houyhnhnm*; and conversely, the Houyhnhnm is equally monstrous precisely because he has suppressed the "material" half of his composite self.

The Yahoo is meant to function in the story not only as a revelation to Gulliver but as a warning to the Houyhnhnm – a warning the noble horse fails to heed, instead concocting a fanciful myth to explain the Yahoo's mysterious presence in Houyhnhnmland. But the other face of "the perfection of Nature," of cool, impeccable rationality and serene self-regard, is nothing other than instinctual ferocity and malevolence. The Yahoo is the caricature of the Houyhnhnm, the twisted reflection of pure reason, an image both Houyhnhnm and Gulliver blithely misconstrue. Gulliver, as we know, does see himself in the Yahoo but resolutely misinterprets the significance of the apparent reflection. Accordingly, he strives to emulate the unapproachable Houyhnhnm, with the absurd result that he spurns his wife and children and decides to live in a stable. But the Yahoo reflects not man as such or man as beast but man mutilated and self-divided – precisely as does the drab, complacent, unsympathetic Houyhnhnm. The central irony in the fourth book resides in the fact that Houyhnhnm and Yahoo, brothers under the skin, fail to recognize their common pedigree.

From the perspective we have adopted here, we may see Houyhnhnm, Yahoo, and Gulliver as intimately related along a sartorial spectrum. The Yahoo represents nakedness or matter relatively undeveloped; the Houyhnhnm, unashamed of cantering in the buff, is really all clothes, cerebral elaboration, or form thriving at the expense of matter, of the physical and emotional self; Gulliver, situated between the Houyhnhnm dwelling and the Yahoo stable, misapprehends his condition as involving a choice between one or the other, when what is required of him is a reunification of the sundered halves and their eventual reconciliation.[23] Instead he soles his shoes with Yahoo skins and proceeds to trot like a horse. At the end of the story, fulminating in his misanthropic retirement like Alceste on his way toward his precious "rustic solitude," Gulliver is nothing more than an "abstracted fop,"[24] improperly dressed for his human occasion.

Applying the same extensive trope *formally* to *A Tale of a Tub*, one might diffidently suggest that the entire performance can be construed as the textual embodiment of the sartorial metaphor. The Narrative line represents the "body" or physical substratum attired with increasing elaboration in the extravagant garb of the Digressions, each instalment of the latter corresponding to another piece of ornamentation: gold-lace repartee, periwig humour, embroidered wit. The result is a bravura performance in which form has *ostensibly* flourished at the expense of matter, providing us with an illustration of entelechy on the run, of interminable exegesis, and of a kind of political subversion in which the hack, a declassé *roi soleil*, imposes his own rampant sensibility on the "body politic" of the text. The principle of irony, however, which determines the performance, allows us to read the text in an unAristotelian way, since what we have called "deformity" – form gone mad, energeia out of control – is in fact the subject matter of the *Tale*.[25] The ironic principle at work is really the principle of imitative form, but rigorously controlled, held in aesthetic check. So the *Tale*, for all its appearance of unruly exuberance and rambling disorganization, exhibits its own content and achieves its own species of functional harmony, its entelechial perfection. It is properly dressed for its thematic occasion.

Notes

PREFACE

1 A less subtle but of course equally important such "analogue" is the political freedom to choose one's themes without fear of censorship. As this right or privilege effectively exists in the West, we are providentially free to investigate the ontology of the self as both manifested in and generated by the passion for stylistic flexibility – perhaps the greatest of all luxuries.

With respect to the question of versatility, F.P. Santangelo, baseball's current virtuoso supersub, said recently in an interview: "I want people to think that wherever on the field I'm playing, that's my everyday position." This sleight-of-mind may involve the ability to pretend well enough to deceive oneself as well as others, i.e., to apply a kind of mock-Boolean logic to one's heteroclite practice: if x is false, assume it is true; if x is true, execute. Joking aside, this is more or less what Yeats in a late essay recommended as "the emotion of plenitude" and Baudelaire in his reflections on literary dandyism called "greatness without convictions" – but clearly, not without conviction. The extent to which deception (especially of the self) functions as an integral component of authenticity or competence still needs to be explored. Poets in particular, as specialists of the general, are like Disney coyotes racing off cliffs who need not plummet to the ground and splat into the Real – until they look down.

2 This kind of writing has already become indelibly stereotypical, reproducing itself endlessly in a condominium style of fantastically minimal differences. As Bhabha claims, “the stereotype requires, for its successful signification, a continual and repetitive chain of other stereotypes. The process by which the metaphoric ‘masking’ is inscribed on a lack which must then be concealed gives the stereotype both its fixity and its phantasmic quality.” Like many of his ilk, Bhabha appears serenely unaware that pomo represents not so much a breakthrough in discursive convention as an intellectualized form of colonialist discourse itself. (See Homi K. Bhabha, *The Location of Culture*.) When it begins to approximate a distinct form of expression and acquire paradigm status, the postmodern mode inevitably invites or *becomes* parody. There isn't much to choose, these days, between pomo and paro. (See this volume, “On the Essay,” for an attempt to develop a serious theme in a parodic mode and to treat the postmodern style as merely one among many possible forms of discourse, though not an altogether legitimate one.) Even so astute and reasonable a commentator as Gerald Graff in his justly celebrated *Beyond the Culture Wars* does not see that the “postmodern” idiom has pretty well become an institutional aberration. Graff argues that “the most clearly written criticism will be gibberish to people who have not been socialized into the literary and intellectual community,” and that “talk of ‘traditional moral themes’ will not be much less intimidating than ‘hegemonic discursive practices’” to anyone who has not entered that discourse community. My own experience in the classroom suggests otherwise. The students I teach may indeed struggle with F.R. Leavis, C.S. Lewis, or Gerald Graff himself, but nevertheless manage to arrive at some degree of understanding and partial mastery. They make *absolutely no headway* with Homi Bhabha and the legion of contemporary exemplars of the School of Night. Curiously, Graff himself implies, by using the phrase “clearly written criticism,” that the other term of his comparison may be described as “unclearly written criticism,” which demolishes his argument at the outset.

3 Jean-François Lyotard in *The Postmodern Condition* defines postmodernism as “incredulity toward metanarratives” (and thus as resistance to the institutional “apparatus of legitimation”) and approves the consequent “dissolution of the self into a host ... of contradictory codes and ... instabilities.” I would have no problem with this definition, which is very close to the notion of elective

criticism I am advocating here – if the so-called postmodern style had not hardened into a set of academically vetted protocols complete with mandatory dialect and an attitude of destabilizing relativism which, oddly enough, has not even remotely shaken the absolute self-assurance of its practitioners. In any case, what we now call the "postmodern" has become so vast and nebulous a category that it has lost all denotative meaning and hangs out mainly in the region of the connotative.

4 As a lexical correlate of what I am getting at, consider the following well-known instance, which can only be a determinate or "codified" accident. In 1610, while the King James Bible was in process of translation, Shakespeare was forty-six years old. If you turn to Psalm 46 and count down forty-six words from the top (skipping the instructional Selah), you arrive at the word "shake." Count up forty-six words from the bottom and you stop at the word "spear." Although Shakespeare does not appear to have collaborated on the project, his name was somehow "in the air," coming to rest via a complex numerology in another dimension or element, print. This notion bears a certain structural resemblance to Ferdinand de Saussure's theory of the hypogram, which refers to clusters of letters distributed throughout a text that articulate unanticipated meaning, embedded names and nested anagrams, textual forces and traces at work beneath the level of overt signification. But here I am thinking not so much of lexical correlates, fascinating as these may be, which strike me in the last analysis as onomastic metaphors for the mystery of correspondence, but rather of that curious and sudden catch of recognition or unexpected apparition of a half-intuited self one experiences over and over again in literary works, like seeing one's profile reflected in a brace of angled mirrors. There is also, then, a hint of Goethean affinities in this strange dynamic, provided the "other" is understood as a textual projection, simulacrum, or possibility which must be essayed and tentatively denominated.

NEVER ON SONTAG

1 One recalls in this connection Ben Jonson's character in *Tale of a Tub* (1633), whose plaintive lament is applicable to many historical periods: "I, Miles Metaphor, your worship's clerk, / Have e'en been beaten to an allegory."

2 What I call symptomatic criticism is that familiar mode of thought which treats the text as a stalking horse or smokescreen for an underlying symbolic meaning or as a structure of ideas and compulsions governed by forces of which the author is not entirely conscious. Thus the critic feels constrained to penetrate the disguise or ideological camouflage that the text mischievously (and ostensibly) constructs.

3 Despite the imposing array of scholarly names to shore up her deposition at this point, one tends to remain unconvinced. Frye and Barthes are intensely prescriptive writers, and Walter Benjamin on Nicolai Leskov may sound impressive to urban intellectuals – that touch of the dry, the esoteric, the dandiacal, the farouche – but gritty-minded writers respond more vitally to poverty, sex, and baseball. Besides, as suggested above, the descriptive mode tends to slip into the mode of the rescriptive and thence into the fully prescriptive: the discussion of form leads to analysis, argument, and, yes, interpretation.

4 In section 4 the allegorical and, by implication, the polysemous approach is rather brusquely jettisoned; in section 9 it is accorded a somewhat grudging respect as having once been useful and even avant-garde – in its time. But what is its time? The fact that the technique was approximately a thousand years old when Dante adopted it apparently escapes Sontag's attention. In fact the Augustian hermeneutic goes back through the *Collationes* of John Cassian (370-435) to the threefold interpretive schemes of Origen and Clement in the third century, which were themselves founded on the dyadic exegesis of Philo of Alexandria in the first century. One might go further and suggest that the Christian evolution of textual exegesis is shadowed and constrained by the ancient Jewish tradition known as "Pardes" (acronymed as PRDS), a secular tetragrammaton referring to the four interpretive levels of the obvious, the sinuous, the homiletic, and the mystical. And we are still working with hermeneutic quadratics today – for example, Norman Holland's transactive analysis with its emphasis on the four essential reading functions: Defense, Expectation, Fantasy, and Transformation, or what he calls DEFT.

5 Sontag's "luminousness" very much resembles Stephen Dedalus's concept of *claritas* or radiance in the elaboration of his Thomist-inspired aesthetic theory. Cf. Joyce's *Portrait*, which impinges on the development of Sontag's argument in more than one place.

6 Or perhaps they are like Swift's industrious flappers drawing the attention of their masters away from rapt aesthetic (or mathematical) communings and toward the heresy of subject-matter – which tells us something about the Laputan nature of Sontag's central thesis. But, in effect, interpreters are neither climenoles nor *shiroshisan*, but *mystagogoi*, initiators into mysteries whose founders they complement.

7 The Buddha was known as *tathagata*, "thus-come," since his essential nature transcended all categories of explanation or intellectual inquiry. We find the identical notion in the Old Testament in which the divine name is rendered as "I Am That I Am." Art, we might do well to remember, is a product of the human mind.

8 This is a good example of what we may call the "ontological fallacy," the belief (as David Daiches writes in his *Literary Essays*) that a work of art "fulfils its purpose and achieves its value by *being*, so that the critic becomes concerned only to demonstrate the mode of its being by descriptive analysis."

9 Cf. MacLeish's "Ars Poetica" ("A poem should not mean / But be.") – a poem that violates its own anti-semantic premise (if I may so phrase it). The essays and the poem self-destruct in different though complementary ways, the former by condemning what it seeks to preserve, the latter by preserving what it affects to condemn.

10 As Browning's Fra Lippo Lippi instructs us:

Don't object, "His works
Are there already; nature is complete:
Suppose you reproduce her – (which you can't)
There's no advantage: you must beat her, then."
For, don't you mark? we're made so that we love
First when we see them painted, things we have passed
Perhaps a hundred times nor cared to see;
... Art was given for that.

The objection to which our painter objects would appear to reproduce the anti-reproductive argument I mobilize against Sontag, but of course the point we are meant to get is that Fra Lippo is not reproducing Nature. Nor, for that matter, is he restoring it by putatively resurrecting our entombed sensitivities. On the contrary, art performs a *mnemonic* or donative function, not a restorative or recreative one. It is *ordinary* forgetfulness, our universal distraction, that art corrects, not the industrial and technological devastation of the senses. The issue has nothing to do with the *sfumato* and craquelure of the jaded contemporary eye, as Sontag's thesis implies.

I might also note here that Paul de Man's well-known argument in *Blindness and Insight* (chapter 2) which denaturalizes the work of art while not entirely intentionalizing it – he proposes the concept of "structural intentionality" to turn the natural object into which the New Criticism has inadvertently reified the poem back into quasi-intentional object – touches on my critique of Sontag only at a tangent. The notion of structural intentionality, since we are after all dealing with poems and pictures and not with tables and chairs, merely begs the question, albeit tactfully. The notion of intention cannot be dissociated from the notion of use, and aesthetic objects do indeed have an undeniable use, like de Man's chair, but this use is not somatic or instrumental or structural. The use of the aesthetic object is precisely *to be interpreted*, to be integrated into the texture of one's living and thinking and remembering, to modify one's habitual mode of discourse as it alters *the way* one sees the world, to enter the harbour of intimacy and enrich the substance of one's dreams, and also, unashamedly, to help us make contact with great souls (who may not always be beautiful). A world in which art is defined and "appreciated" as either a natural object or an instantiation of structural intentionality is no longer a human world – and certainly not a civilized one – which is resolutely and inescapably an intentional world. Aesthetics, as it seems to me, is neither a self-consistent part of the natural world nor an immanent, structurally autonomous world-in-itself. It is one of the languages in which the "conversation of mankind," as Michael Oakeshott understands it, is pursued and transmitted across the centuries. This should be clear to all of us, provided we are not distracted by our own theoretical facility, the moment we pick up a book or put pen to paper. You cannot get away from the empirical self who constantly negotiates with other empirical selves (occasionally sublated as "imaginary" or "fictional" selves) if you wish to avoid autism or psychosis, or at the very least, the dandiacal affectation of the "aesthetic self" or the philosophical exhalation of the "ontological self" – both of which latter, at any rate, flourish mainly in literary criticism and therefore enjoy the minimal virtue of being reasonably harmless.

But perhaps the time has come to admit openly to one another, despite our cherished complexity and sophistication, the following, very real possibilities:

1 the self is not a brute datum, though it is always in danger of becoming one;
2 there is no such thing as a transcendental self, or any of its congeners and displacements (aesthetic, ontological, etc.);
3 the self, or what we understand as the self, comes into being in the intersection between a nexus of desires and a world of reified process, and is constituted as a communal artifact hiding a core of perishable awareness which accounts for the savour, joy, terror, and reflexivity of our existence;
4 art is, accordingly, neither a brute datum nor a transcendental object but a kind of language – glossolalia aspiring to prophecy – requiring interpretation and translation, and intended for the fallible communings of forgetful, discrepant selves who are neither monads nor thoroughfares but permeable bubbles of solitude.

CULLING AND DEREADING

1 For example, consider these typical, twitching Derridean distinctions from "Plato's Pharmacy" in *Dissemination*: "the disappearance of truth as presence, the withdrawal of the present origin of presence, is the condition of all (manifestation of) truth. Nontruth is the truth. Nonpresence is presence. Differance, the disappearance of any originary presence, is *at once* the condition of possibility *and* the condition of impossibility of truth. At once. 'At once' means the being-present (on) in its truth, in the presence of its identity and in the identity of its presence, is *doubled* as soon as it appears, as soon as it presents itself." But the reader should perhaps be thankful for the expository blessing of a passage that closely precedes the above. Since the "disappearance of truth as presence" is tantamount to the disappearance of the "forbidden intuition of the face of the father," we learn more or less in the nick of time that the "disappearance of the face is the movement of differance which violently opens writing or, if one prefers, which opens itself to writing and which writing opens for itself." Whew! The reader has narrowly averted the danger of misunderstanding. But what would Dr Johnson have said?

2 By such "works" I refer mainly to the swarm of reviews and articles in which the term proliferates, and not to fascinating and important studies like Deleuze and Guattari's *Anti-Oedipus* or Kristeva's *Desire in Language*.

3 See Henry Staten's *Wittgenstein and Derrida*. What we would now seem to need is a spontaneous rising of literary bailiffs or repo men who would do us the inestimable favour of repossessing a language that bespeaks little more than vehicular ostentation – a language for which we cannot make the payments.

4 As M. Dupin attests, "The French are the originators of this particular deception." And as John Caputo says, albeit honorifically, in *Radical Hermeneutics*: How they do things in Paris. For Camille Paglia in *Sex, Art, and American Culture*, the French semioticians are completely dispensable: Lacan is a "fog machine," Foucault is a "vacuum cleaner," and Derrida is a writer whose method is "masturbation without pleasure."

5 Naturally a poem can echo or resonate in many ways. It can echo the words, phrases, lines, attitudes, and subjects of other poems – "inscription" and "intertextuality." Marvell's famous "green shade" gleamed duskily in his garden without being further shadowed by quotation marks, which did not prevent it from being recognized as Virgil's "viridi ... umbra" in Eclogue 9 or from decorously "inscribing" itself within a venerable tradition at the same time as it incorporated a "fragment" of that tradition within its own "text." A poem can also echo itself, reproducing its own thesis or craftily identifying itself with its ostensible subject – "doubleness," "self-reflexivity," and "self-inscription." Consider the seventh idyll of Theocritus and its technique of bucolic masquerade for a celebrated classical example. Or does one really need to be told that a poem flanked by quotation marks "create[s] a diacritical relationship between the voice cited and the voice citing it" [Kamboureli]? Is this not precisely the relationship that obtains between the confessional voice and the invisible transcriber in Browning's "My Last Duchess"? The "perverted commas" (as Joyce called them) were always *understood* as a part of the ordonnance of the dramatic monologue. All this supersubtle theorizing reminds me a little of Thomas Adams's warning in *The Soules Sickness* (1630) against the "dangerous Prognosticator" who "suffers the skimme of his braine to boile into the broth." In any case the entire question was definitively and simply clarified by Bakhtin in *The Dialogic Imagination* where he demonstrated how both alien and authorial discourse may be embedded in the same syntactical unit.

6 I am not referring here to the acknowledged existence of the blind spot in every deconstructive text, so that it can be "aporetically"

deconstructed in its turn (which has the additional merit of insuring continual employment) but to its self-devouring, Erisichthian tendency, so that it must ultimately find itself walking up its own asshole.

7 See Stanley Fish (whom Camille Paglia calls a "totalitarian Tinkerbell") writing in the guest column in PMLA for October 1988.

8 One deconstructor who is refreshingly candid about the "takeover" is Joseph N. Riddel, whose radical textuality dispossesses literature and raises criticism to equal status. For Riddel, texts are too "intertextually" promiscuous, as well as racially miscegenous, so to speak, to keep their modal purity and distinctiveness intact. And, of course, Geoffrey Hartman, the champion of "crossing over," has taken criticism and metacriticism across the textual Rubicon toward a literary Imperium. A "reversal must be possible whereby this 'secondary' piece of writing turns out to be 'primary.'" (Not only the "secondary" piece of writing, but the "tertiary" as well.)

9 Or to renovate the image: criticism, having programmed literature into the deconstructive system like a simulator game, gradually begins to program itself, becoming its own species of software. Thus it is radically "problematized" (to use that barbaric word).

10 Lacan is not generally regarded as a deconstructor and was himself deconstructed by Derrida, but he is an arch-practitioner of what I have here been calling the deconstructive style, the fashionable obscurantism whose "profundity" is to a very large degree a function of its opacity. (Althusser and Jameson are perhaps even more infuriating than Lacan for the tantalizing gleams of lucidity they have not entirely succeeded in repressing. And, of course, Derrida, himself, in such texts as "The Double Session," or (most devastatingly) in *Glas* (the putative *Wake* of contemporary critical writing) is probably the chief offender in this regard, the master of near-absolute occultation.)

11 For example, see J. Hillis Miller's 1986 Presidential Address in PMLA 102, no. 3, May 1987.

12 I presume most of these "critics" are writing for and perhaps to one another through the medium of the scholarly essay, updating a traditional form into a species of literary modem. Readers are cast unwillingly in the edgy and often baffled role of eavesdroppers. They preserve their integrity in one of two ways: by leaving or by hemming loudly. (Cf. Hazlitt's classic statement on the subject in his essay "On Criticism": "A critic does nothing nowadays who

does not try to torture the most obvious expression into a thousand meanings ... His object indeed is not to do justice to his author, whom he treats with very little ceremony, but to do himself homage and to show his acquaintance with all the topics and resources of criticism.")

13 Something, perhaps, that resembles what Douglas Coupland in *Generation X* calls the AVD (or Anti-Victim Device): "a small fashion accessory worn on an otherwise conservative outfit which announces to the world that one still has a spark of individuality burning inside," like earrings for men. One may also recall Laurence Sterne's meditation in *Tristram Shandy* on the latus clavus, a mysterious sartorial ornament that distinguished the Roman aristocrat in a time of vestimentary sameness.

THE AUTOEROTIC TEXT

1 Note Jane Gallop's comment (in *Reading Lacan*) on the parapraxic misprint, "La phallus," which appeared in an early edition of Lacan's *Ecrits* – a slip that "propels us, if but for a moment, into an epicene utopia." Gallop goes on to consider favourably Jacqueline Rose's proposal (in *Feminine Sexuality*) that such parapraxes are important and contribute to a "double agenda for reading." I concur. Inscribing the feminine or rather the epicene into the phallocentric thrust of language, I choose to read the name of the author of *Ecrits* as Jacqueline Lecon.

(At the same time, one can't help remarking the idiomatically phallarchic dedication of Gallop's book, which if taken literally renders the feminist or epicene project of reading a trifle dubious: FOR DICK.)

2 As Thomas More said of scholastic philosophy, it is one of those things "without which it is possible to live."

3 Jane Gallop in *Reading Lacan* calls the essay I am commenting on here "a brilliant reading of the Derrida-Lacan confrontation around Poe."

4 The purloined letter as the mother's missing phallus? As a (male) friend of mine remarked after reading Bonaparte and Johnson: "I have trouble keeping abreast."

5 A typical example of this species (specious?) of writing is the opening of Derrida's "The Purveyor of Truth," quoted by Johnson: "Psychoanalysis, supposing, finds itself." Dupin has no trouble finding the letter because "he knows that the letter finally *finds*

itself where it must *be found* [i.e., between the legs of the fireplace] in order to return circularly and adequately to its proper place. This proper place ... is the place of castration." And so on. (A more appropriate image in Poe would be the ourang-outang shoving poor, dead Mlle L'Espanaye up the chimney.) This is how far we have come from the genuine *laine* of critical writing. The current practice of wiredrawn literanalysis reminds me of an elderly gentleman I once observed in a tailor's shop, testing a pullover and remarking that it was 100 per cent acrylic. He intended no irony, buying two of the articles.

6 The clinching paradox is that these supersubtle theories of reading, writing, and the nature of textual analysis appear to proliferate in proportion as fewer and fewer people read. Who is kidding whom? It is as if a new variety of craft literacy is developing, a new hieratic and "calligraphic" scribal culture, in which a tiny minority of the elect is in possession of textual secrets that differentiate it from the vast, agrammatic majority incapable of achieving a sense of intellectual continuity and historical purpose. But this agrammatic mob is slowly being alphabetized in another direction as it becomes increasingly computer literate. Between postmodernism and computerism falls the shadow of a dispersed social literacy.

The problem for the innocent reader is how to disentangle the snarled futhark, to decipher the corrupt chirographum, of this species of writing – a problem without an available solution. Perhaps it should just be allowed to die out. One day we will forget about *texts* and start reading *books* again. And regard, to quote Julian Barnes in *Flaubert's Parrot*, these "contemporary critics who pompously reclassify all novels and plays and poems as texts" with historical bemusement.

7 David Cooper's definition of (true) orgasm in *The Language of Madness* as "the cancellation of the mind" is ironically appropriate here. He is referring, of course, to the annulment of alienated experience, but goes on to advocate a *political* change in our endocrinological structure as the condition for orgasmic joy and social liberation. This solution to the problem of repression, which also involves the proscription of mere procreative sexuality, is perhaps a trifle implausible.

8 Naturally, it is much easier to control the existing penis than the missing phallus, but the problem is really not so much anatomical or psychological as terminological. The same point is made by

Camille Paglia in *Sex, Art, and American Culture*: "And sometimes a penis is not a penis. A phallus, in Francobabble, is just a power tool. But since only men have such tools, we have somehow to circle back and admit it *is* a penis after all. It's a case of Aaron's rod as the incredible shrinking dildo."

Ultimately, what we are dealing with here is a form of obsessional neurosis whose debris, a collection of amputated signifiers, is cleverly if disingenuously hidden behind the opaque surfaces of the text. One longs for a little transparence. As a young student contemplating a career in medicine, I underwent the ordeal of several visits to the anatomy room. One of the exhibits in the foyer of the dissecting theatre was a large Mason jar crammed with severed penises pickled in formaldehyde – an image that in the current context generates a curious emotion somewhere between nausea and nostalgia.

9 Such scientific immunity is the cherished and indispensable fiction of the contemporary effort in the field. All criticism is really a sort of personal confession. A critic like Barthes, for example, moves from one position to another. What, then, guarantees the authority of each individual text in which a given position is articulated? We read not to discover what structuralism or post-structuralism is or to adopt a constitutive perspective on a subject but to find out where an interesting critical thinker has arrived in his or her critical itinerary. The Barthes of *Writing Degree Zero* is not the Barthes of *S/Z*, who in turn is not the Barthes of *The Pleasure of the Text*. We don't read deconstruction; we read Derrida. Criticism can never be an objective or dispassionate mode of inquiry. It is always a sort of confession or epiphany, either deliberate and self-acknowledged, or as is the case with the material under discussion here, unintentional, symptomatic, and self-revelatory, like the squeaking of the fingers on the frets behind the cascading guitar melody.

10 We construct and project our own ideals, Daniel Boorstin argues in *The Image*, in the attempt "to contain our own emptiness." Boorstin defines our world as one "in which the image has itself become the original, the shadow has become the substance." This subject constitutes an intellectual territory more recently opened up by the work of Jean Baudrillard (see especially *Simulations*).

11 "What has become of seduction today, of passion ...?" asks Jean Baudrillard (once again) in *The Ecstasy of Communication*, and answers: "it can only have found refuge ... in covert dysfunction ...

in the rule of the hidden game, in the secret. The sublime has passed into the subliminal." If, that is, the subliminal realm continues to exist.

Of course, my essay may be aporetically deconstructed in its turn, since the subject of autoerotic textuality necessarily requires a steady focus on precisely the vocabulary and mindset it opposes. The only way around this problem is simply not to write about what one is writing – by which I do not mean to write about the (Lacanian) text as not-to-be-read but not to write at all.

12 I am using terms like "autoerotic," "narcissistic," "hedonistic," with a certain degree of latitude, since I have not embarked on a psychoanalytic investigation in which it is important to adduce and name various categorial entities and thus bring them into existence by nominal fiat. Jean Laplanche and Jean-Baptiste Pontalis point out in *The Language of Psychoanalysis* that autoeroticism and narcissism are not to be identified. The first is associated with the early stage of the *corps morcelé*, the unintegrated body, while the second is a function of the mirror stage that provides a totalized image of the self and occurs at a later time in the child's development. If I wished to apply this distinction it would be easy to work up an argument for one or the other. I could suggest that what I am calling the psychocritical text corresponds to the *corps morcelé* as the expression of the *esprit morcelé*, its psycholinguistic doppelganger – as, that is, the production of a mind that has not experienced its secondary or higher mirror stage, its integration as a "practical" or "realistic" human being in the world outside the nursery of the university and the academic journal. Thus it remains condemned to autoeroticism. Or, to "speculate" further, one could posit an indefinite number of mirror stages (avoiding the problematic realm of the "symbolic" for the nonce) which allow for various levels of integration, each more embracing or enframing than the other, and claim that narcissism is a function not, to be sure, of the "body in bits and pieces," but of a *partial* totalization, a totalization in process. However, none of this is necessary, unless one is trying to impress one's peers and colleagues by analytical *pilpul*. Autoeroticism, understood as an undifferentiated lust for the "self" (whether fully, partially, or un-constituted), that is, as desire for *the body that is no one else's body* (i.e., the body as the felt locus of being); and narcissism as the rapt preoccupation with the body that is no one else's body, are, if not equivalent affections, inextricably associated.

But why hackle and scutch the hemp, as Villon so aptly says? This sort of theorizing can become as complex and intimidating as it remains essentially null, resembling as it does the rarified excesses of scholastic disputation that preconstitutes its object, legislates it into existence. Once the *corps morcelé* is posited, narcissism is logically contra-indicated until the self has been totalized in the mirror stage. One has simply to redefine narcissism.

13 This problem, at the heart of contemporary critical theorizing, defies resolution. The basic structuralist principle, in the concise formulation of Frank Lentricchia (*After the New Criticism*) regards the self as "an intersubjective construct formed by cultural systems over which the individual ... has no control." To this Lentricchia opposes the basic traditionalist principle, which claims that the self "at its highest pitches of self-consciousness can cut itself free of cultural determination."

It seems to me that, in the first case, one is entitled to ask: who (or what) is speaking, self or system? The systemic voice, accredited in structuralist theory, is without authority in human contexts and produces only scepticism or derision. But if it is self and not system that speaks, the principle self-deconstructs. On the other hand, who (or what) is responsible for the framing of the second formula? If it is in fact culturally determined, the principle is self-contradictory and the structuralist can smile benignly at the deluded traditionalist. The independent self is a cultural or systemic fiction. Nevertheless, the structuralist cannot *prove* that the proposition is not the independent insight of a free ontological subject. If the semiotician is speaking *personally*, his opposition may be put down to competitive animus; if he is speaking systemically, he is without authority, a mere puppet on the knee of the systemic ventriloquist that must itself constitute a prior subjective entity capable of generating such interested statements. The dispute is, logically, without foundation or issue.

The phenomenon is curious indeed. Having surrendered the autonomy of the subject to the semiotic dimension of language, each one of these critics, unfazed by his or her analytic operations, continues to write out of the same, old, tremulous, uptight self, each one generating his or her own monogrammed construct usually ending with the suffix "eme." After the introduction of the seme, the sememe, the classeme, the mytheme, the vesteme, the grapheme, the ideologeme, the glosseme, the catagoreme, the matheme, etc., I am waiting for the critic who will propose the systeme and, finally, in a blaze of taxonomic splendour, the phalleme and the clitoreme. And one need not, of course, stop thereme. For a particularly egregious example of this tendency, see Joel Fineman (*Shakespeare's Perjured Eye*), whose poststructuralist prattle struggles to achieve the state of transcendent unintelligibility "colonized," "appropriated," and "instantiated" by his European masters. His efforts culminate in the magisterial "Shakespeareme," which he defines as "the smallest minimal [sic] unit of Shakespearean self."

14 In part, like Joyce's Shem the Penman who "wrote over every square inch of the only foolscap available, his own body, till by its corrosive sublimation one continuous present integument slowly unfolded ..." Yet, despite being "transaccidentated through the slow fires of consciousness into a dividual chaos," Shem finally brandishes "his bellbearing stylo" to create from suffering and isolation the vast "cyclewheeling history" of rich, messy, sprawling, ever-productive life. (*Finnegans Wake*, book 1, chapter 7.) Compare also Lyotard's notion in *Libidinal Economy* of the "*grande pellicule éphémère*," which, however, does not enter into the history of dialogue or reciprocity but functions as a mere "conductor of intensities."

ON THE ESSAY

1 See Wassily Kandinsky, *Concerning the Spiritual in Art*, for a discussion on the geometry of spirit. See also Lacan's alphabetical hijinks in *Encore* involving the a and the A, the lower case representing the representable object and the upper case signifying the *Autre*, the radical, non-objectifiable Other. The former, writes Lacan, "sets itself in the place of that of the Other which cannot be glimpsed." While this formulation corresponds to the thesis I am developing here and accounts for the ultimate success=failure of the essay project, the representation of the non-presentable, I should reiterate that the A figuring in my own pages is not the Lacanian A but the Greek *lambda* transposed iconically, with handrail, into the common alphabet, performing the signifying function of the Hebrew lamed and finally identical *in intent* with the sigma=S, though representationally as well as ontologically distinct – and thus producing the eventual catastrophe (which generally goes unremarked). This inevitable process of striding, climbing, and hanging on precariously as one prepares to fall may be

regarded as alphabetically implicit in Victor Hugo's description of the letters in question, given in his *Travel Notebooks* of 1839, in which L is "the leg and the foot" and A is "the gable with the crossbar."

2 Derrida in *Speech and Phenomena* also notes the connection made by Hegel between the letter A and the pyramid, "keeping in mind not only the capital form of the printed letter but also the passage from Hegel's *Encyclopaedia* where he compares the body of the sign to an Egyptian pyramid." Commenting on Derrida's celebrated portmanteau, *différance*, Gregory Ulmer suggests in *Applied Grammatology* that the term "should perhaps be written 'DifférAnce' in order to retain the visual image of the pyramid."

3 See Viktor Frankl, *Man's Search for Meaning*. Frankl's concept of logotherapy, as a technique for conferring meaning upon life and filling the "existential vacuum," thematizes the essay project as "noodynamics." Frankl believes that the valuing process is founded biologically and constitutes "a pre-reflective axiological self-understanding" which can also be defined as "a will to meaning." But it is very doubtful whether such a process can be characterized as ophthalmological, seeing the world *as it really is*. Rather we should regard it as parallactic, fictive, and radiantly occlusive. Or (to change metaphors), as Sven Birkerts puts it in *The Gutenberg Elegies*, the essayistic method is "predicated not upon conclusiveness but upon exploratory digressiveness." It is "a method which proposes that thinking is not simply utilitarian, but can also be a kind of narrative travel that allows for picnics along the way."

4 Every person structures his or her life narratively, a process that comes, so to speak, naturally. But from the perspective we are taking here, the narrative is regarded as nothing more than the poor man's essay, that is, the easy way in. (Compare Stephen Greenblatt's remark in *Renaissance Self-Fashioning* about Montaigne, who "invents in effect a brilliant mode of *non-narrative* self-fashioning.")

5 Absolute knowledge of the Analogical self is, of course, a logically untenable concept, since Absolute knowledge of *anything* is clearly unattainable. The logical formulation of its impossibility would involve, as the Finnish logician Jaakko Hintikka has schematically demonstrated, having to suppose a probability distribution P(x), based on background information – e_o – further supplemented by new evidence – e_i. What, Hintikka asks, "is the probability distribution which now represents our epistemic state?" The answer,

plainly, is $P(x/e_o + e_i)$. Our problems, however, are only beginning, since e_i must "be thought of as codifying literally *all* one's pertinent information." But as the universe, or even any particular aspect of it, resists conceptual as well as quantificational closure, e_i must remain potentially infinite. And infinities that do not cancel tend to unbalance or disrupt the (otherwise) most elegant solutions. Moreover, apart from the theoretically inexhaustible contents or "sample-space points" of all possible knowledge, the principle of total evidence collapses before the necessarily *fallibilistic* nature of human knowing. Between the compressor arms of fallibilism and e_i, Absolute knowledge is crushed out of existence. For our purposes, however, the notion of *analogicality* (rather than "analogy") allows us to postulate an "Absolute" knowledge for the simple reason that it permits of arbitrary or *imagined* closure. (Cf. Jaakko Hintikka, "Sherlock Holmes Confronts Modern Logic," in *The Sign of Three*, ed. Umberto Eco and Thomas A. Sebeok.)

6 "We Derrida admirers," footnotes Richard Rorty in *Contingency, Irony, and Solidarity*, "are tempted to write learnedly on the relation between the S-p relation in 'Envois' and the S-a relation ('Savoir absolu,' Lacan's 'petit a,' and all that) in *Glas* – but such temptations should be resisted." The specific target of these remarks would appear to be Geoffrey Hartman. I plead extenuating circumstances here, since I am neither writing learnedly nor surrendering to any temptation other than the lure of the mathematical sublime which, as Kant would tell us, arises out of sheer cognitive exhaustion.

THE END OF POETRY

1 Paul Fussell argues that, since the traditional lyric subject is time, mutability, and evanescence, the "rigid poetic forms" with which the lyric is associated "provide tension and technical irony – they provide a fixed element as an ironic counterforce to the verbal argument of the poem." This would suggest that the lyric's dependence on rhyme and metre is a thematic constituent of the traditional mutability motif. But in modern poetry, Fussell continues, the mutability theme is virtually defunct, which explains the absence of the countervailing, binding element of rhyme and metre: "The technique of unrhymed and loosely structured verse can now be seen to be one powerful bulwark against [the] tragic sense." Fussell's analysis of poetic form is in its own way a "mutability lament" as well as

a passionate critique of the banalization of the contemporary spirit. (See *The Southern Review* 29, no. 2 [April 1993].)

2 This is a point stressed, perhaps overstated, by Wilde in *The Decay of Lying*, which claims that art in no case reproduces its age. "So far from being the creation of its time, it is usually in direct opposition to it." Similarly, for the Frankfurt School (in particular Adorno and Horkheimer), art was not only the expression of actual social tendencies but also the source and lieu of *critical negativity*, the projection of the utopian "other" or theoretical alternative to the repressions, contradictions and cruelties of social existence. Art generates a negative resonance, a denial of present reification in the name of that other, heterocosmic society.

3 Richard Bradford takes up a similar position in *A Linguistic History of English Poetry* in which he cites Walter Pater's argument (in *Appreciations*) that the "chaotic variety and complexity of the modern world" cannot be mediated by "the restraint proper to verse form" – an argument Bradford regards as a misrepresentation. On the contrary, the presence of metre, and by implication the entire conventional register of poetic devices, serves to "maintain a sense of continuity with the (imagined) order of the past, against the unpredictable contingencies of the present." I find it instructive to reflect upon the putative originality of many contemporary poets who are given to repeating Pater's thesis almost verbatim without realizing that its formulation goes back over a hundred years. These same issues are also powerfully addressed in Matthew Arnold's 1880 essay, "The Study of Poetry." It would appear that a certain dimension of poetic experience and speculation has remained constant, predictable, and, yes, traditional to the point of unconscious plagiarism.

Bradford very sensibly contends that poetry "can only be accepted as poetry if it supplements the organisational framework shared by all another linguistic genres with a continuous pattern of effects drawn primarily from the material, non-signifying element of language." Otherwise poetic language merely surrenders "either to the institutional imperatives of prose discourse or to the unstructured localised patterns of speech."

THE WORD AND THE STONE

1 See Scholes's *Structuralism in Literature* as well for a thoroughgoing discussion of the subject.

2 Theorists revel insatiably in drumsticking new terms for this process. Abraham Maslow, for example, in *Religions, Values, and Peak-Experiences* comes up with "anti-rubricizing" and "rhapsodic isomorphic communication" and Jerome Bruner in *Actual Minds, Possible Worlds* tucks in with "subjunctivizing." (Literature, he says, "subjunctivizes, makes strange, renders the obvious less so.") See Craig Raine's "A Martian Sends a Postcard Home" for a contemporary example of this defamiliarizing procedure. Raine's poem, however, is compromised by a conceptual flaw: the Martian, who knows neither what a book is nor the common word "book" (he compares books to birds and refers to them, oddly enough, as "Caxtons") is nevertheless quite at home with the adjective "bookish" and the verb "read."

3 Johnson was with his usual astuteness commenting on the *double* function of metaphor, which constitutes "the two most engaging powers of an author. New things are made familiar, and familiar things are made new." Formalism does not for obvious reasons focus on the first or *domesticating* function of metaphor.

4 Cf. Mandelstam's extraordinary book of poems, *Stone*.

5 Austin's work is pointedly applicable here, especially his essay "A Plea for Excuses." In fact, the value of his work in this connection is triply relevant, as it not only compels us to reconsider the ways in which language negotiates the world but to refresh our awareness of the ways of language itself; and finally and inadvertently, its deconstruction at the hands of Derrida tends to place that renewed understanding in an even stranger, more auroral light.

6 See the *Attic Nights* of Aulus Gellius (c. A.D. 123–170), which is devoted in large part to the study of etymologies and the right use of words in Latin poetry to avoid the twin perils of the ridiculous and the redundant. The erudite and belletristic Gellius provides an extreme example, perhaps, of the philological preoccupation, but the study of the right use and application of poetic language as such runs from classical antiquity through the entire western literary tradition. Interestingly, the twin attitudes I am discussing here, the emphatics of Shem and Shaun, were already represented for the Romans by two emblematic personalities, Gellius on the one hand and on the other, the polymathic Terentius Varro whose study of literature stressed the primacy of subject matter. In the words of R.M. Ogilvie in *Roman Literature and Society*, Gellius manifested "a very different attitude from that of Varro, who searched earlier writers for knowledge."

7 The by-now standard distinction between metaphor and metonymy is not appropriate to our discussion, as the language/world polarity cuts right across such tropological discriminations. Though metaphorical language, especially in its more "conceited" forms, tends to draw attention to itself, to revel in its conspicuousness, it does not follow that metonymical language is necessarily compromised. See David Lodge's discussion in *The Modes of Modern Writing* of Forster's *A Passage to India* for a good example of how the principle of contiguity or linearity can generate a rich and *apparently* metaphorical language. The polarity we are working with is more a question of the writer's focus, attitude, instinct, or interior "set" toward his material.

8 See Robert Hillyer's *In Pursuit of Poetry* for a rather different application of the metaphor of the stained-glass window. Hillyer identifies the poet *in himself* with "the stained glass window that transmits sunlight just as ordinary windows do, but colors it as it passes through. And the poet should rest content with that; no man is great enough to be both the window and the sunlight." See also Sartre's celebrated formulation in *What Is Literature?* "For the ambiguity of the sign implies that one can penetrate it at will like a pane of glass and pursue the thing signified, or turn his gaze toward its *reality* and consider it as an object."

9 The world as "discourse" is, of course, an idea with a respectable pedigree in Neoplatonism, in the Smaragdine Tablet of Hermes Trismegistus, the doctrine of "signatures" in Boehme, the "correspondences" of Swedenborg, and the poetry of Blake, Hopkins, and Yeats.

10 I use the nuptial metaphor advisedly, as if to say: poetry cannot celebrate its complex marriage with the world unless it pursues at the same time its love affair with language. There is no question of infidelity here but the mature sufficiency of an "Italian" arrangement.

More seriously, this relation of language and reality should not be miscontrued as a Hegelian dialectic of reciprocal negation or as implicated in the workings of a deconstructive strategy in which the one undoes its representation of the other. Rather, the relation is one of mutual subsumption, perhaps even of mutual need. Poetic language, in fact, is the authenticating imprint, the ISBN number of the Real, which is at the same time and paradoxically an *event* in itself, thus demanding its registration in consciousness and memory.

11 I often think of language not only as a phenomenon but more particularly as a *phonemenon*, the other face of the world. Each requires the other in order to survive. "To call the ship 'ship' is merely to utilize language as a mediator of signification, therby killing both object and word. To call the ship 'sail' is to fix our attention on the word, giving language a value of its own and the world a chance of surviving" (Tzvetan Todorov, *The Poetics of Prose*).

12 The same idea *mutatis mutandis* which Tolstoy develops in *The Death of Ivan Illyich*.

13 Some notable current exceptions: James Merrill and Richard Wilbur in the U.S.; Seamus Heaney (in part) and Medbh McGuckian in the U.K.; Eric Ormsby and Tim Lilburn in Canada.

14 I wish to go on record here and state that Harris and Geddes are, in my estimation, both excellent poets, among the finest of their generation in this country, and in their best work manage to stay clear of what I am calling "the ideology of the real," word succumbing to stone. See, for example, Harris's "The Gamekeeper," "Uncle Edward," and "The Dolphin" among many others, and Geddes's *The Terracotta Army*. I have chosen to subject some of their poems to critical scrutiny here precisely because they have, as poets, produced an impressive body of work. If *their* work has in part failed to resist realistic petrifaction, what shall we say of their confreres? (I cannot refrain from suggesting, however, that Michael Estok's praise of Geddes, recorded on the book's last page – namely, that the poet's elegiac power "puts him on the same level of poetic intensity (perhaps he surpasses it) of Milton's 'Lycidas' and Tennyson's 'In Memoriam'" – may be a trifle premature.)

The essential drift of my argument, however, has to do with *tendencies*. Owen and Thomas, for example, have produced a certain amount of undistinguished work in which the language element may appear flat, archaic, tedious, redundant. But the perceptible effort or *nisus*, more often than not successful, is towards that "intercession on behalf of language" that renders their work memorable *on the whole*. The corresponding tendency in contemporary English-language poetry is towards the intervention on behalf of the world, at the expense of linguistic specificity, which produces that strange quality of anonymity or transparency to which the *works themselves* generally succumb.

By contrast, the "strategy" of poetic commutation, or the balancing of pathos and craft through narrative indirection and discretionary rhetoric, is movingly demonstrated in the recent work of the Sarajevan poet Goran Simic, for example, in his "The Sorrow of Sarajevo":

Someone lobs a child's shoe
into the furnace, family photographs spill
from the back of a garbage truck ...

There's no way of describing these things,
not really...

Simic then concludes with a tense and subtle restraint that is almost explosive by describing not "these things" but *other things* delivered in the mode of implication:

Each night I wake
and stand by the window to watch my neighbour
who stands by the window to watch the dark.

It is this double principle of semantic transfer and lexical diffraction (e.g. especially the resonant or incremental phrasing in the last two lines whose effect is primarily *rhetorical*) and not the reporting in isomorphic detail of the world's atrocities that is a major source of Simic's poetic power. (Originally published in the *Times Literary Supplement* of London; reprinted in the PEN Canada newsletter for November 1995.)

15 The experience of aesthetic joy seems to be regularly misunderstood by professional philosophers. I refer not only to Aristotle's emetic theory of tragedy but to Kant's Third Critique in which the pleasure of "fiction" is interpreted in the somewhat naïve sense of displacement therapy, as if art were a universal recreation centre, part of the Sunday pottery syndrome. "We entertain ourselves with it when experience becomes too commonplace," writes the renowned Königsberger, solemnly insensible to the jocoserious (to quote Joyce, who got the word from Browning's *Jocoseria* of 1883) enchantment of the mind produced by the aesthetic medium. The aesthetic pleasure has a serious cognitive function in helping us face up to and not merely circumvent or betray our experience of reality. It *braces* the mind, opposing both the insidiousness of sentimental diffusion and the paralysis of radical despair. As Browning writes in "Ixion" from the *Jocoseria* volume:

What is the influence, high o'er Hell, that turns to a rapture
Pain – and despair's murk mists blend in a rainbow of hope?

16 Such language gives the impression of concrete *entasis*, pleasing because it convinces us of the poem's solidity, the words bulging

under the compressive stresses that support its deposition – like Doric columns. In this connection one recalls Jakobson's answer to the question, "How does poeticity manifest itself?" in *Question de poetique*: "In that the word is felt as word and not as a simple substitute for the object named."

This is also what Wallace Stevens meant when he wrote in "The Noble Rider and the Sound of Words" that "A poet's words are of things that do not exist without the words." Similarly, Michael Oakeshott in his essay on "the voice of poetry in the conversation of mankind" claims that "truth," properly speaking, "concerns propositions, and while practical statements" – that is, statements of desire, aversion, approval, and disapproval – "may constitute propositions and scientific and historical statements always do so, poetic images are never of this character ... In short, when you know what things are really like you can make no poems." Oakeshott's argument seems rather too extreme, but his distinction between the practical, scientific, and historical modes of activity on the one hand and the character of poetic diction and imagery on the other ("In poetry words are themselves images and not signs for other images") is certainly well taken.

17 Or in the antinomial formulation of Jean Baudrillard, the language we manipulate is not simply that of analysis: "It seeks to preserve the enigma of the object through the enigma of discourse." We must resist the temptation of defining and relating to the object as "the subject's mode of disappearance." (See *The Ectasy of Communication.*) Interestingly, Baudrillard's warning works as an updated, linguistic (and defamiliarized) version of Augustine's *concupiscentia oculorum*, the temptation of *seeing* rather than experiencing, which is also taken up in Mallarmé's famous quip that "all poetry has gone wrong since the great Homeric deviation." Eliot would seem to date this "deviation" somewhat later, though the idea remains:

Where shall the word be found, where will the word
Resound? Not here, there is not enough silence.

18 What I am here calling "poetic language" the American poet Oscar Mandel denominates simply as "music," which, he writes in his *Book of Elaborations*, "signifies a patrician order of words victorious over words as amiable rabble." When "stern stucture and high music" go out of poetry, what is left is a typical combination of "slouch in the form, bric-a-brac for the matter, and decayed statement in the message."

19 The test of recitation strikes me as a telling one, and one moreover that has nothing to do with the phonocentric impulse, the privileging of voice over writing, that Derrida has made a career out of deconstructing. What moves us tends to seek utterance, to outer itself. This is a fact of whatever "nature" we may still be said to possess in our deconstructive and psychocritical times – to which, for example, any non-celibate may persuasively attest. But the vast proportion of our poetic productions is perfectly compatible with an encrypting silence. I have rarely seen or heard my literary acquaintances in this country joyfully or compulsively *reciting* the work of their contemporaries, whereas in Greece I have listened to hotel clerks and restaurateurs movingly declaim passages from Seferis, Elytis, and Gatsos. This is not because – or *only* because – the Greeks may happen to be a more lyrical and effusive people than we are, but because – or *also* because – their poets still tend to write a more incantatory, significant, and *linguistically compelling* poetry than ours. (Two Nobel prizes for poetry in one generation may not be an accident.) This property of their verse will often come across even in translation. One need not, of course, cede this privilege or monopoly exclusively to the Greeks. I think of the work of Yehuda Amichai and Abraham Sutzkever in Israel; Gaston Miron, Sylvain Garneau, and Jacques Brault in Quebec; Eugenio Montale, Mario Luzi, and Valerio Magrelli in Italy; and anyone familiar with other languages or traditions will readily come up with similar examples. The point remains, however, that a certain kind of poetry tends spontaneously to utter itself *through our voices* in a sort of benign yet demonic possession. I find myself reciting or at least reading aloud in the works of Layton, Thomas, Garneau, Seferis, Merrill, partly *taken* over by the gift of rich, passionate, elegant, tensile, or marmoreal language which these poets exhibit and deploy. I cannot say the same for the great majority of my strict contemporaries.

The citation incorporated here is from Seferis's celebrated signature poem, "In the Manner of G.S.," of which the first line, repeated toward the end of the poem – "Wherever I may travel, Greece wounds me" – has become part of the "cultural literacy" of contemporary Greece.

20 See Tzvetan Todorov in *Literature and Its Theorists* for an illuminating study of Russian Formalism and its distinction between heterotelic or practical language and autotelic or poetic language. Todorov goes on to consider the relation between Döblin and

Brecht, a discussion to which I am indebted for some of my citations. (The now-"classic" study on Russian Formalism is, of course, Fredric Jameson's *The Prison-House of Language*.)

FELLATIOTICS

1 Barzun, writing in 1959, uses the term "philanthropic," which I replace here by "pornosophic." But the point remains.

2 This is an important aspect of the bizarre dialectic of reprographic certification. What is imagined in depth must ultimately be re-imagined either *on and as* the surface if it is to persuade the contemporary new-sceptic of its veridical existence; or what is actually perceived is relentlessly consumed in the voracious quest for depths, requiring in a secondary epistemic act to be *imagined as it is* in order to assume its own dative existence. As Andrei Codrescu argues in *The Disappearance of the Outside*, "imagination ... has become the custodian of the real."

3 In the original sense of "imagination," as defined by Philostratus in the second century A.D., in his discussion of the great sculptures of antiquity: "Imagination made them, and she is a better artist than imitation; for where the one serves only what she has seen, the other carves what she has not seen" (quoted in C.S. Lewis, *English Literature in the Sixteenth Century*).

One can trace the complex expansion of this notion in Kant's *Critique of Judgement*, especially section 49 of the "Analytic of the Sublime," in which we find the following passage: "If now we place under a concept a representation of the imagination belonging to its presentation, but which occasions in itself more thought than can ever be comprehended in a definite concept and which consequently aesthetically enlarges the concept itself in unbounded fashion, the imagination is here creative, and it brings the faculty of intellectual ideas ... into movement." It is the unconscripted or "creative" use of the imagination that generates what Kant denotes as the "aesthetical attributes of an object," whose result is to "enliven the mind by opening out to it the prospect into an illimitable field of kindred representations." The imagination was never intended, if I may so phrase it, to reproduce the given but to disclose and extend the parallel, analogous, and consanguineous – that is, the "aesthetical attributes" or "kindred representations" that, by a kind of feedback loop, "stimulate the imagination, so that it thinks more by their aid."

4 "Whoever thinks that fantasy consists of leaps and pirouettes is a prisoner of a notion that opposes imagination to the everyday, workaday world; that supposes it to be a form of entertainment. True imagination is hard work. It implicitly criticizes the prevailing version of reality" (Ariel Dorfman, *The Empire's Old Clothes*). In terms of the argument I am pursuing here, imagination in its contemporary form is not so much a matter of "leaps and pirouettes" as it is a reverie of endlessly containing depths, like that experienced by Verdant dreaming on the lap of Acrasia in *The Faerie Queene*.

5 As witness this bit of dialogue from Eco's *Foucault's Pendulum*, an updated version of the Swiftian polemic and a long footnote to *The Name of the Rose*:

> "You live on the surface," Lia told me years later. "You sometimes seem profound, but it's only because you piece a lot of surfaces together to create the impression of depth, solidity. That solidity would collapse if you tried to stand it up."
>
> "Are you saying I'm superficial?"
>
> "No," she answered. "What others call profundity is only a tesseract, a four-dimensional cube. You walk in one side and come out another, and you're in their universe, which can't coexist with yours."

It is precisely this passion for depth, this need to fill the ontological void (one of the characters in the novel is a taxidermist) and reify the fiction of *profound* existence, that drives the army of mad occultists to absurd and extremist acts of violence. "And it was my fault," says the protagonist, "I made them believe there was a depth that they, in their weakness, desired." The passion anatomized in the novel may be conceived as another form of what Stephen Greenblatt in his analysis of Marlowe's characters in *Renaissance Self-Fashioning* calls the perverse inability to "desire anything for itself," a flaw which derives from "the suspicion that all objects of desire are fictions, theatrical illusions." This disabling recognition paradoxically impels the Marlovian hero to create a fictitious object of desire even more elusive and destabilizing than the questionable contents of ordinary experience. The intense preoccupation with an illusory and recessive depth which characterizes so much of contemporary life may thus be understood as a process of fictionalization homologous with the Marlovian projection of identity into the perpetual unveiling or reconstruction of the object of desire. From a more limited and specialized viewpoint, one can detect the same structure of perception reproduced in the protocols of contemporary narratology with its investigation of the underlying invariant elements and organizing principles of narrative artifacts. But as Lubomir Dolazel notes, even Propp conceded that the interest of a tale resides in its "variable properties," in its surface complications. "It appears that aesthetic effects are somehow associated with variability, individuality, uniqueness ... any semantic theory or model which reduces the variable 'surface' meanings to invariant semantic categories" is regrettably partial (Lubomir Dolazel, "Invariant Function, Invisible Worlds, and Franz Kafka," *Style* 17, no. 2)

In the last analysis, reading, as Barthes would agree, is very much like making love, a thwarted exploration of interiors that continually recede in disclosing themselves as an endless sequence of impenetrable surfaces. See John Dryden's lines in his translation from Book 4 of Lucretius:

> They gripe, they squeeze, their humid tongues they dart,
> As each wou'd force their way to t'others heart:
> In vain; they only cruze about the coast,
> For bodies cannot pierce, nor be in bodies lost...

In reading, we also "cruze about the coast," but that is where the variety, richness, and fabled ampullosity of the text reside in fractals of renewed delight. Thus, as James Clifford writes in *The Predicament of Culture*, "there are no more ultimate depths ... What remains are surfaces, mirrors, doubles – an ethnography of signs without essential content." An ethnofellatic study of contemporary attitudes to the act of penetration, whether violent, surgical, erotic, or textual, would no doubt arrive at the same profound, that is, superficial conclusion.

6 For the record, I am not suggesting that Barthes and Robbe-Grillet cannot be enjoyed at face value. Barthes is a brilliant, supple, and engaging author whose work is meant to be enjoyed but not taken too seriously, too "deeply." (Barthes's own zigzag itinerary makes this pretty clear.) He remains an author, not a scriptor. Robbe-Grillet can also be great fun to read, largely because the mind insists on recuperating the tangential and integrating it into a diegetic structure – the higher Agatha Christie.

Learning to manage and enjoy the surface demands both the devotion and the equilibrium of the surf ace, a condition to which the "reader" may legitimately aspire. As Helen Vendler argues in

The Music of What Happens, "an ultimate disregard for 'surface' in favour of a presumed 'depth' goes absurdly counter to the primary sensuous claim of every work of art, the claim made precisely by its 'surface' (these words, these notes, and no others)." This thesis is a variation on the standard trope – which can be traced back through such writers as Swift (*Tale of a Tub*) to Quintilian (*Institutio Oratoria*) – comparing figurative language and eloquence to an exterior covering and content or subject-matter to the body. But the equation is sometimes deliberately skewed, as in the *Tale* when Swift in section 2 compares the body to "inward Cloathing," thus setting up the spectre of an infinite regress which, as it eliminates the possibility of a final *terminus ad quem*, requires us to remain permanently on the surface. His warrant for this mischievous displacement derives from Cicero's *Orator*, where the body is understood as a metaphor for metaphor, a figure for figurative language, a tropical substitute for eloquence – in short, as simply another veil or envelope, another surface. (See Todorov's *Theories of the Symbol* for a thoroughgoing discussion of these ornamental runcinations.) Carlyle's Circumspective plays with the same sartorial paradox, as we move from the "outward vulgar, palpable Woollen hulls of man" through his wondrous flesh-garments, and his wondrous social garnitures; inwards to the garments of his very soul's soul, to time and space themselves! And now does the spiritual, eternal essence of man, bared of such wrappages, begin in any measure to reveal itself?" Precisely Wittgenstein's point in the *Tractatus* [4.002], in which language is understood as "clothing" for thought, with the added twist that this linguistic apparel is a disguise, "because the outward form of the clothing is not designed to reveal the form of the body." In any case, depth, which is nothing but a perpetual recession of the surface, reveals itself as the fictitious projection of desire, Lacan's demand for love minus the appetite for satisfaction – if we allow "knowledge" to deputize for "love." Ultimately, this metaphysical figment only distracts, hinders, and impedes wherever we may happen to find it. As Barthes writes in *Image-Music-Text*, clothing these venerable notions in the spandex of contemporary rhetoric, the "play of signifiers is not a process of deepening, but a serial movement of metonymic dislocations." Metonymy, of course, licenses an authentic superficiality, now called endless contiguity along the chain of signifiers. To adapt Jakobson's joke: everywhere it is surface.

NOTES ON LUCIANIC SATIRE

1 Pertinent here would be the passage in *Utopia* in which Raphael speaks of the Utopian predilection for the fool: "They are very fond of fools. It is a great disgrace to treat them with insult, but there is no prohibition against deriving pleasure from their foolery."

2 It is only fair to bring in the case for the opposition. Charles Sears Baldwin, in his *Renaissance Literary Theory and Practice*, contends that Rabelais's purpose in sending Gargantua's pedagogical letter to Pantagruel was not to pierce "medieval ignorance, but Renaissance complacency," and that he was by no means "forecasting modern education," as has been frequently maintained. He points out that the abbey of Thelème, the experimental "university" in which the new scheme of education is developed, takes its name from the preposterous allegory, *Hypnerotomachia* (1467) by Francesco Colonne, in which the hero forsakes the guidance of Reason (Logistica) for that of Will or Desire (Thelemia). Its community of privileged, titivating men and women are required to speak six languages: Greek, Latin, Hebrew, French, Tuscan, and Spanish. "Certainly," Baldwin argues, "he did not mean to propose Thelème for adoption as an idea, much less as a scheme. Do as you please, provided you live in luxury and command six languages ... Is that an educational idea?" Thelème may in fact be "a shrewd satire on the Renaissance." In my own reading of Rabelais, I tend to understand Thelème more as an extravagant wish-fulfilment fantasy than as intentional satire.

3 I mean by this something different from the idea of literal duplicity suggested by Ronald Paulson in his *Satire and the Novel in Eighteenth-Century England*. Paulson tells us that the aim of the Lucianic satirist "is double – to expose the real ... and to discomfit the reader ... disrupt his orthodoxy." Nor do I intend the distinction drawn by Empson, "double-irony," expounded later by Paulson as giving "some credence to both 'the contrary' and 'what one means.'" Curiously, the same notion is developed in Dostoevsky's *The Idiot* in which Prince Myshkin maintains that it is perfectly possible to be loyal to the person one betrays, that is, to entertain what he calls the "double-thought" (which obviously bears no relation to Orwell's "doublethink"). The satirist is aware that human beings tend to live in a state of contradiction: for one species of satirist, this means hypocrisy and for another, complexi-

ty. Paulson indicates, in connection to Lucian and Fielding, that satire may very well be "a technique for suggesting the complexity of reality." The idea of "doubleness" which I have in mind has to do, as I hope is reasonably clear, neither with the satirist's objective, remedial purpose – the sense intended by Paulson – nor with Empson's binomial form of irony that points to the intricate and plural nature of our experience, but rather with the subjective flexibility, the psychological resilience, of the satirist in himself.

THE TRIAL AS JEWISH JOKE

1 The doorkeeper figure probably derives from the tract of the *Greater Hekhaloth* (compiled between the second and sixth centuries) where gatekeepers are stationed beside the entrance to the doors of the heavenly hall which the aspiring soul must negotiate in its mystical ascent to the realm of self-transcendence. Kafka's theme may be plausibly regarded as a demotic or textual rendering of the Merkabah mystical motifs associated with the Hakhaloth treatises. Here, of course, it is the author who does not permit immediate or even eventual access to his work except to the reader for whom it is designed. Thus the "intensional macrostructure" of *The Trial*, as an expansion of the Legend, is not an indeterminate world about which no information is available, as Lubomir Dolozel argues in "Intensional Function and Franz Kafka," a world which is "inaccessible by necessity." At the same time, neither is it "a door open and intended for each and every one of us," as George Steiner claims with his usual midrashic flair in *No Passion Spent*. On the contrary, it permits entry to the chosen few for whom epistemological eagerness is always a function of ontological regret.

2 Kafka agonized for years over having to choose between "marriage and the community" on the one hand and "solitude and writing" on the other, being unable to combine in his personal life, as did his great medieval precursor, Jehudah the Hassid, the intense privacy of introspection with concern for the welfare of the community. When he did find the woman with whom such a reconciliation became possible, the aptly named Dora Diamant, irony intervened in the form of tuberculosis.

FRAMING LAYTON

1 It is only now that it strikes me how curious it is to find Layton expounding the intricacies of metaphor when his own work is

characterized, in Eli Mandel's words, by "his odd preference for simile over metaphor (analogy rather than identity)," a stylistic bias Mandel inscrutably traces to the "god's presence" in the poems. Layton's most recent reprint, for example, "The Madonna of the Magnificat," gives us in very short compass three similes and no metaphors. I haven't figured this one out yet.

2 There are times when Layton most reminds me of Hasek's Colonel Kraus, always prone to embark "on interminable conversations about omelettes, sunlight, thermometers, puddings, windows, and postage stamps." To which must be added: philistines, cultural decline, desiccated professors, and *zaftig* wenches.

3 So that I sometimes think of "Layton" as the poetic representative of the Montreal construction company that goes by the name of Salvati & Spurio.

4 Or as the poetic equivalent of Milorad Pavic's Khazar Jar, which may look like any other jar but is to-the-count-of-70 deep, and which "serves to this day, although it has long ceased to exist" as a veridical object.

5 Like a certain bus driver I know on the Greek island of Kalymnos who regularly toots his horn and waves when passing the cemetery.

6 As does, e.g., Norman Sacuta, writing in the *Edmonton Journal* of 28 June 1992, who looks forward to the publication of *Fornalutx* because it will presumably give our poet the chance "to invent new – even more stupid – cover notes." There is a lot of this ultra-crepidarian stuff around.

It is interesting in this connection to chart Northrop Frye's changing assessment of Layton's work over the years, as documented in *The Bush Garden*. In 1953, Frye could deride with patrician *hauteur* something he called Laytonese: "forced language and flaccid rhythm." A few years later, Layton was suddenly hailed as "an erudite elegiac poet, whose technique turns on an aligning of the romantic and the ironic." By 1959, "no poet has written more good poetry in Canada in the last decade than Irving Layton." The cool and virginal, quintessentially Canadian Frye was evidently waiting for the barbarian against whose reproductive afflatus he could raise no more than token resistance. But the new critics and reviewers of the school of Lobo, Busto, and Blot, who tend to regard themselves as cultural custodians, no doubt feel they are taking on an institution that needs to be contained rather than an eldering poet who should be encouraged or at the very least respected for an accomplishment they can scarcely hope to emulate.

PRONOMINAL DEBRIS

1 Among Canadian poets writing today, Don Coles is a master of the meditative sweep, the reflective letting out of the long breath which generates its own syntactic authority and sustains the reader's confidence. The same is true of Michael Harris and Robert Bringhurst. When reading a poem one should not feel that one is being repeatedly stabbed by a serial killer.

2 One of the few poets I am aware of in Canada who can handle the "list poem" or anaphoric structure with deft assurance and unfailing verbal energy is Peter Van Toorn. Tim Lilburn also shows impressive signs of possessing this gift, as does Eric Ormsby.

3 The test of memorizability is at least as valid a criterion for determining the value or quality of a poem as are the various somasthetic phenomena beloved by the poets themselves, like scalp tinglings, spine chills, scrotum contractions, and what not. But it should be understood that memorizability means more than one thing. Some poems seem inherently memorizable, as if the words came covered in Velcro, as is the case, for example, with certain Shakespearean sonnets, the beginning of "My Last Duchess" and the conclusion of Tennyson's "Ulysses," portions of "Thirteen Ways of Looking at a Blackbird," and so on. Anyone can cite dozens of such instances. But there are other poems or texts that do not for whatever reason lend themselves readily to absorption or mnemonic inscription (as Morris Zapp might wryly put it), yet the reader feels compelled to invest considerable effort in order to possess the poem in question: certain parts of *The Waste Land* or the Jeoffry portion in Christopher Smart's *Jubilate Agno*, or passages from *Paradise Lost* (other than the self-memorizing invocation). But if a reader is presented with a poem or part of a poem that is not memorizable in either of these two senses, which does not either write itself (or a part of itself) into the memory or *demand* that it be (wholly or partially) retained, then it is a safe bet that one is dealing with journeyman or merely competent material (in the dyslogistic sense of "competent," what Hopkins meant by "Parnassian"). This will be true of vast segments of the work of even the very greatest poets. *But*, as every reader knows, there are poems – perhaps the overwhelming majority of poems – that *resist* incorporation to the hilt. This is the supreme test of the bad poem, the criterion of forgettability or memory-resistance, as if the words squirted about like greased pigs at the proverbial

country fair. Try as one might, the poem simply escapes retention. (The exception here is the poem that is so bad that it becomes ludicrous, a parody of itself, and therefore *representative* of all such efforts, in which case a few lines may tend toward survival. Yet there must be something crisp and distinctive in its phrasing, syntax or imagery – e.g., certain stanzas from Crashaw's Magdalene poem). Or, if after herculean labours one does manage to get it down, a form of temporal evaporation rapidly takes over. The thing just doesn't remain in the memory for long. It seems likely that the Ebbinghaus curve – which specifies that up to 80 per cent of disconnected elements (i.e., a sequence that strikes the memorizer as arbitrary) will be lost to memory within a twenty-four hour period – adequately defines the instance under consideration.

I introduce this concept of memorizability as a kind of heuristic device, a rule of thumb procedure on a level with the somasthetic phenomena poets and readers are fond of citing or deploying. It is a rough device that works up to a certain point but depends, of course, to some extent upon the sensibility in question. The real issue goes much deeper and has to do with what Eugenio Montale called "the second life of art," the continued circulation of an artistic work in the life of the reader, viewer, or listener after the initial *production of* or *encounter with* it. Montale's distinction is a seminal one. "An art which destroys form while claiming to refine it denies itself its second and larger life: the life of memory and everyday circulation"; the species of poem that cancels its, so to speak, posthumous existence in the conscious or intuitive life of the reader is that "in which each line moves on its own, has a meaning in and of itself, but is not linked to the others [and] is sustained by a mechanical association of ideas" – the kind of poem in which the reader "has to create the poetry for himself [because] the author ... has not willed something for him ... has limited himself to providing a possibility for poetry," and not much else. Montale goes on the castigate the breed of modern artists who "deliberately exclude every pleasant sound from music, every figurative element from painting, every syntactical progression from the written word," and prophesies the eventual failure and inanition of these artists who "do not have the courage to speak words that can go back into the street again." On the level of Montale's distinction, we can easily forgo the test of memorizability and exercise patience instead, waiting to see whether the sort of poetry we are anatomizing here (i.e., the poetry which is busy atomizing itself) does in fact enter into or deprive itself of the memorial life which recuperates its mere *occasional* existence, translating it from the dimension of the momentary into that of the momentous. (See Montale's essay, "The Second Life of Art," in the collection of that title.)

4 A subject for a doctoral thesis – frugian thematics in Canadian verse; or perhaps for a psychological study – holetic cathexis and Canlit. The recent proliferation of fruits, tubers, and vegetables in Canadian poetry is a phenomenon that still needs to be explained. Every reader can no doubt cite cartloads of examples, or find them by turning the pages of any literary journal. Not long ago a series of poetry books appeared in which the reader was invited to scratch or pluck the vegetable essences taped on the covers. Like Timon we are busy rejecting gold and digging for roots.

5 One is also reminded of Joyce's Mr Duffy, who would from time to time compose "a short sentence about himself containing a subject in the third person and a predicate in the past tense."

6 There is another sense in which this work may be characterized as derivative or Derridative. It sounds like so much other deconstructico-feminist writing replicating furiously in the literary community today, in both poetry and prose – which in turn *sounds like it*, so that at times it is difficult to distinguish or locate the idiolect. It has become a question now of reciprocal derivability.

7 A more tactful, or tactical, way of dealing with (touchy) issues of this sort would be to apply the psychoanalytic distinction between "introjection" and "incorporation," the two modes of internalizing external objects – in this case, literary objects – and locating them unextraditably in the self. One could then scumble the matter by considering it as standard psychological procedure. As Derrida writes in "Fors," interpretation, like incorporation, "is a kind of theft to reappropriate the pleasure-object." Incorporation leaves the encapsulated text reasonably intact; introjection assimilates it thoroughly. What form of internalization obtains – if it does at all – in the Mouré piece is beyond my competence to decide. See Cary Nelson's discussion of the problem (in which the quote from Derrida appears) in "The Psychology of Criticism," collected in Geoffrey Hartman's *Psychoanalysis and the Question of the Text*.

8 The same applies to the more common homoerotic display of selective passion, as in Kent Stetson's popular play, *Warm Wind in China*, which is to be made into a movie. The play relies to a great extent on its shock value, not only in terms of an intimate look at

the family life of a gay couple, one of whom is suffering from AIDS (refried beans by now), but in terms of its copious sensational elements: the passionate kiss guaranteed to make the audience squirm, the erotic curiosity of the AIDS victim's mother (totally implausible in or out of context), and so on. Sensationalism always depends on what falls outside the range of current social expectations, tastes, and values, or of the larger normative discourse shared by both author and audience alike. It does not address what is permanent or basic in collective experience but feeds parasitically off convention alone in an effort to create an effect. As soon as the sensational element begins to fall *within* the range of the collective, as soon as it ceases to be an issue or to be perceived as a violation, the work dates and becomes obsolete. A good example would be Ibsen's *Ghosts*: syphilis is a dead letter, and the play now enjoys only a retrospective life. Delete the sentimental rhetoric and rampant sensationalism from *Warm Wind in China* and what is left? A minority version of *Kramer vs. Kramer*, a gay lover battling for child custody. Shock value is always schlock value.

9 This particular issue has already been addressed in Gertrude Stein's "Poetry and Grammar," in which it turns out that the lowly preposition is Stein's favourite part of speech: "Prepositions can live one long life being really nothing but mistaken and that makes them irritating if you feel that way about mistakes but certainly something that you can be continuously using and everlastingly enjoying. I like prepositions best of all ..." Stein goes on to deprecate adjectives and nouns as being uninteresting and inadequate, checking the flow of reported experience, and concludes: "So you see why I like to write with prepositions and conjunctions and articles and verbs and adverbs but not with nouns and adjectives." It does not escape the reader's notice that all these words designating parts of speech are, in fact, poor, contemptible nouns. Of course the logical result of all such linguistic speculation was aptly specified by Swift in the post-verbal colportage practised by the academicians of Lagado.

10 Unlike Ritsos as well, if we want to get picky: the great proletarian poet in his finest writing deploys a subtle and intricate, highly flavoured, non-enchorial Greek. The last thing to be found in the best work of Ritsos – or, for example, in the genuine democratic vistas of Whitman, or in the raconteur-like prodigies of James Merrill (in his *The Changing Light at Sandover*), or even in the

taut confessional tracts of Sharon Olds – is precisely the "perfect flatness of ordinary language" or the intention of "us[ing] this flat surface to open the deep emotional current that lies just beneath its surface" ("The Acts"). In those passages where the language of these poets lapses audibly into flatness, the "emotional current" fizzles right out. It is, in fact, just where the prose "hypogram" ruptures the "poeticality" of a text (to apply Riffaterre's terminology) that the language of a poem suffers painful and embarrassing herniation. Or to put it in the idiom of Arthur Golding's unique translation of Ovid's *Metamorphosis*, orpid buggs sty awkly in the queach and flackering pookes ensue.

11 We find a similar idea expressed in the metaphor of the Tuscan ring, from which Browning derived the first half of his title, *The Ring and the Book*. The ring is fashioned from a mixture of pure gold and alloy. After the shape has been formed, the alloy is dissolved with acid and the gold remains in its purity. The "manageable mass" once "effect[ed]," worked with hammer and file, there follows "repristination." This notion is, in turn, a variant of traditional alchemical procedure, a kind of textual cupellation.

12 "Pulling the old poem through the new, making the old lines a thread thru the eye of the words I am sewing." The play on a traditional feminine occupation does not redeem – apart from the fact that the metaphor is hopelessly mixed. The "new" poem, obviously composed of "lines" or "thread[s]" of "words" as is the "old," cannot be both fabric and needle at once. The image in question is properly and consistently handled in W.S. Merwin's little poem "Separation":

> Your absence has gone through me
> Like thread through a needle.
> Everything I do is stitched with its color.

– which I find interesting *in context* not only because the simile is appropriate but because the absence which it concretizes is a real, not an abstruse, "deconstructive," absence.

INTOXICATED WORDS

1 See Wallace Stevens's "The Man with the Blue Guitar":

> And they said then, "But play, you must,
> A tune beyond us, yet ourselves,
> A tune upon the blue guitar
> Of things exactly as they are."

2 Or, as Sebastian defines it in *The Tempest*, "It is a sleepy language," a speech that languishes away from both pastoral simplicity and poetic renovation. Stephano, pouring wine down Caliban's throat, plays on the same set of associations: "Here is that which will give language to you." Mutatis mutandis, this is effectively the same language which the First Devil in Henry Purcell's opera *The Tempest*, in the aria "Arise Ye Subterranean Winds," inflicts upon the proud, the ambitious, and the tyrannical: "let them howl and languish in despair."

3 Ferdinand and Miranda are naturally idiophonic, citizens of Gonzalo's golden commonwealth. "My language?" Ferdinand inquires in the surprise and joy of understanding and being understood without labour of translation. Caliban and Antonio-Sebastian represent the two sides of hedonic speech, the blunt and the insidious, together comprising what Stephano calls the "backward voice" whose function is "to utter foul speeches and to detract." Prospero's is the language of metamorphosis, discipline, beneficent power – of theurgic commands that Ariel performs "to th' syllable."

DUKES AND DUCHESSES

1 This perception of the duke reminds me a little of Lloyd Alexander's Gast the Generous (in *Taran Wanderer*), a warlord who finds his justification in his hoard of stolen objects and whose magnanimity reduces those around him to near-starvation.

2 I should say here that I am not attempting a deconstructive reading of the poem, since I do not claim to have disambiguated its marginal, hidden, or supplementary elements. My analysis, which attempts only to clarify the obvious, to enucleate what perhaps should have been self-evident – the 911 signal which the duke composes – can be considered a "minority" reading only in the sense that few readers have chosen to notice or emphasize what is an important and possibly the "major" theme in the poem.

3 It need hardly be mentioned that Browning is working within the venerable tradition of the gallery poem or device. See for example Farquhar's *The Beaux' Strategem*, Marvell's "The Gallery," John Gay's *Trivia* and Pope's "Epistle to a Lady," *inter alia*. A thorough account of the device may be found in Jean H. Hagstrum's *The Sister Arts: The Tradition of Literary Pictorialism and English Poetry from Dryden to Gray*.

4 We need not enter here into a Propp/Greimas functional analysis of the poems in question, which would take us into another *explication de texte* – one that would be based, moreover, on the set toward the subject (to modify Jakobson) developed here. But from this point of view, one may suggest that neither Pompilia nor the duchess articulates the underlying seme of mere "outraged innocence." Pompilia represents the idea of innocence combined with the faculty of spiritual development, the duchess that of a static pastoral simplicity that disregards, as we would say today, the complexity of the interface.

5 As Browning himself remarked, "the commands were that she should be put to death, or he might have had her shut up in a convent" (quoted in Lionel Stevenson, "The Pertinacious Victorian Poets," *University of Toronto Quarterly* 21 – an article that derives Browning's duke in part from the historical Duke Alfonso II and his father, Ercole II, and in part from Shakespeare's Leontes). Moreover, if the "murder" is considered as part of the *metaphorical* rather than the historical context of the poem, it clearly functions as a correlate of the crucial importance of the theme itself – spousal negligence is no laughing matter and justifies an irreversible response. As Ted Hughes puts it in his *Shakespeare and the Goddess of Complete Being* with respect to *Troilus and Cressida*, "Murder ... as everybody understands, lifts the situation into a bigger theatre: it expresses the mythic stature of the original love, and of the injury it has suffered, and of its weird justice."

6 Browning received the "riband" of sonnets (the "Portuguese" of the title, the poet explains in a letter to Julia Wedgwood, "was that Catarina who left Camoens the riband from her hair") in 1849, seven years after the composition of "My Last Duchess"; yet there is both a kind of poetic justice and proleptic irony at work here. Browning received from his wife a latreutic adoration, amounting to a species of idolatry, that far eclipsed the considerably more modest affection the duke would have been content to enjoy. (I do not discount the gnomic twinges of resentment that Browning may have "felt" on the level of the unconscious cf. note 11.) Browning saw himself reflected in his wife's verses wearing "purpureal tresses," anointed with precious chrism, filleted in kisses, protected by Venice-glass, exalted, belaurelled, and graced with "divine sufficiencies":

> And I who looked for only a God, found thee! (27)

> Yet still my heart goes to thee (ponder how)
> Not as to a single good, but all my good. (34)

And of course the celebrated "I love thee with the breath / Smiles, tears of all my life!"

Browning was not insensible of these eulogistic devotions and reciprocated hyperdulically; for example, in the Invocation to *The Ring and the Book* he addresses the spirit of his wife (as he must frequently have addressed her in the flesh) to invoke

> some interchange
> Of grace, some splendour once thy thought,
> Some benediction anciently thy smile

– presumably a smile of a different order of significance from that of the duchess. And in the lovely line in "By the Fireside," the poet defines himself as "One born to love you."

Also in this connection, one cannot disregard the speaker in "Any Wife to Any Husband" whose dedication, exemplary and restorative, persists in the face of complications any *other* wife might find disabling. Unlike the duchess, her portrait, requiring little empirical detail to render the constancy and purity of soul that animate it, provokes no disquiet:

> That is a portrait of me on the wall –
> Three lines, my face comes at so slight a call.

7 The social presuppositions of the time and place were manifestly different – raw, "primitive," residually feudal – from those we share. Yet one cannot reasonably argue that Browning conceived his poem as a critique of Renaissance cultural attitudes – neither, for that matter, as a form of historical mitigation nor as an imaginative reconstruction of the episode in question. The duke and the events he sets in motion serve a completely different purpose within the theoretical construct of the poem. They represent what has now come to be called the "enabling fiction," the pretext that allows the poet to project, set up, and explore his real subject. (I say this in full awareness of the dubious status of intentionality in contemporary criticism.)

8 A good example of the rotarian vehemence that the duke seems to provoke may be found even in presumably astute commentators like Robert Langbaum, who in *The Poetry of Experience* gives ample vent to his moral outrage: "When in the last two-and-a-half lines the duke of 'My Last Duchess' makes his insolent, trivial, egotistical and hyperaesthetic pause before that bronze by Claus of Innsbruck, he manages to add a new shock to the shocks we have

already endured." Northrop Frye in *Words with Power* adopts a basically similar attitude though his formulation, while equally shallow, is typically more adroit and elegant: "The narrator of Browning's poem 'My Last Duchess,' who had his wife murdered because she smiled at other people, but cherished her picture which smiled only at him, was what is known as a cultivated man, but that cultivation had not done much for his moral sense." If Frye is right, why would the duke expose the portrait of the smiling duchess to the fascinated gaze of others? Why would the duke collaborate in his own misprision? And so on.

9 See the 37th sonnet in the Portugese volume, with its "sculptured porpoise ... within the temple-gate."

10 Me, made because that love had need
Of something irreversibly
Pledged solely its content to be...

("Johannes Agricola in Meditation")

The possibility that this poem may be a study of religious fanaticism or, indirectly, a portrait of the gnostic pseudo-deity, as Harold Bloom appears to suggest, does not affect the larger appositeness, the citability, of these lines.

11 One recalls Browning's reaction to the adverse criticism of his personal poem, *Pauline* – a resolution never again "to lay my soul bare." Interestingly, in *Pauline* the word occurs twice in an honorific sense: in the phrase "some wild bird stoop for its freshness" and, similarly, to describe Pauline "from heights above, / Stooping beneath me."

Pauline is a strange, hybrid production, laced with some fine passages but mainly, as John Stuart Mill witheringly said, morbid and pre-convalescent. The "stooping" that goes on in this poem accords well with the general stupour – pardon the pun – of its rhythms and the insipidity of its doctrinal content – just as the refusal to stoop corresponds with the muscularity of the verse in "My Last Duchess."

But a relation (both direct and inverse) between these two poems may be detected. The duchess is no Pauline, whose beauty, innocence, and gentleness exist, within the situation as it is portrayed, *solely* for the hero's education and "conversion." He is "one so watched, so loved and so secured" – as the duke would have wished to be. But although the latter plainly does not share the flushed and saccharine rhetoric of the young Shelleyan (much as it may have been an expression of Browning's state of mind at the time), he does share the confessional mode as well as a smattering of claims and assumptions. For example:

> The soul would never rule;
> It would be first in all things, it would have
> Its utmost pleasure filled, but, that complete,
> Commanding, for commanding, sickens it.

The differences, however, are clear. The duke does command, not the duchess but her execution; and Pauline, the ministering angel all men desire, is depicted in a rather humiliating or, shall we say, "Roman" posture.

Also, for what it's worth, we may note the ambiguous apposition of the word in Browning's description in *Sordello* of the first of the two temptations incident to the second of his two classes of poetic temperament (the unself-conscious and the self-conscious, clarified twelve years later in his essay on Shelley as the objective and the subjective):

> Ah, but to find
> A certain mood enervate such a mind,
> Counsel it slumber in the solitude
> Thus reached nor, stooping, task for mankind's good
> Its nature ...

– where "stooping" might imply either that Sordello *should* stoop to the level of common humanity or that he is stooping *now* in his state of slumbrous enervation.

We may summarize by suggesting that this little word, whenever it appears in Browning's text, is almost always loaded, problematic, disturbing. It is rarely neutral or innocuous, used merely to fill out a measure or a rhyme, as for example in his wife's "A vision of Poets":

> who dares to stoop
> Where those dank branches overdroop,
> Into his heart the chill strikes up.

12 Nor does he exhibit the inferior taste and indiscriminate appetite of Pope's Philomede who

> stoops at once,
> and makes her hearty meal upon a Dunce.

13 Browning, in addressing the domestic question, has worked the stuff of history into what has now become a legendary or mythic complex whose function is to resolve a contradiction (in Lévi-Strauss's sense); that is, we may regard the state of mind that produced the poem as a form of *pensée sauvage* which grapples with

a perennial and very possibly transcultural dilemma: how to reconcile the need for domestic tranquillity at almost any price with the equally urgent need to feel oneself chosen and exalted by the beloved.

The political formulation of the same problem would involve the following question: how to square democracy with monarchy, a latent contradiction in the minds of all those, for example, who would lay down their lives to defend the Democratic State but who are at the same time profound believers in the Lord's prerogative, the dispensation of the Heavenly State. A linguistic version of this same problem occurs in Vico as the conflict between the "poetic language" of "heroic man" (read: the duke's language) and "human" or democratic speech, the domestic vulgate (read: the duchess's language). In Vico the transition from the former to the latter is regarded as a fall. But Vico's formulation turns on the ambiguity of "human," which could equally well designate the universal quest for uniqueness and recognition. We may thus revise Vico's nomenclature and suggest a transposition of terms in which "human" language now refers to ducal speech whereas the duchess deploys what we may call the prelapsarian tongue. Duchessarian speech, we may surmise, consists of a syntagmatic string in which silences, smiles, formulaic expressions, speaking looks, soft tones, and unexceptionable rejoinders reflect a vernacular of prelapsarian response, a world in which social and existential distinctions need not be made. The introduction of the prelapsarian mentality into the human world inevitably complicates an already complex situation (except in pastoral romance, where it simplifies). It would probably make home life unbearable.

With respect to the poem, if it is permissible to read the domestic predicament as thematized in the text, then it is no giant step to assess "My Last Duchess" as a displaced psychography, the recording of an inner conflict (as in Kafka's "The Judgment"), allowances for "a changing epistemology of the subject," in the words of Paul Jay in *Being in the Text*. The ambiguity in which the poem is drenched, its ironic destabilizations, may be accounted for as a reflex of the aesthetic problem "of translating a psychological subject into a literary one." This thesis implies that Browning's domestic relations were considerably more complex than the poetic postal shuttle between husband and wife would seem to indicate

– which is plainly the case. On the level of affirmation, the poems articulate an undoubted truth; at the same time Browning certainly registered a subtle play of tensions in his relationship with Elizabeth, who was a far stronger personality than her early biography and the content of her Portuguese donation would betoken. It is possible (I say this with extreme tentativeness) that on the barometric level of the sensibility, Browning may have felt an element of constraint, little pinches of coercion, writing as he did in part to his wife's specifications. The portrait of the duchess might then function as a parodic analogue, a reverse simulacrum or protective distortion. Coercion is the other face of neglect, and both conduce to the sense of disenfranchisement, of misprision.

But we are on shaky if fascinating ground here. Whichever way we are predisposed to read the duchess (as ironic counterpart or straight antithesis), it seems to me far more likely that Browning regarded her, at least consciously, as the just the sort of wife he was fortunate enough to have escaped. In either reading, however, the duke would continue to function as a fictive surrogate, asserting the fundamental claims of conjugality.

JOYCE'S CHOICES

1 In a letter of 31 May 1927 to Harriet Weaver, Joyce says that he has never read Rabelais – a curious omission in so erudite a writer, and one there is no point in questioning. But I think we can safely assume that Joyce must have come across extracts and excerpts in the course of his voluminous reading, and that he must have been at least partially familiar with the celebrated Rabelaisian technique. In any case he certainly knew it from Defoe, on whom he lectured in Trieste. Oddly, Joyce apparently came late to Lewis Carroll as well, though it is hard to believe he would not have been familiar with the magisterial Humpty Dumpty.

2 The difference between them, perhaps, is analogous to that between Newton and Einstein, the one positing an "objective" and universal non-perspectival space, the other a time-space continuum the description of which must take the observer into account. Yet both were superb mathematicians, and Einstein once considered calling his work on relativity "invariance theory."

3 "Having given up God's world, the godlike artist will create its aesthetic counterpart, round, solid, and crammed with every-

thing," writes William York Tindall in *A Reader's Guide to James Joyce*. He is referring to Stephen but evokes, inevitably, the figure of "word-loving Joyce."

4 One might permute these terms and suggest that the imagination in its creative potency sires twins: the privileged self and the validating text, both of which turn inevitably on the father at the same time as they engage in complex, fraternal strife – in which the text usually emerges triumphant. The textual Shaun generally enjoys the advantage over the introspective Shem. But this is merely another way of formulating the problem.

5 "The real problems of *Finnegans Wake*," says Anthony Burgess in *Joysprick*, "are not semantic but referential. Joyce loves to mystify, and the mysteries yield less to the language scholar than to the diligent enquirer into the facts of Joyce's life, or the lives of his friends." He goes on to develop this thought. "Soon ... all the linguistic problems of that book will be solved ... But the real riddles of the book derive from its subjective, autobiographical quality, the private world of so many referents." Colin MacCabe makes the same point in his *James Joyce and the Revolution of the Word*: "The text cannot be regarded as a closed and self-sufficient unit of meaning, for it constantly refers outside itself in a set of random allusions." *Ulysses*, while more accessible than the *Wake*, is open to the same critique. Burgess's comment on the "Oxen of the Sun" chapter may apply equally well to the complete, cephalopodic *oeuvre*: "Joyce makes it appear that *Ulysses* not merely continues the line of literature in English but encloses it as well." Ellmann, in *Ulysses on the Liffey*, sees a sort of referential takeover in the making: "*Ulysses* was in fact designed to be related to other large works, encyclopedias and dictionaries."

We can appreciate the ingenuity, the intellectual complexity, the fey self-deprecation ("his usylessly unreadable Blue Book of Eccles"), yet there is a sense in which both *Ulysses* and the *Wake* are like a *game*, a multi-dimensional crossword puzzle (or "crossmess parzle") rebus and charade, fascinating and addictive, costing not less than everything to invent and very steep dues indeed to play. One begins to live for the sport, as with racing, golf, or squash. Or does one tend to justify the work as a kind of supersonic language primer, instructing us in the infinite possibilities and resources of the *ursprecht* that is potentially ours to manipulate – the higher Berlitz?

6 As Joseph Campbell and Henry Morton Robinson (the latter aptly named) write in *A Skeleton Key to Finnegans Wake*, "One of the chief tasks of the creative artist is to provide new sustenance for the insatiable gorgon within him," but they do not seem to see how problematic and indeed petrifactive such an enterprise may eventually become – as the word "gorgon" unintentionally implies.

7 Proust's *À la recherche* ... is, after the *Wake*, the century's other great example of the encircling and devouring text. *Ulysses* is in a sense the expeditionary force that precedes its "Manchurian" successor.

8 Close readers of Joyce may imagine that *they* are doing the nibbling. As John Ralston Saul comments in *Voltaire's Bastards*, "there's a lot of flyfood in *Ulysses* and it was put there for the flies." But if we are the flies, the text is ultimately a kind of Venus flytrap. Any way we look at it, the joke is still on us.

SWIFT AND SARTORISM

1 Ricardo Quintana, *The Mind and Art of Jonathan Swift* (Swift's *Letter of Advice* is quoted herein).

2 Nigel Dennis, *Jonathan Swift: A Short Character.*

3 By the word "lying" in this context is intended something other than its psycho-literary correlative. Swift understood perfectly well the Polonian conception of the lie – "By indirections find directions out" – which is, in effect, the functional basis of his ironic art. Lying as a literary technique or as the very definition and essence of fiction, in the sense intended by Wilde in *The Decay of Lying* or implied by Carroll in *Alice through the Looking-Glass* (Alice reaching the looking-glass hill only when she advances in another direction); or lying as a technique of survival, as in George Steiner's concept of "counter-factuality" in *After Babel*, is implicit in Swift's entire satiric practice. In fact Steiner's notion of language reads like a partial clarification of Swiftian procedure. "The human capacity to utter falsehood," he tells us, "to lie, to negate what is the case, stands at the heart of speech ... Language is the main instrument of man's refusal to accept the world as it is." Man is indebted to the "unboundedness of falsehood" for his imaginative liberty. Deprived of the "fictive, counter-factual, anti-deterministic means of language ... to articulate possibilities

beyond the treadmill of organic decay and death," it is unlikely, Steiner thinks, that man would be able to survive. "Language is centrally fictive because the enemy is "reality," because unlike the Houyhnhnm man is not prepared to abide with the thing which is." (One recalls that not only the Houyhnhnms but the Laputans as well, the latter an unmistakable satiric butt, possess an impoverished language. Linguistic richness or complexity is plainly not the satiric target but the asymptotic ideal).

It seems to me that Swift might have been in at least partial agreement with the content of a "metaphysical" analysis of this kind, although this does not mean that he would have approved of lying in the non-metaphysical sense of deceit or fraud. It is precisely these latter vices he strenuously and consistently opposed. As a satirist, Swift was plainly no Whinny, impeccable but limited; as a man, he abominated the personal and social lie by means of which we deceive others as well as ourselves. Swift would probably have endorsed Steiner's notion of "alternity" up to a certain point and recognized the intimate and necessary bond between language and fiction. (We remember that the Houyhnhnms conceive of language, or speech, as an instrument for the communication and reception of "Information of Facts" and that the pixilated Laputans cannot express even the concept of Imagination.) Swift knew that the prelapsarian agreement between word and thing had expired as the Sprat-like linguistic projectors in Lagado, hauling their vocabularies about on their backs, had not, to their eventual befuddlement and exhaustion. (For a brief but lucid discussion of stylistic "simplicity," especially Bishop Sprat's dictum of "so many things almost in an equal number of words," see Quintana. Also, in a similar vein, see Ian Watt's consideration of the influence of John Locke's enjoinder "to convey the knowledge of things" in *The Rise of the Novel*).

But fiction exists, Swift would have surely contended, not to create an alternative or counter-factual universe of discourse but as a way of pointing up, articulating, and discovering truth. One determines one's position by "takeing observations" with respect to a distant, celestial body which transcends the horizontal plane of four-footed factuality, yet permits the establishment of earthly coordinates.

Or to put it another way: the Houyhnhnm (or literalist) understands latitude, the satirist (or fictionalist) longitude as well. Both readings are required to plot a topographical grid in which "truth" can be more or less accurately localized. One of the benefits of Struldbruggian immortality that Gulliver mentions is the privilege of seeing "the Discovery of the Longitude," a scientific feat that was not accomplished until the mid 1760s with Pierre Le Roy's marine chronometer and John Harrison's fifth, miniaturized chronometer based on the isochronous hair spring. In terms of the analogy I am *tentatively* suggesting here, standard time would correspond to the existence of the satiric norm; the complex device for obtaining standard time from which the longitude could be calculated would correspond to the satiric fiction itself. We attempt to determine the satirist's position *vis à vis* his subject, though with a lesser degree of accuracy than is allowed by geodetic calibrations, by observing his latitude – the "facts" he is putatively treating – as well as measuring his longitude – his attitude toward the "facts," the psychological meridian on which he is located, his manipulation of language and plot to reveal an underlying state, stimulate response, and effect persuasion. The Houyhnhnm-mind is bound to the world of the "Information of Facts," to mere latitudinal movement; the longitudinal mind is aware of perspective, distance, interpretation. The genius of language in its post-lapsarian condition resides in its longitudinality, the imaginative or fictive co-ordinate of which both the Whinnies and the linguistic projectors of Lagado are ignorant. Thus, the literalist is concerned with the dissemination of "facts," the satirist with the approximation to "truth" in social, political, and spiritual life.

But to return to the beginning of this excursus: lying as the presentation of a fictional construct that incorporates the author's vision of "truth" must be rigorously differentiated from lying as social deception in order to gain an advantage or as exaggeration in the form of self-aggrandizement. This is the "lie" Swift's "truth" exposes.

4 Compare "William Cleland" in the prefatory apparatus to *The Dunciad*: "Deformity becomes an object of Ridicule when a man sets up for being handsome; and so must Dulness when he sets up for a Wit."

5 Now dextrously her Plumpers draws,
That serve to fill her hollow Jaws.
Untwists a wire; and from her Gums
A set of teeth completely comes.

"A Beautiful Young Nymph Going to Bed"

6 Swift's studies at Trinity would have been pursued within the traditional Aristotelian framework. (See Phillip Harth, *Swift and Anglican Rationalism.*) The references to Aristotle's *De Interpretatione* and *Dialectica* in the *Tale* and the resurrection of Aristotle at Glubbdubdrib in the *Travels* would argue for (at least) a passing acquaintance with the Stagirite on the part of a writer who was not, self-admittedly, philosophically inclined. ("To enter upon causes of philosophy is what I protest I will rather die in a ditch than go about" [*The Correspondence of Jonathan Swift*, ed. F. Elrington Hall.]) But Swift's familiarity with the major aspects of Aristotelian thought cannot be doubted.
7 A.E. Taylor, *Aristotle.*
8 Mary Douglas, *Purity and Danger.*
9 Quoted in Taylor, 47. All subsequent quotations from Butler's poem are taken from the Laurel *Restoration* volume, edited by Alan S. Downer and Arthur C. Kirsch.
10 William S. Sahakian, *History of Philosophy.*
11 Marjorie Grene, *A Portrait of Aristotle.*
12 That is, the Anglican rejection of the blind faith of Catholicism and the charismatic inspiration of Puritanism on the one hand, its acceptance of revelation as opposed to the critical rationalism of deism on the other.
13 Robert M. Philmus, "Swift, Gulliver, and 'The Thing Which Was Not'," *English Literature History* 38, no. 1.
14 Opie, Iona and Peter, *The Classic Fairy Tales.*
15 We see the same discrimination at work in the notion of book *titles* as opposed by implication to *content*, in *The Mechanical Operation of the Spirit*, whose "author" ransacks Fleet Street, etc., for convenient and proper titles for his ostensible letter to a friend. The title clearly represents the *outside* of the literary artifact (or of the thought that generates it). In terms of the dialectic we are examining here, we would have to say that title and content should exist in functional correlation or unity if the book is to attain its *quidditas.*
16 Castiglione's *The Courtier* was published two years earlier in 1528, but its purpose was somewhat different in its attempt to present the indelible image of the perfect courtier.
17 All quotations from Erasmus are taken from this volume.
18 For example, "right conduct is incompatible with excess or deficiency in feelings and actions." *Nichomachean Ethics*, 2. 2

19 It is important, even crucial, to note that the Aristotelian conception of matter is radically different from the vulgar conception of matter as "thing" or "object." Matter in the original sense is the undifferentiated and internal constituent of substance; form is what provides for its "external" manifestation.

20 See Tacitus's *Germania* as a source text in this "Romantic" symbology. The Germans wear "a cloak fastened with a brooch, or failing that, a thorn ... They also wear the skins of wild animals – the tribes near the river frontiers without any regard to appearance."

21 See Ralph Cudworth, in his *True Intellectual System of the Universe*, 1678, with which Swift would have been familiar. Cudworth speaks of the infirmity of "Hylomania," whose sufferers "madly dote upon Matter, and devoutly worship it," and are dismissed as atheists.

22 As an ironic sidelight, we may note that the militant dissenter could look back to a martial tradition in which sartorial appointment was highly developed and sensibly adapted to conditions. "At his Restoration Charles II was so impressed by both the men and their accoutrements that many of the disbanded Cromwellian troops were immediately re-enlisted for his own service." (See *Modesty in Dress* by James Laver.) We may also cite here Laver's definition of modesty as "an inhibitory impulse directed against either social or sexual forms of display. It is opposed both to the wearing of gorgeous clothes and to the wearing of too few clothes."

23 Split off from the whole, each constituent becomes grotesque, all-inclusive, and destructive. See Pope in the *Essay on Man*:

> Two principles in human nature reign;
> Self-love to urge, and Reason, to restrain.

Self-love and Reason are necessary and countervailing forces.

24 See the Epilogue to *The Way of the World*.

25 The concluding chapters of McLuhan's *The Gutenberg Galaxy*, while treating primarily of Pope's *Dunciad*, are pertinent in this connection as well. McLuhan's point, as is by now common knowledge, is that print induces us to forfeit the bulk of our experience to the unconscious (which in its hypertrophic state is represented by the goddess Dulness). The significant portion of experience which is not linked either literally or metaphorically with the visual sense re-enters the tribal, non-literate world of Chaos and

Eternal Night. The artist or intellectual now becomes not the director of "individual perception and judgment" but the hierophant of the unconscious. As a result McLuhan laments, "literature will be at war with itself ... For the matter of literary vision will be collective and mythic, while the forms of literary expression and communication will be individualist, segmental, and mechanical. The vision will be tribal and collective, the expression private and marketable." This radical cleavage or disjunction between form and matter is persuasively illustrated in the logical scheme of the *Tale*, in which what we might call a privately deregulated sensibility, pursuing its idiosyncratic "vision," expresses the seething and inchoate inwardness of an entire culture.

Interestingly, Hugh Kenner makes a similar point in *The Stoic Comedians*, written at about the same time as *Gutenberg* (1962 is the copyright year of some of the articles in Kenner's book, the same year that saw the publication of McLuhan's). Kenner sees the *Tale* as the great hymn to encroaching discontinuity between – though he does not use these terms – consciousness and unconsciousness. The distinct person is disappearing into the swamp of technological anonymity. The *Tale* "is anonymous because it is written by nobody, by no person, but by the autonomous book-compiling machine itself" – shades of the automatic word-frame in the Academy of Lagado – "and it addresses itself ... to the public at large and to posterity – that is, to no one." Form and matter, in forcible separation, are destructive of entelechy, which is to say, the person, the *unified sensibility*, is dismembered or aborted.